Contents

Part 5 Design and Text Processing

Part 6 Finance and Business Structure

Part 7 Student Study Guides

Introduction

This book is aimed at those students who are embarking on a GCSE course in Business and Communication Systems. It aims to develop a strong knowledge base, which is then built on and extended through written exercises, and a series of practical tasks directly related to the content of the syllabus.

The book has been divided into short, manageable units of work. Each unit concludes with a series of practical tasks which have been designed to develop the understanding and knowledge necessary for successful completion of the course. Whenever possible, these tasks seek to reinforce the theoretic base of the syllabus with the skills and abilities required by the practical aspect of the course. Extension material has also been included at the end of each section to provide some progression for more able students. This material may also provide a basis for homework assignments and supported self-study. This second edition includes a series of written exercises in each unit which are designed to reinforce the theoretic elements of the courses and provide stimulus material so students are not dependent upon access to a computer to complete some of the work necessary for successful completion of the course.

At the back of the book is a section that details the practical skills that all students need to develop during the course. You may find it helpful to photocopy this and use it as a checklist against which progress and development can be charted. This will help ensure that you can carry out all the practical tasks required in the practical examination.

There is also a section on revision and revision techniques that you may find useful as your course progresses. It is worth reading this section now so that you are aware of its content and will know where to find help and advice when it is needed.

Suggested answers to the exercises and other information to help students with the practical tasks, together with additional resources and materials are included in the companion teacher's book.

Bill Owens
20 February 2001

PART 1

Computers

- Computer systems
- Computer input devices
- Computer output devices
- File management systems
- Word processing skills
- Spreadsheets
- More on spreadsheets
- Databases
- Databases: Searching and Sorting

Computer systems

Computer technology is an everyday part of our lives. Microprocessors are used to manage traffic lights, to operate electronic equipment in the home and to control the engine in a car. In business they are used to manage levels of stock in supermarkets, to operate automated welding equipment in a car factory and to maintain patients' records at the local health centre. Everyone today has part of their life managed by a computer and most people will have used one, probably to play games, possibly to prepare text, notices or posters, perhaps to learn how to do some programming or to control a device using Logo. Computers consist of two elements: hardware and software.

Hardware

This is the term used for the electronic equipment itself. Most computers consist of several devices linked together. The main items of a stand alone computer are shown in figure 1. Some of these devices, or peripherals, will allow you to put data into a computer (see Unit 2), others will allow you to get information out (see Unit 3).

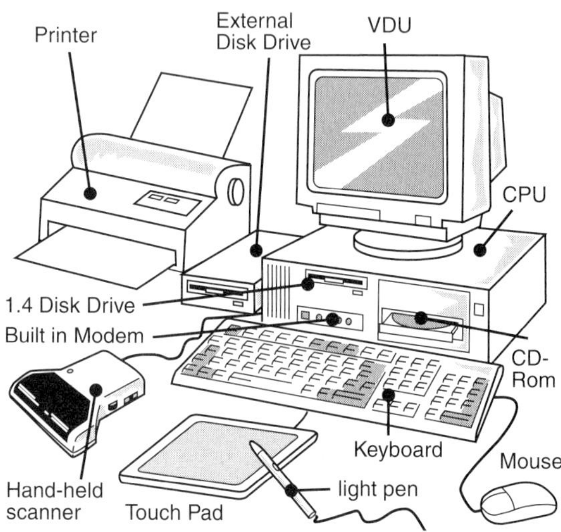

Figure 1 Diagram of a computer

Software

This is the term used for the programs which run on the computer. A program is the set of instructions the computer uses to carry out specific tasks. As most computers are reprogrammable, these instructions can be changed so the computer system can perform many different tasks.

Computer Networks

In businesses and other organisations, it is quite common for all the computers to be linked together electronically to form a network. This allows computers to 'talk' to each other so that data can be exchanged between them. Linking computers can be done with or without cables. The most common communication which uses cables can either be with wires, which are relatively cheap to install and use, although the signal may require 'boosting' over longer distances, or with fibre optic cable. This consists of a thin glass fibre encased in a protective sheath and although expensive to install, has a number of benefits:

- it can carry several different signals at the same time
- it does not suffer from electrical interference
- the data transmitted through it is secure
- the cable does not suffer from corrosion, so has a longer life.

Linking computers without cables is becoming more common as the technology develops and becomes cheaper to install. Satellite communication allows communication between continents but is extremely expensive to set up and use. Secure communication can be established using microwaves but these are expensive to set up and require direct line of sight between transmitting and receiving stations.

Recent developments have seen the introduction of infra-red and short range radio communications. Infra-red technology allows machines to be freely moved (as in the case of laptop computer terminals) but they still require a direct line of sight with the receiver to ensure a strong connection. Short range radio waves, which have a range of up to ten metres are now being used to connect a mouse or keyboard to a computer without wires, or to allow the use of wireless headsets to mobile phones.

Whichever method of transferring data is used, when computers are linked together, they form a network. A network requires one computer to act as a controlling device or file server. Usually the file server is a more powerful computer on which the software is held, this is shared by all other computers or work stations on the network. This computer 'manages' the network and controls the distribution of data to the other work stations or terminals. On smaller networks, one of the work stations may carry out this function but with the demand for all members of staff to have their own individual email facilities. There are a number of significant benefits to networking computers within an organisation:

- fewer peripherals such as printers are required, as each one of these can be shared by several work stations
- data input onto one work station can be recalled on another, often in another part of the building
- information stored centrally on the file server can be shared with other users on the network
- work stations can be of a lower grade and specification than a stand alone computer, which can save money as less expensive equipment can be purchased
- expensive software is not needed on every work station. Only one copy need be purchased with a licence for its use on a number of work stations.

Computers can be linked together in a number of ways depending on the requirements of the organisation and the finance available. The simplest and least expensive method is known as a 'bus' network. This links the terminals with a single cable rather like the stops on a bus route. See figure 2. Although cheap and easy to use, as the number of terminals increases, the transfer of data on this type of network will slow down and if the main cable fails all the computers will be affected.

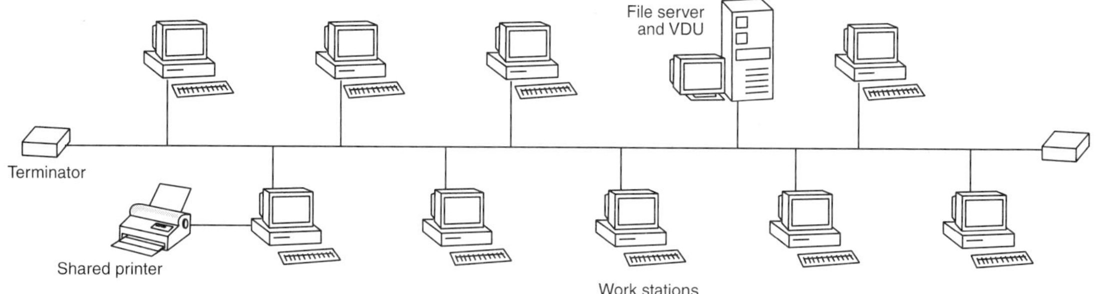

Figure 2 Bus network

To overcome some of these disadvantages a 'ring' network can be used. See figure 3 below. Terminals are linked together on a ring of cable and as data is transferred in one direction only, it improves the speed of communication. However, as with a bus network, if the cable fails all terminals are affected.

Larger organisations set up their networks using a 'star' system. Cables radiate from the file server to local hubs or switches through which other terminals can be connected. This allows a high performance as the data flowing through any one part of the network is limited to the number of terminals on that one section and if there is a cable failure, the other sections of the network will remain operational. However, this type of network is expensive to install as it requires more cabling as well as a number of hubs or switches to control the terminals on each spur of cable. An example of the layout of a star network is given below in figure 4.

To prevent unauthorised use of an organisation's

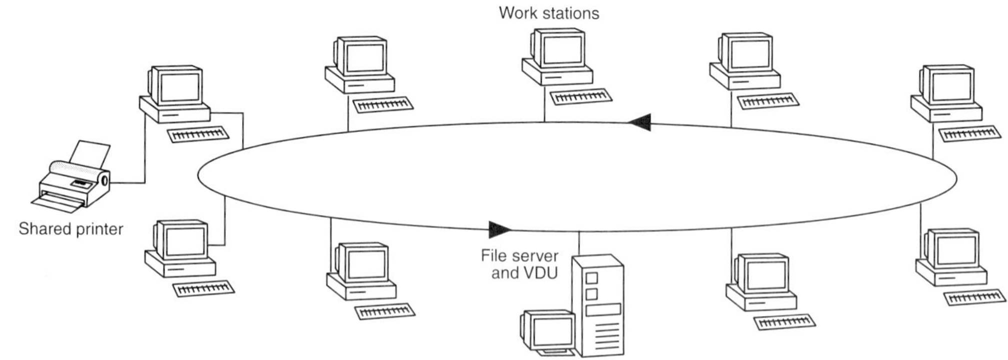

Figure 3 Ring network

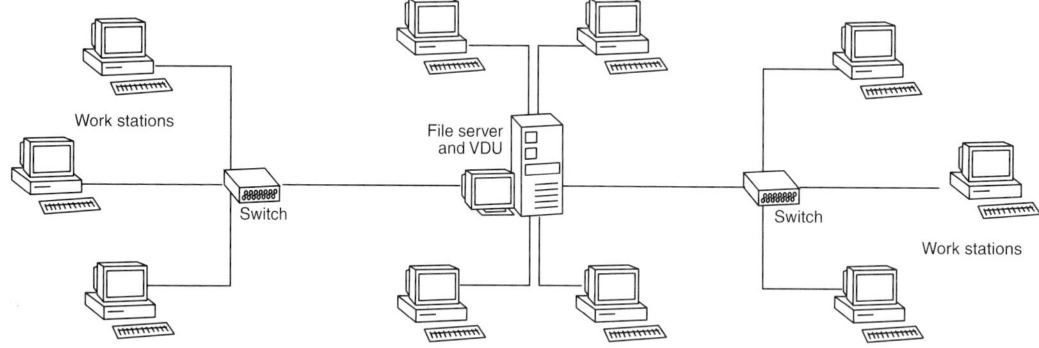

Figure 4 Star network

network, all users are required to 'log on' to a network system using a user name and password. These are usually set up and managed by the Network Manager who is able to determine the level of access each user has to the information on the system. Within a school or college, staff will have a higher level of access to facilities on the network than students. But only the Network Manager or the IT technicians will have sufficient access to allow them to install or remove software.

Exercises

1 Explain the difference between hardware and software in a computer system. (2)

2 List the benefits to an organisation of using a computer network rather than a number of stand alone computers. (4)

3 Explain the differences between a bus network, a ring network and a star network. (3)

4 What are the benefits of using a dedicated file server on a network? (3)

5 List the advantages and disadvantages of linking computers with and without cables. (4)

6 Why do networks require all users to have a password? Explain what may happen if a password becomes known by other users on the system. (4)

Your employer is considering replacing all the computer hardware in your office. Word process a report which compares the advantages and disadvantages of purchasing stand-alone computers with a network.

Carry out a survey of all the computing equipment in your school or college and plot the position of each computer or work station on a plan of the area. Mark any peripheral items, such as shared printers, scanner and CD Roms.

Extension material

Your school or college has just been awarded a £100,000 lottery grant to upgrade its computer facilities. You have been asked to draw up an outline plan of the school showing where best to spend the money. You should consider installing both a network and stand-alone computers. Your plans should include installing equipment in all departments or faculties as well as the library and resource centre.

Using the information below prepare a table of the costs of the installation using a spreadsheet. The cost of cabling is £1,500 per room. A file server costs £5,000, each network work station costs £750 and stand-alone computers are £1,000 each. A printer cost £500, a CD Rom stack £1,250 and a scanner £120.

Computer input devices

Computers need to 'capture' or receive data quickly and accurately and there are a number of methods by which data can be input. They can be divided into five main categories: by touch, by magnetic means, by light, by sound and through control switches.

Touch Input Devices

- Keyboard

  A standard keyboard is the most commonly used method of entering data into a computer. The letters on the keyboard are set out in a layout that is standard for most countries in the world. It gains its name, QWERTY, from the top line of alphabetic characters. Because the layout is standardised, it is possible to learn the keyboard so that data can be entered quickly and accurately using the touch-typing method. Here the position of the keys is memorised and certain fingers use certain keys. In this way a word processing operator can enter data into the computer without having to look at their fingers on the keys as they work, which speeds up the process of data entry. However, in recent years concern has grown about the increasing incidence of repetitive strain injury (RSI) in the wrists and fingers. This is caused as the muscles and joints become inflamed by frequent short repetitive movements of the hands such as those necessary in the use of the keyboard. To help overcome this, manufacturers are now designing keyboards that slope towards the operator, or have wrist rests to support the hands and, in some cases, are curved to make them more comfortable to use. More information on learning how to use a QWERTY keyboard is given in Unit 60.

- Mouse

  First marketed in 1983, the mouse has rapidly become the second most frequently used input device with a computer. It is essentially a pointing device which allows the operator to move a

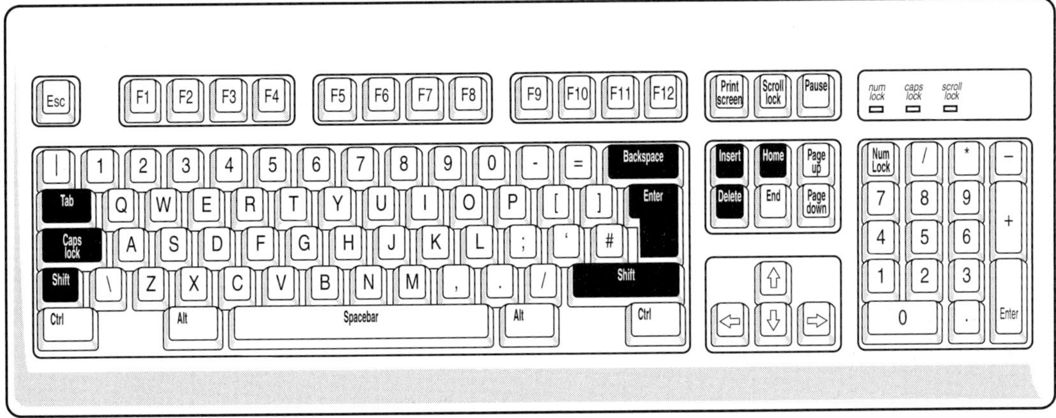

A standard computer keyboard

pointer on the screen over a menu or icon and then click a button to enter that information into the computer's memory. The mouse is a hand-held casing which covers a weighted ball that drives two sets of rollers: one moves the pointer up and down the screen and the other from left to right. Most mice have two buttons which, when clicked, activate a menu from which a selection or activity can be made. Buttons can be clicked, double-clicked or dragged to create different activities on the screen. Some mice also have a scroll wheel which allows the operator to move quickly up and down a document on screen. Modern technology has now devised a mouse which does not require a cable attached to the computer but makes use of infra-red or wireless links in the same way a remote control device works with a television or video recorder. The use of a mouse allows the operator to input data rapidly when working from set menus or on-screen icons.

 Concept Keyboard

A concept keyboard allows the operator to enter pre-programmed information at the press of one button. It is a flat-bed of contact switches which are covered with a sheet of flexible plastic on which an overlay of symbols and pictures can be placed which represent what each button stands for. They are commonly used in retail outlets where a range of standard products is sold, such as a burger bar or a public house. Each button is programmed with the details of a single product. When a button is pressed, not only does it ensure that the correct price is charged, it also allows the computer to monitor stock movements and record sales statistics for the business. Where several employees use the same till, these keyboards can be programmed to record the activities of each operator. However, concept keyboards are limited in the number of keys available which can be programmed and it is more difficult to implement any changes to products and prices.

Magnetic Input Devices

 Magnetic Stripes

These are the narrow strips of magnetic material usually found on the back of plastic debit and credit cards. Imprinted on the magnetic strip is data relating to the card holder, such as the bank account reference number and PIN (Personal Identification Number). When the card is passed through a reader, rather like those used in tape cassette players, the information is read and transferred to a central computer where it can be processed. Cards with magnetic stripes are now commonly used to withdraw cash from cash dispensers and to make payments in shops instead of using cash.

A credit card

Smart Cards

These are similar to cards with magnetic stripes but they also contain a tiny microprocessor chip on which more data can be stored, for example further details of the card holder or a list of recent purchases made with the card. Because of the extra information smart cards can hold, they are more secure than the standard bank cards, however, they are not yet used extensively in this country because of the high cost of altering all the card readers currently in use in cash dispensers and shop tills.

Light Input Devices

Optical Mark Readers (OMR)

These are probably the earliest form of input device which made use of light. They detect marks made on paper, usually by a soft leaded pencil, when the page is scanned by an infra-red light. When there is no mark on the page the white sheet gives a strong light reflection, whereas, when a dark pencil mark is detected, the light reflection is reduced. If you have completed any multiple-choice examinations, your answers will undoubtedly have been read and marked using an optical mark reader.

As technology has improved, simple marks identified by optical mark readers have gradually been extended to include other characters. Probably the largest users of what is known as Optical Character Recognition (OCR) are the Post Office and the banking system. The postcode on each letter is encoded onto each envelope using a series of light blue dots which enable machines to read and sort letters into their correct delivery areas. Banks record account details and amounts onto cheques and

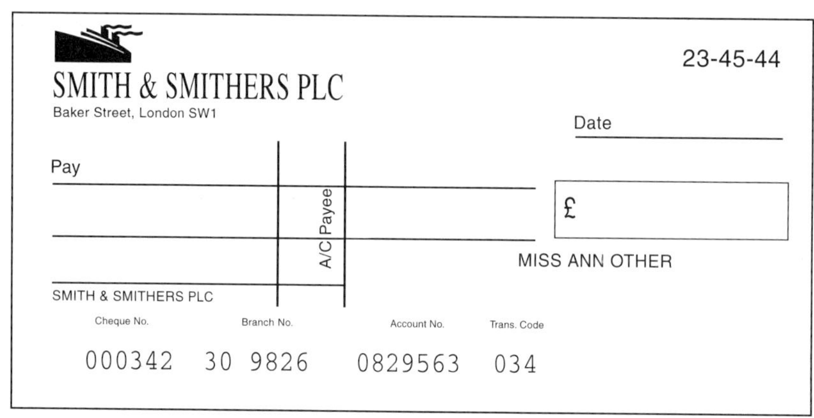

A cheque

paying-in slips, using those oddly-shaped numbers, to enable computers to process the transactions.

Barcode Reader

Almost every product you purchase today will have a barcode printed on it. These are made up of different width black and white stripes which represent numbers. When passed over a laser light reader these numbers are converted by computer into the product description and price. The advantages of the barcode reader include more accurate product information so customers are unlikely to be charged incorrectly, and simplicity of operation as the shop does not have to price every item and assistants do not have to remember lots of different prices! Stock control too is easier as the computer maintains a list of products sold and can advise on when reordering needs to take place. However, careful checking is important to ensure all the information entered into the computer about a product code is correct otherwise every item sold will be incorrectly described and/or priced!

Barcodes

Scanners

The concept of optical character recognition has been developed further and most computer systems now include a scanner. This enables a computer to read both text and pictures. They work in the same way as optical mark readers, where the light passed over an image or page of text, is reflected back using mirrors and lenses to a series of light sensors. These then convert the signals they receive into digital codes which the computer can identify. Once created, a scanned picture can be manipulated using a number of image editing programs and then input into a word processing or desk top publishing system.

Digital Cameras

A picture taken with a digital camera is stored on a removable chip rather than film. The colours of the picture are converted into digital signals by sensors behind the lens. These can be quickly and easily transferred to a computer for further processing, storage and printing. Most digital cameras have their own LCD display screen which enables the operator to view the picture as soon as it has been taken which allows it to be deleted if it is not required.

Digital Video

Technology now allows digital camcorders to download and manipulate a video image, using a Firewire interface, directly onto a computer. However, video capture and editing requires computers with a very large hard disk drive as the files containing video data tend to take up large amounts of memory. Once edited, however, these files can be compressed to reduce the storage space they require with only a slight loss in picture quality.

Sound Input Devices

Voice Recognition

There are now a number of successful speech or voice recognition systems available on the market. These allow the user to input data to a computer using their own voice which is then converted directly into text by a word processor. When first installed, time has to be spent 'teaching' the computer the sound variations in the user's voice and speech patterns. Once this has been done, these systems have proved to be very successful, however care needs to be taken to ensure words sounding the same but with different meanings are the ones required. For example 'mail' and 'male' or 'whether' and 'weather'. Some later versions of voice recognition software are now able to determine the required spelling of a word from the sense of the text being input.

- Musical Instrument Digital Interface (MIDI)
  The MIDI system was developed to link musical keyboards with computers so that music being created and played can be stored digitally on a hard drive. Once stored the music can then be displayed on screen as a musical score, edited as required, and also played back through the computer's sound system.

Control Switches

The two main types of control switch are those which operate by measuring light and those which measure temperature. Light Dependent Resistors or LDRs are sensors that alter their electrical resistance depending on the amount of light they pick up. As the light gets brighter, so the resistance decreases. This type of switch is often used to automatically inform a computer that controls street or motorway lights to switch them on or off as natural light conditions change. Temperature changes can be measured using thermistors. These are switches which react by changing their electrical resistance as temperatures fluctuate. The main use is in computer managed heating and air conditioning systems in houses, factories and warehouses where they can be used to regulate the temperature automatically.

Other switching devices which can be used with computerised systems include those which sense movement to inform a central computer of unauthorised activity on business premises, and mechanical switches, such as push button or slide switches, which may be activated by computer controlled machinery.

Exercises

1. List the different methods of inputting data into a computer system using touch. (6)
2. Explain the differences between a magnetic stripe card and a smart card. (2)
3. List the different types of computer controlled switches. Give an example of where each could be used. (3)
4. Light is being increasingly used as a means of inputting data into computer systems. Select and explain three ways in which light can be used. (3)
5. Write a brief list of instructions explaining to a small child how to use a mouse to enter data into a computer. Remember to keep your explanation easy to understand. (3)
6. What are the advantages to a retailer of using a concept keyboard? Explain why they are only used in a small number of retail outlets. (3)

Using your word processor create a table as shown below in which you list all the different types of input device together with the other information shown.

Type of Devices	Method of Input	Advantages	Disadvantages

Select either a scanner or a digital camera or digital video system and, using your word processor or desk top publisher, prepare a set of easy to understand instructions on A4 paper which explains how to use it.

Extension material

In recent years there have been a number of significant changes in the ways in which data can be input into computer systems, for example the development of voice recognition software. Write a report to your Office Manager suggesting how the main method of keying in data, i.e. using a keyboard, will change in the next five years. How will the change affect the equipment used in business? What will the effects be on office design? What will the implications be for staff training?

Computer output devices

Once data has been input into a computer and processed, it is of little use unless it can be retrieved quickly and easily from the system. There are several ways in which information can be output, some are permanent, such as printed sheets, others are transient, such as a screen display.

1 Visual Display Units or Monitors

This is undoubtedly the most commonly used form of output from a computer system. It displays information in a similar way to that shown on a television screen. Standard monitors consist of a cathode ray tube in which a built-in electron gun 'fires' electrons at phosphor dots coated onto the inside of the screen. The dots are arranged in threes – consisting of dots for three colours, green, red and blue – to form a pixel which when 'hit', glows to give the colours seen by the operator. The size of a monitor is measured diagonally across the screen and the most popular sizes are currently 15 and 17 inches. The larger the monitor, the easier it is to work with. Information can be seen more clearly on the screen and this makes design and graphics work simpler and reduces eye strain for frequent users. Although larger monitors are now available, at present they are considerably more expensive.

Recent developments in monitor design have produced a thin flat screen. These can be of three types. Liquid crystal display screens, or LCDs have been available for a number of years. They consist of tiny crystals that are electrically charged to polarise the light passing through them and are commonly used in calculators and digital watches. Most laptop or notebook computers use a system of thin film transistors or TFTs. These are a more advanced form of display which gives a sharper quality output and allows greater use of colour, contrast and resolution. The most recent development in screen technology is the use of field emission displays or FEDs. These provide a bright sharp image on screen based on a system using two thin sheets of glass narrowly separated by a vacuum. Electrons are fired in the vacuum from the rear sheet at phosphor dots on the inside of the front sheet which, when hit, glow to produce a clear bright image. This modern type of screen is now being used more in industry where desk space is at a premium and they can, for example, often be seen in use by cashiers in many high street banks and building societies.

- Printers

Printers provide the operator with a permanent record of the output from a computer. This has the advantage of being able to be taken away and studied at leisure, or passed on to another individual. There are three types of printer currently in use with most computer systems, each with their own advantages and disadvantages.

1 Dot Matrix Printers

These produce a black and white output made up of a series of dots passing the print head, in which there are a series of pins which strike a continuous ink ribbon and imprint on a sheet of paper. The advantages include:

- they are inexpensive to buy and cheap to run
- they can produce several copies at the same time if self-carbonating paper is used
- they can be used in dirty and dusty situations and will continue to operate where other types of printer may not.

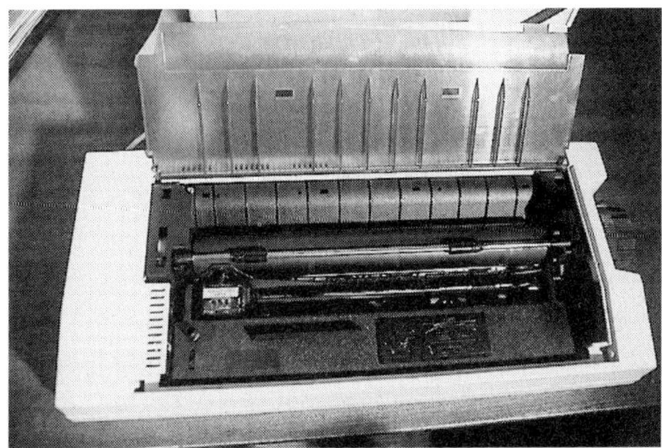

A dot matrix printer

However, these printers cannot produce colour work and the quality of the printed output is poor. Many firms feel it is not of a high enough standard for work to be sent out to customers.

2 Inkjet Printers

A Hewlett Packard Inkjet printer

Probably most commonly used with a home computer system, this type of printer has tiny nozzles in the print head which spray ink in a thin 'jet' onto the page to form characters or graphic images. They have the advantage of being relatively cheap to purchase and are able to print work in both black and white and colour and produce a much higher quality than the dot matrix printer. There are some disadvantages:

- high volume output is costly as the ink cartridges they use are quite expensive
- relatively slow output especially when printing in colour – usually no more than three or four pages per minute
- output is ink based therefore will smudge if the printout gets wet.

3 Laser Printers

Laser printers are very similar to photocopiers in the way in which they operate. They contain a powdered ink or toner which is transferred and 'burned' onto the paper using the processes of heat and pressure. See the diagram overleaf. The image to be printed is transferred using the laser to a negatively charged photosensitive drum.

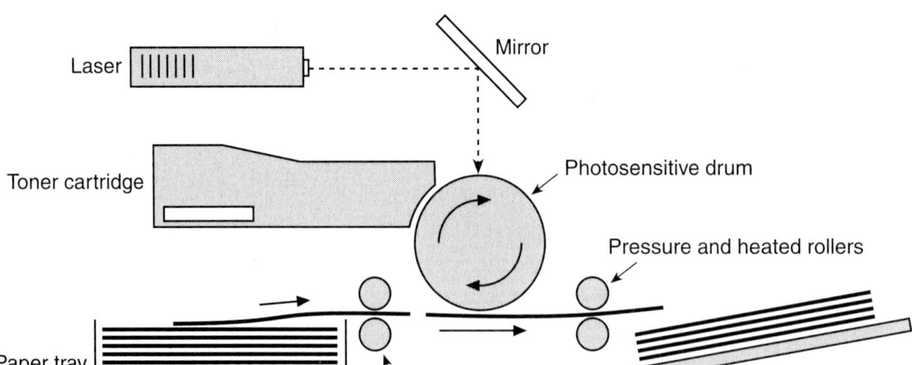

A laser printer

When the drum passes the toner reservoir, the powdered ink is attracted to the charged areas which are then imprinted onto the paper and 'fixed' by heat and pressure.

Laser printers, especially those which produce colour output, are expensive and the replacement toner cartridges are often two or three times more expensive than those for inkjet printers. However, despite these cost disadvantages most organisations now make use of laser printers in their work because of the high quality, permanent output they generate. Once the printer has been purchased, the running costs are considerably less than those of inkjet printers and a black and white copy can be printed for little more than 1p a sheet. Colour laser printing, however, is more expensive as four toner cartridges – black plus the three primary colours – are required to create the overall printed image.

Plotters

These are output devices often used by engineering and scientific organisations to draw plans, diagrams of machines, machine parts and printed circuit diagrams. An electronically controlled pen is moved across the page by two computer-controlled motors. The pen is lifted on and off the page by switching an electromagnet on and off. In recent years, however, the introduction of cheaper printers that can handle A3 and A2 sized paper has resulted in a decline in the need for smaller more expensive plotters.

Sound and Voice

With the increasing use of voice recognition software, machines that talk back to you are becoming increasingly commonplace. Programs have been written and are used to help support students with special learning requirements and to assist with learning correct pronunciation of foreign languages. The advantage that they provide allows groups to receive 'individual' tuition on their own PC rather than having to wait to speak to the teacher or lecturer. Other uses in industry are provided by any system which requires standard answers. British Telecom's Directory Enquiries uses speech synthesisers to give out telephone numbers and many companies now use similar telephone systems to route callers through a menu of computer generated options to save staff having to handle routine enquiries. Argos and IKEA have both introduced a computer automated stock control and information system, which uses the telephone network, which potential customers can dial into with enquiries prior to visiting their stores.

Music too has been revolutionised in recent years with the development of music software that allows compositions to be created on and then played back through a computer. To help with this the development of MP3 computer files has reduced the storage space required by digitally created music files so they are only one tenth of their original size without any appreciable loss of sound quality.

 Magnetic Disks and CD Roms

Although these are technically storage devices, their use as a means of getting large data files out of a computer system is becoming more widespread. Traditionally data could only be transferred between two stand-alone computers by saving it to floppy disk from one and then reading or inputting it to the other. With the increasing use of computers especially for graphics, music and photographic applications, data files are often too large to fit onto floppy disks. The development of the CD Rom drive has now enabled many computers to read from and write data to CD Rom. Up to 650 Mb of data can be stored on one CD compared with only 1.4 Mb on a high density floppy disk.

Using a CD Rom as a means of output allows much larger files to be created much more quickly and at a very low cost. CD writers, which are compatible with most PCs, can now be purchased for less than £100 and CDs cost less than £1.00 each.

Exercises

1 List and explain the terms LCD, TFT and FED. (3)

2 Explain briefly how a dot matrix printer works. Although they produce low quality output, explain why they are still in common use. (4)

3 What are the advantages and disadvantages of using an inkjet printer? (4)

4 Although they are the most expensive type of printer to purchase, explain why most businesses now use laser rather than inkjet or dot matrix printers. (2)

5 Why are many businesses now beginning to make use of TFT or FED screens in the work place even though they are considerably more expensive to purchase than the standard monitor? (3)

6 Explain how output devices other than monitors and printers can benefit individuals and businesses with their work. (4)

Using your word processor create a table as shown below in which you list all the different types of output device together with the other information shown.

Type of Device	Advantages	Disadvantages

Using your word processing system or desk top publishing package create a copy of the diagram which shows how a laser printer works.

Extension material

Using a computer suppliers catalogue or an appropriate Internet site, obtain details of six different printers which are available for sale using the following headings:

Make	Model	Type inkjet/ laser	Cost	Pages per minute	Cost of replacement cartridges

Include any other information which you feel may be relevant.

File management systems

Organising and managing documents within a computer system is vital if information is not to be lost or misfiled. All Windows based systems allow you to set up different folders or directories in which you can store related information. For example, you may have a folder (or directory) for word processed documents, another for spreadsheet files and a third for databases. Alternatively you may store your documents by subject, so you would have one folder (or directory) for Business and Communication Systems work, another for English, a third for Maths and so on.

Folders and sub-folders

You are not restricted to the number of folders you can have. They can be equated to filing cabinets within an office. Also, within each folder it is possible to have sub-folders to help divide up your work. For example within your Business Communication and Systems folder you may have sub-folders for word processed files, another for spreadsheets and so on.

The number of folders and sub-folders you need will depend upon the number of data files you create and store. The diagram (Figure 5) shows a series of folders and their associated sub-folders. The open sub-folder is named 'Exams' and the names of the files stored within it are shown on the right.

File management

All files stored on a computer system are automatically given a three character suffix preceded by a full stop. This indicates the software in which the file has been created. Some of the most commonly used suffixes and the software they relate to include:

- .doc – Word word processing
-  .wps – Works word processing

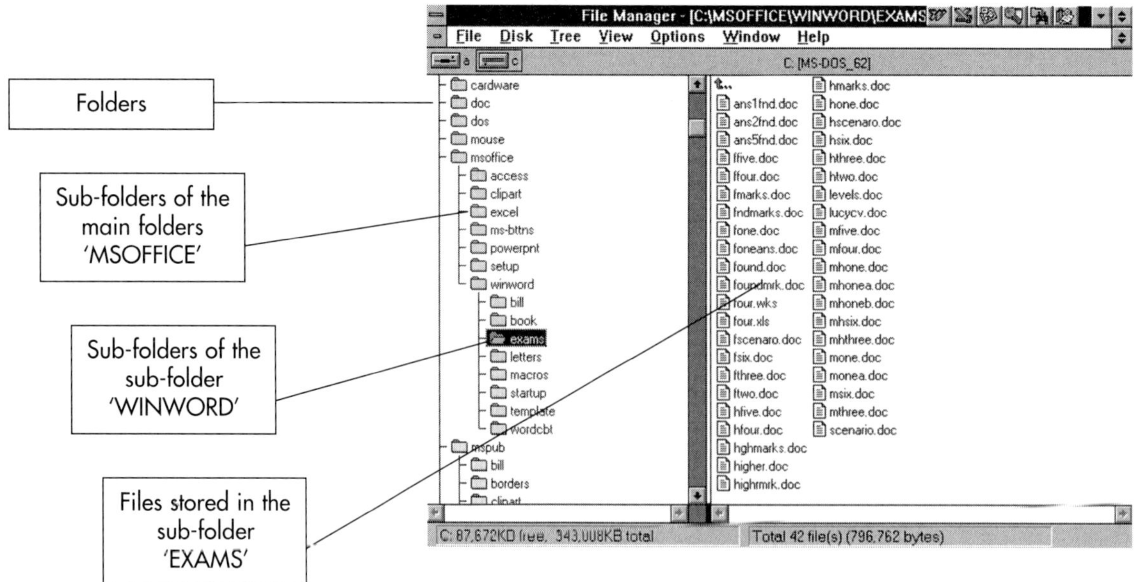

Figure 5 Folders and Sub-folders

- .mdb – Access database
- .xls – Excel spreadsheet
- .wdb – Works database
- .ppt – Powerpoint
- .pub – Publisher DTP
- .wks or .xlr – Works spreadsheets
- .bmp – bitmap graphics

It is important that your files are managed correctly so that you can always find what you need. When you save a document to disk it will ask you for a name. Windows 95 and subsequent versions will accept file names up to 255 characters in length. You should try to give your documents fairly short names, so you can easily see the name in the folder when it is called up on screen. It is also important to give your document a file name which will enable you to remember what it contains. If you gave all your documents file names using your own name – Mary1, Mary2, Mary3, Mary4, etc. – as your files built up you would quickly forget which file called Mary contained what! Similarly, if you name your files after what they actually are – Report1, Report2, Report3 etc. – the same problem would arise.

Try to give your files a name which will prompt you to remember what they contain. A garage database could be called 'Cars'; a spreadsheet calculating pay called 'Wages'; a word processed file on the advantages of an open plan office system called 'Openplan' and so on. This use of file names and files stored in appropriate folders will ensure information can be easily and quickly retrieved when it is needed.

It is also important to weed out any unwanted files on a regular basis. You will probably save most of the work you complete throughout this course – but do you really need to keep it forever? Deleting unwanted files, say every half term, will save on disk storage space. It is good practice to save work every 5 minutes or so as you key it in. Should there be some unforeseen problem, such as a power cut, you will at least be able to recover most of the work lost. But you may not want to store these files permanently. Regularly checking through and deleting out-of-date or unwanted files will make it easier to find the work you do wish to keep.

Copying files

Files can be copied using the facilities of the file

manager. If you store your data files on a floppy disk it is advisable to make a second copy of them to ensure they will not be lost if the first disk fails for any reason. It is also good practice to do this if your files are stored on the computer's hard disk, although failures are much less likely to occur. If your computer work station is part of a network, files will be stored on the hard disk of the file server. Check that there is a backing up system in use and how frequently it is used. You can always save any files you have created or amended on a floppy disk for safety.

Exercises

1 Make a list of all the suffixes which the software you are using creates when saving data. (3)

2 Explain the difference between a folder or directory and file. (3)

3 Write a paragraph explaining to a new word processing operator how to use **File Manager** to make a copy of a file. (4)

4 Outline the advantage of setting up folders and sub-folders in which to store your work. (4)

5 Explain (a) how you would set up file names for your work to ensure you could identify what each contained and (b) how you would weed out any unwanted files. (4)

6 Why do most networked computers have a backup system? (2)

Think carefully about when and where you use computers in your school work. Set up working folders for each of the main subject areas where you regularly use IT. Plan a series of file names which will allow you to recognise what your data files contain. You could keep a list in your folder of the file name used and a one line description of its contents.

Use your word processor to create a table in which you can write down the file names you allocate together with a description.

Using the Screen print facility print a copy of the contents of your folders (see Figure 5) to help you decide which of the files listed you would like to retain and which you no longer require. Delete those files no longer needed.

Extension material

Make a copy of your data files on a floppy disk. Check that you know how to do this and that you are able to back up your data files when necessary.

If you are using a network system, find out how and when the system backs up your data files.

Word processing skills

The one real benefit which a word processor provides when displaying text on the page is the large variety of additional features which you can use to enhance the look of your work. With a manual typewriter, the operator was limited to the use of capital letters, spaced capitals and underlining work. As technology developed, electronic typewriters introduced the use of emboldened typefaces and, when the golf ball or daisy wheel could be changed, an italic font.

Modern word processing systems have revolutionised keyboard display. The style of the typeface can be varied, the point size of the font increased or reduced, text can be emboldened or set in italics and blocks of text can be centred, left or right aligned on the page or rendered in a fully justified format. All of these features enable the operator to produce work which contains much more variety and looks more stylish.

It is important however, that these facilities are used with discretion and that the reader of a notice or advertisement is not presented with too much variety. This can render a piece of work as ineffective as if it had been given no emphasis.

When preparing text using a word processor it is advisable to key in the material using a standard typeface appropriate for business use, such as Times New Roman (if you want serifs) and Arial (if you want your work sans serif), and a normal point size such as 12. This makes the work easy to read and facilitates proofreading and spell checking. It is advisable also at this point to save a copy of your text to disk (see Unit Two).

Spell-checking

This is an automatic process carried out by the word processor. It compares words keyed in with a computer held dictionary to check for accuracy. When it finds a word not in the dictionary, it is highlighted and a list of possible alternatives given.

However, a spellchecker will not pick up every incorrect word. Very often proper names, such as people's names, are not included in the dictionary. Neither will the computer be able to distinguish between incorrectly used words – for example if there is used instead of their – or when keying in creates errors which form other words in the dictionary – for example from instead of form, or in instead of is.

Proof-reading

It is essential, therefore, that all work is not only spell-checked, but also proof read as well. This visual check on the accuracy of work ensures that errors not identified by the automatic spell-checker may be identified and corrected.

Emboldening

This is the facility which makes type appear heavier or darker than normal. It is an excellent way of making one word or a short phrase stand out in a text passage, or to draw attention to a particular word in a sentence.

> Please do **not** take any of the material on this table.

Bold text can also be used to give emphasis to main headings in reports and other documents and for paragraph headings as an alternative to using capitals.

Italics

Text in italics is usually used to show a word or phrase which is slightly different from the rest of the passage in which it appears. It is often used to indicate a quotation or a reference such as a book title. Text in italics is best used to indicate an item which is different rather than something which needs emphasis.

> Everyone was surprised to see how the book entitled *The Spinning Wheel* had sold so many copies in such a short space of time.

Point size

This is the height of the characters in the font. Each unit of point size represents one sixty-fourth of an inch. The standard point size for business letters is 12. Occasionally it may be reduced to 11 or 10 to reduce the size of text to get more text on a page. Larger point sizes can be used to give emphasis to different items within a document.

Point size 10

Point size 12

Point size 16

Point size 24

Point size 36

Point size 48

Font

Word processors are supplied with a range of different styles of typeface called fonts. Some of these are traditional such as Arial, which is a font without serifs or tails on the individual letters. Others create a script or hand written image such as Vivaldi *which looks like copperplate handwriting* or Mistral *which looks like a more modern script*. Others are suitable for headings which need to stand out from the page, such as Stencil. **THIS STANDS OUT IN A PASSAGE**. Some fonts are not suitable for posters and notices, such as Matura, especially when used in capitals which MAKES IT DIFFICULT TO READ. Whatever your choice of font it should improve the presentation of the material being displayed and not detract from it.

One of the main faults which many word processor operators make when first displaying information is to use too many different facilities in one document. As a basic rule you should use no more than two different fonts in any one document. It is far more effective to vary the point size to give emphasis to the important aspects of a notice or poster than to use a variety of fonts. You can easily have too much of a good thing!

Line spacing

One of the least used but most effective of techniques for setting out work is to vary the line spacing within a display. Clear space either side of the name of a band, an event or a job title will set it apart from the rest of the text. Then using a larger point size, to give more prominence, will make it stand out more clearly from the rest of the document

Mail Merge

A key feature of any word processor is the facility to merge or insert elements of text from one computer application into another. Mail merge is the process where a document, usually a form or standard letter, and a list of say, names and addresses, can be combined to produce personalised letters. This can be particularly useful where a standard letter has to be sent out to customers by a company. Although every letter has the same content, each customer receives a personally addressed copy.

When the standard letter is written, markers are put in to show where data from a data file, held in a database or a spreadsheet, is to be inserted into the letter. The field names of the data file are used as markers and before the letters are printed, the word processor will read data from the data file and place it in the coded space on the standard letter.

Mail merging documents has a number of clear advantages. These include, the speed with which personalised letters can be produced, information, once entered in the data file, does not have to be keyed in again, accuracy can be guaranteed (providing the original data is correct!) and personalised letters tend to get a better response than general leaflets in a sales campaign.

Exercises

1 Explain the difference between a spell-check and proof-reading. (4)

2 Give two examples of errors spell-checking will not identify. (2)

3 List three ways in which text can be emphasised. (3)

4 In business why is it important for a word processing operator to spell-check and proof-read work before it is sent out?. (5)

5 What are the main problems in using a variety of fonts for a poster? (4)

6 What font size would you use for a standard text document? (2)

1 Key in the following headlines, then proof-read and spell-check your work.

- Mad dog bites vicar in churchyard
- One man achieves his long lost ambition at last
- New department store opens its doors in August
- Storm fells more than one hundred trees in an hour

- Golfer breaks world record by playing his ball under water
- New rules give players more time during the interval
- Car manufacturer opens up a new factory in record time
- London bus found on the moon by astronauts

2 Using the facilities of your word processor, centre all the odd numbered lines and right align the even numbered lines. Now change the text to bold in the centred lines and to italics in those which are right aligned. Display your work in double line spacing and then print a copy on plain A4 paper.

3 Set out the following notice on A4 paper using a blocked display style. Give emphasis to the main points using a variety of line spacing and point sizes. You may wish to leave out some of the information, change line endings and the order in which the material is presented. Spell-check and proof-read your work and then print a hard copy making good use of the paper size chosen.

GCSE students of the Theatre Arts Department of
Bridgwater Community College
present
The Importance of Being Earnest
a play by Oscar Wilde
Starting at 8.00 pm on Saturday 26 October
in the Osborne Theatre
Admission – adults £3.00, Concessions £1.50
All seats are bookable
Refreshments will be served during the interval
Tickets are available from the College Office

1 Set out the following advertisement giving appropriate emphasis to the main points. Use a variety of point sizes and line spacing to display your work effectively. Centre your work horizontally and vertically on the page and then print a copy on A4 paper.

For hire. A 6 berth caravan with three bedrooms, interior plumbing facilities and central heating on a small select site overlooking the Bristol Channel. Five minutes walk to the local shops and post office. Beautiful views of the north Somerset coastline. Available from 1 May to 31 August. Reasonable weekly rates. Write for a brochure to Mrs B. White, 109 Chessel Street, Bedminster, Bristol, BS3 3DG.

2 Re-format your work using different fonts, point sizes and if possible a different variety of line spacing. Use any other forms of emphasis you feel may be appropriate. Print out a copy.

Extension material

The following notice has been produced by the office junior but you feel he has overdone the emphasis and word processing effects. Word process a list of the changes you would like to make to the document giving reasons for your decisions.

Motor Gears PLC Social Club

Football Training Sessions

to start on Saturday 15 August

AT THE SOCIAL CLUB GROUNDS

Teignmouth Road

10.00 am for children

11.00 am for adults

instruction will be given in

general ball skills, dribbling, heading, passing, and goal shooting

Cost Adults £2.00, Children aged 14 or less £1.00

PLEASE SEE PETE PHILLIPS IN THE ACCOUNTS DEPARTMENT FOR FURTHER DETAILS

Now prepare a more appropriate notice which makes good, effective use of word processing and display techniques to show how it could look.

Spreadsheets

A spreadsheet is a computer program which allows you to enter and store data in a grid or matrix. This then allows you to carry out calculations on the data you have entered using the program and the instructions or formula you have also entered. The spreadsheet will then allow you to alter or amend data quickly and easily. Any of the entries can be changed at any time and the effects of these changes will be shown on your calculations automatically.

Data is entered into a spreadsheet in cells. Each cell has a reference which locates it on the grid, a column reference across the top of the spreadsheet is alphabetical (for example, A, B, C, etc.) and a row reference down the left hand side is numerical (for example, 1, 2, 3, etc.). It is rather like the game of Battleships!

There are three main types of data which can be entered into a spreadsheet:

- **Text labels** These are the words and headings which 'label' the parts of the spreadsheet so you can describe what each does.
- **Numeric data** These are the numbers on which calculations will be made by the program.

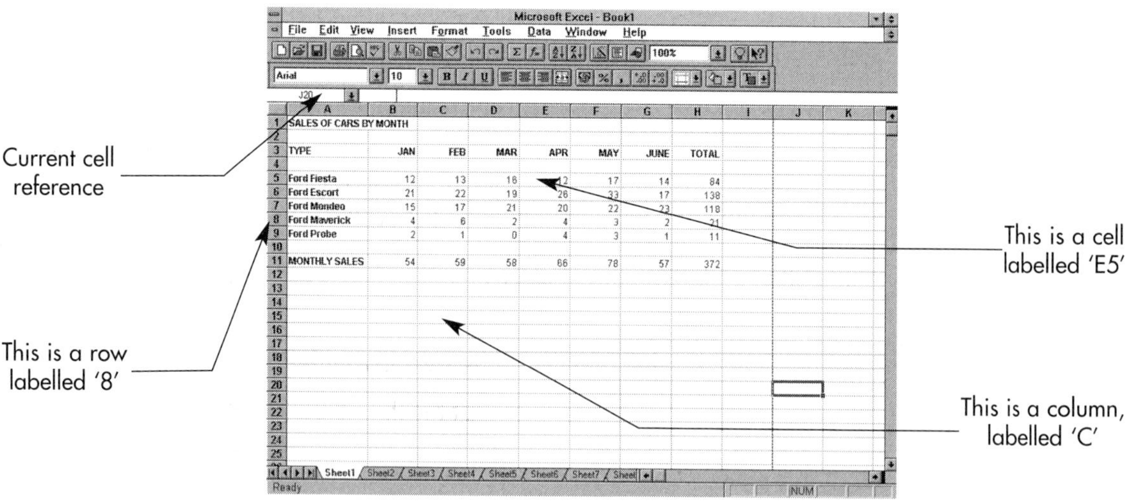

Figure 6 A simple spreadsheet

 Formulae — These are the instructions which the program will use to carry out any calculations.

Figure 6 shows all these elements on a simple spreadsheet.

When text is entered into a cell which is too small, it spills over across the cells next to it until the whole text label can be seen, as in the title 'Sales of Cars by Month' in Figure 6. The title has been entered into cell A1 but stretches across cell B1.

The other labels in the spreadsheet refer to specific columns or rows and you will probably have noticed that column A has been made wider to take the longest of these into account – 'Monthly Sales'. Data within each cell can be left justified, right justified or centred in exactly the same way as text in a word processed file. In Figure 6, the data in column A has been justified to the left of each cell, whereas the data in columns B to H has been justified to the right of each cell. This facility can be used to improve the look of your spreadsheet, especially if it is to be used as part of a formal report.

The content of cells can also be set so the computer automatically formats any data when it is entered. The cells in most spreadsheets are formatted as 'general' cells - where they will accept data in any alpha/numeric format. However, it is possible to format or restrict what will be accepted in any cell. This can be done in two ways. Firstly, one or more cells can be set up so they will only accept data of a particular type, such as numbers or as a date. Secondly, cells can be set so they will alter data entered in one format into another more acceptable form. For example a numeric date entered as 23/3/02 can be automatically amended to show 23 March 2002 in the cell. Similarly cells formatted to contain currency or percentages will automatically insert a '£' sign or a '%' symbol. This can be particularly useful when entering decimals, as cells can be formatted to convert any data automatically so it displays a given number of decimal places.

Editing data

Data in the spreadsheet can be added, altered or deleted using the editing facilities, by moving the cursor to the cell that you wish to edit and then keying in the new data. The contents of a cell can be duplicated into any number of other cells if required. This process, known as **replication**, can save a great deal of time when similar data has to be entered into a number of different cells.

Replication is the process of duplicating a formula

or numeric data any number of times. The program automatically alters the cell references as they are inserted into other rows or columns.

Entering a formula into a cell will enable you to add, subtract, multiply and divide the numbers you have entered. When keying in formulae you can use the following symbols:

- + sign for addition
- – sign for subtraction
- * sign for multiplication
- / sign for division.

The exact instructions you need to enter for a correct formula vary slightly depending on which spreadsheet you are using. Your teacher or the software reference manual will give you the exact format to follow.

To check the accuracy of the formulae you have entered into your spreadsheet, it is possible to print a copy of the sheet showing the formulae rather than the answers. Again, your teacher will show you how this can be done on your program as the procedure can vary. It is an ideal way of being able to check that you have completed the spreadsheet correctly.

Once entered, most spreadsheets will allow you to reorder the data shown on the page. This is usually a simple process involving the click of a mouse and has the advantage of allowing an operator to enter information in any order and then using the spreadsheet to re-sort it into the required sequence. This is particularly useful, for example, when adding a new product to an existing spreadsheet in which the products are held in alphabetical order.

Exercises

1 List the three types of data which can be entered into a cell in a spreadsheet, and explain the purpose of each. (4)

2 List the keys, together with their functions, which you would use in a spreadsheet formula. (4)

3 What is meant by the term *replication*? (3)

4 Explain why you would right justify the column headings over numerical data. (2)

5 Explain what happens when a text string that is too long for a cell is entered. (1)

6 Why would you enter data into a spreadsheet and not use a standard table? (6)

1 Load your spreadsheet program and set up a spreadsheet using the following data in the cells indicated:

	A	B	C	D	E	F	G	H
1	MONTHLY CAR SALES							
2								
3	TYPE OF CAR	JAN	FEB	MAR	APR	MAY	JUN	TOTAL
4								
5	Ford Fiesta	12	13	16	12	17	14	
6	Ford Focus	21	22	19	26	33	17	
7	Ford Mondeo	15	17	21	20	22	23	
8	Ford Maverick	4	6	2	4	3	2	
9	Ford Probe	2	1	0	4	3	1	
10								
11	MONTHLY SALES							

2 Check your work for accuracy and correct any errors in the text labels or numerical data.

3 In the cells at the bottom of column B, opposite the Monthly Sales (row 11), enter a formula to add the contents of the sales for each of the five types of car sold in January.

4 Replicate (repeat) this formula so that you have totals for each of the remaining months, February to June.

5 Enter a formula in cell H5 to add sales for each month for the Ford Fiesta, then replicate (repeat) this formula to give totals for the other types of car.

6 Enter a formula in cell H11 to give an overall total of cars sold for all months. You can do this by either adding up the totals in column H or the totals in row 11. Save your spreadsheet to disk using the filename CARS then print a copy on plain A4 paper.

If you have entered all the formula correctly, any change to the numeric data should also be reflected in the totals without you having to do anything. In cell D9 change the number of Ford Probes sold from 0 to 1. As you do this, watch the effect on the column total (cell D11), the row total (cell H9) and the overall total (cell H11). Are the formulae in your spreadsheet changing the totals for you? Try changing some of the other figures and see the effect on your totals.

7 Save your amended spreadsheet using the filename CARS1, then exit from the program.

1 Load your spreadsheet program and input the following data. Enter formulae to calculate both row and column totals. Save the spreadsheet using the filename MEDALS and then print a copy on plain A4 paper.

Athletics Medal Table				
Country	**Gold**	**Silver**	**Bronze**	**Total**
England	3	8	13	
N Ireland	1	3	8	
Wales	0	6	2	
France	4	6	2	
Italy	6	9	2	
Germany	8	10	11	
Totals				

Table 1 Medals

2 Insert a new row to include Scotland after England. Enter the following medals for Scotland: nine bronze, 12 silver and four gold.

3 Some of the original figures are incorrect. England should have six gold medals; N. Ireland has four silver and six bronze and Germany has five gold, seven silver and 12 bronze. Update the spreadsheet with these new figures. Save your spreadsheet to disk using the file name MEDALS1 and then print a copy on plain A4 paper.

4 Insert two further rows together with their respective medal scores:

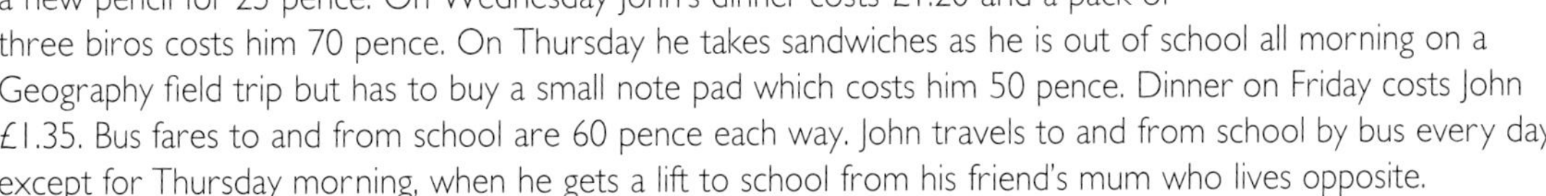

Belgium	**2**	**4**	**7**
Luxembourg	**0**	**2**	**2**

Now print an additional copy of your spreadsheet showing the formulae you have used.

Extension material

John is given £4.00 each day by his dad to cover the cost of buying school dinners, bus fares to and from school and any other items he needs such as pens, pencils and paper. On Monday he spends £1.55 on dinner and buys a pad of A4 paper for £1.10. On Tuesday he spends £1.30 on his dinner, lends his girlfriend, Karen, £1.00 and buys a new pencil for 25 pence. On Wednesday John's dinner costs £1.20 and a pack of three biros costs him 70 pence. On Thursday he takes sandwiches as he is out of school all morning on a Geography field trip but has to buy a small note pad which costs him 50 pence. Dinner on Friday costs John £1.35. Bus fares to and from school are 60 pence each way. John travels to and from school by bus every day except for Thursday morning, when he gets a lift to school from his friend's mum who lives opposite.

Set up a spreadsheet to calculate how much John spent each day on the three different forms of expenditure – Dinners, Bus fares and Other items. Enter a column to show how much money he received each day from his dad and then calculate how much money John had left at the end of each day and at the end of the week.

More on spreadsheets

Spreadsheets are very powerful programs which can be used to carry out complex caclulations if required. In previous units you have used them to complete some fairly straightforward tasks. All formulae are preceded by the equals sign (=) to indicate to the program the need to carry out a calculation on the contents of the cells which follow.

The formulae in spreadsheets allow you to carry out calculations on the numerical data input into cells. They should be entered in to the cell in which you require the answer to the calculation to be stored or displayed. So far, most of the calculations you have used have been to carry out simple addition.

Addition

There are two ways in which an addition formula can be entered into a spreadsheet. The first requires you to enter the address of each cell you would like added. If you were adding together the monthly sales figures for the year (they may be stored in the cells B2 to M2) the formula would look like this:

=B2+C2+D2+E2+F2+G2+H2+I2+J2+K2+L2+M2

This is quite some formula! It is long-winded, takes time to enter and is prone to errors, as this method of addition requires you to enter each individual cell reference. If the cell addresses to be added are consecutive, then the spreadsheet only requires you to enter the reference address of the first and last cells, separated by either two full stops or a colon. This instruction needs to be placed in brackets and preceded by the command 'sum', so the program knows it will have to carry out a calculation. The previous formula could now be written as:

=SUM(B2..M2) or =SUM(B2:M2)

Each of these is much quicker to input into the

computer and far less likely to contain errors. Both formulae will give the same answer.

Some spreadsheets have an 'autosum' facility, indicated by the [Σ] button on the toolbar. This facility will add cells automatically. To use it, highlight the cells to be added ending in the cell where the total is required. Then just click on the autosum button. The appropriate formula will automatically be entered to add the highlighted row or column of data.

Subtraction

To take away or subtract the contents of one cell from another is relatively easy. The equals sign (=) should be entered followed by the address of the cell which contains the data from which the deduction is to be made. The equals sign (=) should be followed by two cell addresses separated by the minus sign (−), the second cell address being that which contains the data to be deducted. The formula will be written as follows:

=D3−F3 (where the contents of cell F3 is deducted from the contents of cell D3)

Multiplication

As with subtraction, the two cell addresses to be multiplied are separated by the multiplication sign (*) and follow the equals sign (=). The formula for multiplying two cells is written as follows:

=C3*G2 (where the contents of cell C3 will be multiplied by the contents of cell G2)

Division

The formula for division follows the same pattern of an equals sign (=) followed by two cell addresses, separated by the division sign (/). The second cell is divided into the first. This formula is written as follows:

=D4/D5 (where the contents of cell D4 is divided by the contents of cell D5)

Multiple formulae

Combinations of mathematical instructions can be carried out in one formula, providing they follow the basic arithmetical precedence. Where more than one mathematical instruction is to be carried out within a cell brackets or parentheses should contain that part of the sum to be calculated first.

For example, if the contents of five cells need to be totalled and then the contents of a sixth cell are deducted from the answer, the formula would be written as follows:

=sum(A1:A5)−A6 (where A1:A5 represents the five cells to be added and A6 is the cell to be deducted)

Calculations (or formulae) which contain multiple parts can be very useful. Two of the most commonly used in a business environment are averages and percentages.

Averages

These are calculated by adding the contents of a number of cell addresses and then dividing by the number of cells added together. For example, if you wish to average the contents of the five cells B2, B3, B4, B5 and B6, the formula would be written as follows:

=sum(B2:B6)/5 (where B2:B6 first adds the contents of the cells and then they are divided (/) by the number five) which is the number of cells added together)

Similarly, if you wish to average the contents of four cells, E4, E5, E6 and E7, the formula would be written as:

=sum(E4:E7)/4

Your spreadsheet may have an average function that will automatically calculate averages for you. The formula usually used for this =average(E4:E7), where E4:E7 is the range of cells to be averaged by the formula.

Percentages

Calculating a percentage using a spreadsheet is no different from using a calculator, with the exception that data is already stored in the cells, rather than being input directly into the machine. To find the percentage that the contents of one cell is of the contents of another, divide the second cell into the first and then multiply by 100. For example, to find the percentage that 30 is of 50, if cell A3 contains 30 and cell A5 contains 50, the formula would be written as follows:

=(A3/A5)*100

Essentially this is a division formula with the answer multiplied by 100 so as to give the answer as a percentage, i.e. out of 100.

Exercises

1 List the four different mathematical functions which can be entered into a spreadsheet formula. (4)

2 Explain why you would not enter all the cell references of a string of consecutive cells to be added in a formula. What alternative method would you use? (4)

3 Write a brief paragraph to explain to a friend how the **autosum** facility works. What, if any, are the drawbacks of using this facility? (4)

4 What formula would you use to create an average? (2)

5 What formula would you use to generate a percentage? (2)

6 Explain carefully what is meant by the phrase *what if calculations*. (4)

1 Load your spreadsheet program and input the following data. Enter formulae to calculate both row and column totals.

CINEMA ATTENDANCES	Odeon Queens Sq.	Odeon Park St	Odeon High St	Total admitted
Monday	97	74	102	
Tuesday	78	65	80	
Wednesday	100	80	120	
Thursday	85	54	46	
Friday	167	148	201	
Saturday	180	175	150	
Totals				

Table 2 Cinema attendance

2 Insert a new column on the right, with the heading 'Price per Ticket'. Enter the price for Monday, Tuesday, Wednesday and Thursday as £2.00 and for Friday and Saturday as £3.00.

3 Insert another new column with the heading 'Sales Revenue'. Enter formulae to calculate the sales revenue for each day by multiplying the total admitted by the price per ticket. Save your spreadsheet to disk using the file name CINEMA and then print a copy on plain A4 paper.

4 Your employer is considering increasing the price of admission by 50 pence on Wednesdays and Saturdays. Enter the new price in your spreadsheet.

5 This increase in price is expected to reduce the number of people who will attend each of the three cinemas by 20 on both Wednesdays and Saturdays. Enter the new attendance figures in the appropriate cells then print another copy of your spreadsheet on plain A4 paper. Use the file name CINEMA1 to save your work.

1 Set up the following data in a spreadsheet. It contains a class list of pupils and the scores they obtained in tests in several subjects.

Pupil	Maths	English	Science	History	Total
Shaheda Ali	45	57	34	60	
Nicola Baker	67	60	68	72	
Joseph Govan	24	45	50	28	
Chris Greenslade	34	33	38	41	
Nichola Kates	53	61	58	71	
Shuheb Khan	23	40	51	42	
Paul Marshall	74	76	80	63	
James McMurry	67	62	50	65	
Alexandra Somers	48	52	37	59	
Jennifer Thomas	26	30	35	25	

Table 3 Test scores

2 Insert and replicate formulae to show the total marks for each pupil.

3 Insert a new column entitled 'Average Mark' and use a formula to calulate the average mark scored in all tests by each pupil.

4 The following scores have been received following the French test. Insert an additional column in the appropriate place in the spreadsheet and enter the data.

Shaheda	23	Chris	31	Paul	22
Nicola	15	Nichola	39	James	27
Joseph	26	Shuheb	28	Alexandra	10
				Jennifer	19

Table 4 French test scores

Check the formulae you have inserted to calculate the average mark for each pupil and amend them if necessary to take account of the new subject data.

5 The total mark for all five tests is 400. Insert a column to calculate the total percentage mark for each pupil. Print a copy of your works.

Extension material

The weather has been abnormally wet recently and various weather centres around the British Isles have been collecting data on rainfall for the past seven days. You have been asked to enter the data onto a spreadsheet in alphabetical order of weather centre, to show the total rainfall measured each day, the average rainfall measured at each centre over the seven days and the percentage of rainfall each centre has measured. All measurements are in millimetres.

CENTRE	DAILY TOTALS						
Bristol	3	10	9	2	16	8	6
Cardiff	4	11	8	3	12	10	7
Manchester	5	15	9	6	18	12	5
Aberdeen	7	13	12	5	13	12	7
Belfast	6	9	12	4	15	9	3
Birmingham	11	6	6	10	13	8	5
Exeter	4	10	7	0	8	5	3
Newcastle	9	8	6	12	13	10	6

Table 5 Daily totals

Databases

A database is a collection of information, usually stored on a computer system. It is also known as an electronic filing system. Traditionally, a business or organisation would have kept all this information on a card index system that was kept up-to-date by amending the cards by hand, a long and time-consuming process. Today, computers can do this work for you.

In this day and age, everyone becomes part of a 'database' from the day they are born. The National Health Service records and stores information about every individual from the moment they are born. At school, your personal details will be held on a computer system to make administration easier. As soon as you apply for a driver's licence, the DVLC retains the details on computer. The telephone network operates the directory enquiry system which holds names, addresses and numbers for all telephone subscribers in the United Kingdom. Every time you purchase something through mail order or catalogue the company will check the goods are available on its computerised stock list.

The structure of a database

If databases are so much a part of your life, then how do they work? The details of each person or product are held on computer as records that are made up of a series of fields. Each field holds one piece of information, for example, surname, date of birth or postcode. These individual fields collectively form a record where all the information relating to one person or product is held. All the related records form a file of data in which all the information is held.

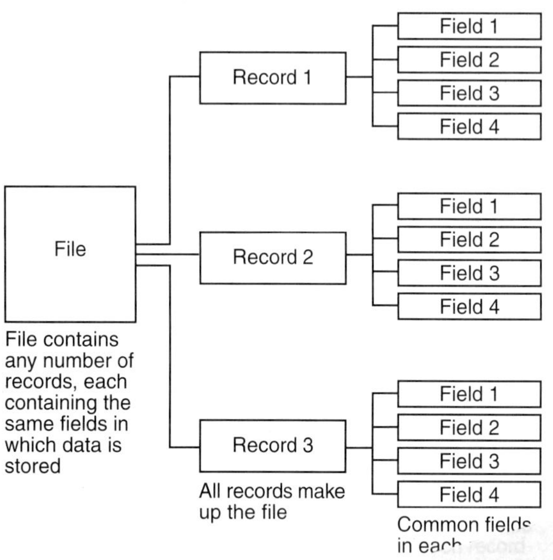

Figure 7 The structure of a database

File

This holds or stores all the records which have a common theme. For example, the data on each pupil in a particular year group would be stored together. Similarly, all the health records of the patients for a particular doctor would be stored in one file.

Record

If the database is about a firm's customers, for example, each record would include details of their names, addresses, when they last purchased goods, what goods were purchased, when they paid for them, etc. If the database is about goods held in stock within a company it would contain the name of the product, its reference coding, the current number held, the date and quanitity of the last order, the name and address of the supplier, etc.

Field

Each record is made up of a series of fields in which the individual items of data relating to the record are held. These fields are given titles, or field names, and each record has the same number of fields. To help with the accuracy of inputting data, fields can be coded to accept only a certain type of data. The most commonly used data types are alphabetic, numeric, alphanumeric and date. Once coded to receive only a certain data type, information entered in the field that does not match, will be rejected by the program. This helps ensure that only correct data is entered into specified fields of the database.

Coding fields

To save time when entering information into a database many organisations use a form of coding, which gives a shortened version of the data. The result is, less data has to be keyed in and less disk storage space is needed. For example, a firm storing information about its customers may code the [illegible] code such as this:

S = South M = Midlands N = North

Alternatively, a garage may code the type of car it is selling as follows:

S = Saloon E = Estate H = Hatchback

This form of abbreviated data can save considerable amounts of time and effort but, when used, it is important that all users of the database are aware of the coding [illegible] information. [illegible] garage [illegible] should not [illegible] as this would lead to [illegible] Regions could be coded numerically, for example, 1 = South, 2 = Midlands and 3 = North.

Database uses

Databases can provide firms with an increasing amount of useful information about their products and customers. The use of customer loyalty cards such as the Tesco Clubcard or the Boots Advantage Card means that every time your card is swiped by the checkout operator, the supermarket's computer database records details of who you are, where you live, the store you are using and all the products you have purchased.

Over a period of several weeks a picture of where you shop and which products you purchase on a regular basis can be built up. The supermarket can then use this information to ensure the right products (i.e. the ones you buy) are in the store nearest to you. They can also target you with information about new products or special offers which may be of direct interest to you. For example, if computer records show that in the course of your shopping you purchase a number of different low fat and healthy eating products, and if a new low sugar soft drink is launched on the market, the company will send you details and possibly a money-off-voucher to encourage you to purchase it, because your shopping profile indicates you buy this type of product.

Advantages

There are a number of advantages to computerised databases, including:

- They allow large amounts of information to be stored in a relatively small space.
- Information can be quickly and easily retrieved from the database due to the computer's speed.
- Data can be re-sorted very quickly into another sequence if required.
- Information can be kept up-to-date with little effort.
- Information not previously available from a manual filing system can be obtained from the database, which will provide management with more effective information.
- Selective information can be obtained quickly, for example a list of customers who live in the London area.

Disadvantages

There are, however, some disadvantages but these are mostly connected with setting up the database rather than operating it:

- The computer equipment on which to store the data can be expensive.
- The cost of setting up a new database can be very high.
- Staff need to be trained in the necessary computer skills to make effective use of the system.
- Information cannot be obtained from the system if the computer fails.

Setting up a database requires considerable thought and planning. What information will be held in each record? How will it be used? Where will the original data come from? How accurate will it be? How can the file, once set up, be kept up-to-date? Does the information come under the control of the Data Protection Act?

It is very costly to set up a new database and it becomes even more costly if it does not contain all the information which the company requires! Some firms will use their existing records as the basis of their database, others may buy in data from a firm in a similar line of business. However the information is obtained, it must be kept up-to-date if it is to be of any real use. Sending advertising literature to the wrong address is unlikely to obtain an order and will cost the firm money for which they will see no return.

Raw data for a database may be collected on a standard form; sometimes referred to as a data capture form. This would contain all the fields in a record together with space in which the data could be entered. Once completed the forms are passed to a computer operator who would key the data into the computer system.

Exercises

1 Explain what is meant by (a) a field (b) a record and (c) a file. (4)

2 Draw a diagram to show the relationship between fields, records and files. (2)

3 What are the benefits of using a coding system in a field? (3)

4 Name two disadvantages of coding data. (2)

5 What is a customer loyalty card? Give an example of one. (3)

6 Explain why firms use loyalty cards. (2)

7 What problems would Vodaphone encounter in trying to maintain a mobile phone directory for all its users? (3)

8 What is a data capture form? Why would a firm use one? (2)

Use your word processor or desktop publishing system to design a data capture form to collect all the necessary information needed to set up a database of all staff cars which come onto your school or college site. You will need to record details of the make, model and registration number as well as the colour and vehicle excise duty expiry date. What other information would be useful? Once you have collected the data, enter it into a database.

The leaders of the local youth club you attend are considering setting up a database of their members. They have asked you to prepare a brief report detailing what information they would need to store on computer in each member's record and explaining the advantages and disadvantages of doing this. Would you recommend the use of coding in some fields? If so, which ones and what form would you suggest the coding takes?

Extension material

1 You have been given the following membership list for your local youth club. Using appropriate computer software, set up a database. Print a copy of the information and check it carefully for any errors.

Surname	First name	Date of birth	Address	Main hobby
Nash	Mike	22.07.88	14 Robarts Street	Ice skating
Germaine	Sue	14.01.90	26 Chessel Road	Reading
Kelly	Connor	29.11.90	29 Robarts Street	Computers
Hughes	Darren	31.08.89	12 Butterfield Walk	Music
Angle	Anna	26.12.92	146 Kenn Road	Craft
Derbyshire	John	25.10.91	207 Station Road	Modelling
Richards	Tim	11.05.91	1 Wordsworth Avenue	Computers
Stevens	Judith	05.06.91	23 Elton Road	Cycling
Landon	Elizabeth	17.10.91	73 Griffin Road	Computers
Morgan	Gary	12.10.91	31 Butterfield Walk	Football
Santino	Patricia	20.02.90	14 Coleridge Lane	Computers
James	David	27.05.89	109 Kenn Road	Football

Table 6 Membership list

2 The following members have resigned from the club. Delete their records.
David James Tim Richards Sue Germaine

3 The following new members have enrolled. Add their records to the database:
Amy Drew, 35 Hamilton Road, 30.06.92, football.
Barry Styles, 67 Old Church Road, 14.03.92, computers.

4 Now save your work using the filename YOUTH and print a hard copy of the membership list in alphabetical order of surname on appropriate paper.

Databases: searching and sorting

Holding information in a database can save a considerable amount of storage space. However, the information held is of little use unless it can be retrieved quickly and easily. The following is a sample database set up for a garage selling second-hand cars. It has been kept deliberately small so that you can pick out the searches to check how they work.

Make	Model	Colour	Price (£)	Mileage
Ford	Focus	Blue	£5500	21500
Volvo	S40	Red	£9800	32100
Vauxhall	Vectra	Blue	£8600	39300
Renault	Laguna	Red	£10750	12600
Ford	Mondeo	Green	£9250	14900
Renault	Megane	White	£9000	19800
Peugeot	406	Blue	£10250	33750
Ford	Mondeo	Red	£6750	41100
Renault	Clio	Red	£6300	11300

Table 7 Second-hand car database

Retrieving information from a database is facilitated through a search or query facility. This requires you to state precisely what you need from the database. Searches can be carried out on the contents of any field, and these can use one search criterion or more than one. Each search criterion is made up of three parts: the fieldname to be searched, the criterion to be used and the value or content in the field being searched (see Figure 8).

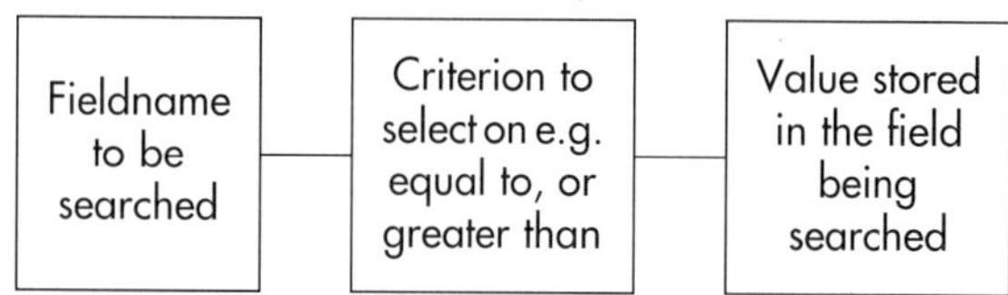

Figure 8 Search

Single search criteria

To find the details of a particular make of car you would use the 'equal to' search criterion. For example, a customer looking for a Renault car would use the following search:

Make → is equal to → Renault

This would then produce the following list of cars, all of which are Renaults:

Renault	Laguna	Red	£10,750	12,600
Renault	Megane	White	£9,000	19,800
Renault	Clio	Red	£6,300	11,300

For another customer seeking a car, who did not want a red one, the criterion 'not equal to' will exclude specific data in a specified field. The search would therefore be:

Colour → is not equal to → Red

This would produce the following list of cars, none of which is red in colour:

Ford	Focus	Blue	£5,500	21,500
Vauxhall	Vectra	Blue	£8,600	39,300
Ford	Mondeo	Green	£9,250	14,900
Renault	Megane	White	£9,000	19,800
Peugeot	406	Blue	£10,250	33,700

Single searches can also be used which will retrieve data that is 'greater than' or 'less than' a specified value. For example a customer may be looking for a car and the minimum price they wish to pay is £10,000. In this case the search criterion would be:

Price → is greater than → £10,000

This would give the following list of cars, which are priced at more than £10,000:

Renault	Laguna	Red	£10,750	12,600
Peugeot	406	Blue	£10,250	33,700

Alternatively, a customer may be looking for a car with a recorded mileage below 15,000 miles, in which case the search criterion 'less than' would be used:

Mileage → is less than → 15,000

This would give the following list of cars all of which have a recorded mileage less than the 15,000 miles:

Renault	Laguna	Red	£10,750	12,600
Ford	Mondeo	Green	£9,250	14,900
Renault	Clio	Red	£6,300	11,300

Multiple search criteria

This form of search can be used to narrow down or limit the records which will be selected, and so help the user to obtain only the information they require. For example, a customer seeking a Mondeo for more than £8,000 would use the following search criteria:

Model → is equal to → Mondeo **AND**
Price → is greater than → £8,000

This would give the following:

Ford	Mondeo	Green	£9,250	14,900

Similarly, a customer seeking a Renault car with less than 15,000 miles would use the following search criteria:

Make → is equal to → Renault **AND**
Mileage → is less than → 15,000

This would give the following vehicles to choose from:

Renault	Laguna	Red	£10,750	12,600
Renault	Clio	Red	£6,300	11,300

Using multiple search criteria, searches in databases can be narrowed down to eliminate what is not required. In the two examples above the criteria have been linked using AND. This reduces the possibilities as more search criteria are added using the AND facility. However, some searches may seek alternatives, in which case they should be linked using the OR facility. For example, another customer may be looking to find either a Volvo or a Vauxhall car. In this case the following search would be used:

Make → is equal to → Volvo **OR**
Make → is equal to → Vauxhall

This examines the same field but for different content. The effect of this when applied to the database would be as follows:

Volvo	S40	Red	£9,800	32,100
Vauxhall	Vectra	Blue	£8,600	39,300

Both of these cars meet the requirements of the customer.

Sorting information

Once selected, information can be listed either on the screen or printed out as a hard copy. When more than one record has been selected it is helpful if the data can be sorted and listed in a particular sequence. This could be alphabetically by surname, numerically by age or by code, relating to a product range.

Output

Most databases now allow you to present information that has been selected in a predefined form. These forms place the information on to the screen in a more user friendly way than in column form listed under the field names in which the data is stored. This makes information much easier to see and understand and still allows the operator to amend information if required. Output can also be obtained in label format. This allows information to be printed out on labels which can then be used for mailing or other purposes. This facility is particularly useful for companies who store details of their customers, or potential customers, on a database and may need to communicate with them, either in total, or just certain categories.

Exercises

1 Draw a diagram to show the three parts of any search criterion you would use in a database. (3)

2 Using the information given in the database of second-hand cars in Table 7 on page 40, decide what criteria you would use to find the following.
   a) Cars which have a mileage of no more than 20 000 miles.
   b) Mondeo cars which are priced at £9 000 or more.
   c) Renault cars which are red and have a mileage below 12 000.
   d) Ford and Vauxhall cars which are blue. (4)

3 Carefully explain the difference between using the terms *and* and *or* to link together two criteria. (2)

4 Write down the steps you would follow to sort a file into descending alphabetical order. (2)

5 Explain with the aid of an example when you would use multiple search rather than single search criteria. (5)

6 Other than alphabetical sequence, explain two other ways in which a business may want data sorted. Give examples to support your answers. (4)

Set up a database using the following information:

Surname	First name	Age	Postal town	Region*	Model bought
Mason	Paul	45	Bristol	SW	D520
Wilkins	Thomas	56	Manchester	N	D240
Orchard	Michelle	33	Carlisle	N	D450
Webster	Michael	26	Bristol	SW	D200
Battersby	Nichola	34	Aberdeen	SC	D200
Crane	William	76	Birmingham	M	D520
Moore	Daphne	67	Truro	SW	B180
McKenzie	Sean	18	Bromsgrove	M	D450
Evans	Rhys	23	Bristol	SW	B280
Bradley	Elizabeth	27	Exeter	SW	B280
Fearst	Malcolm	42	Coventry	M	D450
Gates	Jenny	50	Bradford	N	D240
McCarthy	Amanda	41	Newcastle	N	D240
Kapoor	Raj	37	Birmingham	M	B380
Paterno	Sergio	25	Walsall	M	D450
Winston	Rosemary	65	Newquay	SW	B180
Gatsby	Jonathan	29	Perth	SC	B380
Garrison	Ellen	42	Durham	N	D200
Edwards	Doris	58	Exeter	SW	D520
Madson	Virginia	49	Nottingham	M	B280

* SC = Scotland N = North M = Midlands SW = South West

Table 8 Database data

1 Check your work to ensure that it contains no errors. Save your work using the filename GOODS, then print a copy of the file in alphabetical order on plain A4 paper.

2 The following amendments need to be made to the data:

- Virginia Madson is aged 39 not 49.
- Daphne Moore's surname has been misspelt and should be Moor.
- Amanda McCarthy has now bought a D450.
- William Crane has moved to Bristol in the South West region.
- Malcolm Fearst has purchased a B280.

3 Print a list of all customers living in the South West region in alphabetical order of surname.

4 The Sales Department has asked for a list of all customers aged 50 and over.

5 All D240 models sold in the Northern region need to be recalled for modification. Produce a list for the production department.

6 All customers aged over 50 who own a D520 are to be sent some promotional advertising material. Prepare a list of those involved.

The following information is part of a supermarket product database. It shows the product and its description, the number of grammes in each tin, the cost per tin, the retail price, the supplier (which is coded) and the number of weeks for delivery. Suppliers have been coded using the following codes: Heinz = HZ; Crosse & Blackwell = CB; HP Products = HP.

Product	Description	Grammes	Cost (p)	Retail Price (p)	Supplier	Delivery
Beans	Baked	250	19	21	HZ	2
	Baked	450	29	34	HZ	2
	Baked	650	42	49	CB	3
	Butter	250	45	49	HP	1
	Red	450	55	62	CB	2
	Green	250	67	75	HP	1
	Broad	350	45	49	CB	2
Peas	Garden	350	28	31	CB	3
	Marrowfat	450	25	28	HZ	3
	Marrowfat	650	42	46	HZ	3
	Processed	250	22	25	CB	1
	Processed	450	34	39	HP	2
	Mushy	250	28	35	HP	2
	Petit Pois	250	35	42	HP	4
Carrots	Sliced	450	26	30	CB	2
	Whole	450	32	38	CB	1
	Baby	250	60	69	HZ	1
Spaghetti	Hoops	250	19	23	HZ	3
	Hoops	450	29	35	HZ	4
	Shapes	250	24	28	CB	2

Table 9 Supermarket Data

1 Enter the information onto your database and check it carefully for errors. Save your file to disk and then print a copy of the database in alphabetical order of product.

2 Make the following amendments to the data:

- Marrowfat peas are no longer available in the 650 g size. Delete this record.
- The supplier of 450 g Baked Beans has changed to Crosse & Blackwell.
- The size of the butter beans should be 350 g.
- Sliced carrots now cost 27 pence and the retail price has increased to 32 pence.
- The price of all spaghetti hoops has increased by 2 pence.
- Delivery times for baked beans have been reduced by one week.
- Tinned baby mushrooms are to be added to the stock list. The 250g tin costs 28 pence, sells for 36 pence, and is supplied by Heinz. Delivery takes three weeks.

3 The purchasing department is trying to reduce stock levels by reducing the time taken for the delivery of products. Print a copy of all products which have a delivery time of 2 weeks or more.

4 Management is concerned about high price levels and would like a list of all products which are sold for more than 50 pence or which have a cost price of more than 45 pence. They would also like a second list of tins that weigh more than 350 g and are not supplied by Heinz.

5 The marketing team wish to promote a 'small is interesting' campaign and would like to know which tins are 250 g or less and cost 40 pence or less.

Extension material

You are to set up a database of all the students in your class, recording the following information:

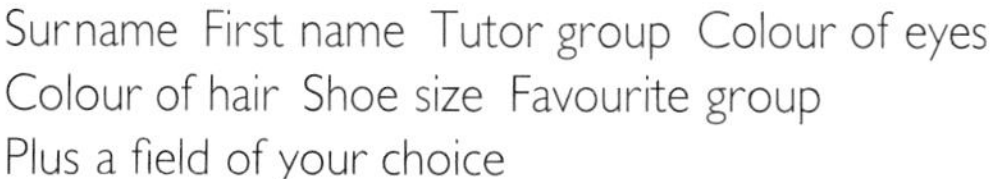

Surname First name Tutor group Colour of eyes
Colour of hair Shoe size Favourite group
Plus a field of your choice

When you have set up the file, check each record for accuracy and then ask your teacher to provide you with some queries or interrogations on the data.

PART 2

The Workplace

The office environment

The conditions and surroundings in which we work are very important to us. They can affect the way in which we approach our work and can act as a significant factor in motivating us to work harder. If you went into a local café for a drink and found the floor dirty, tables stacked high with dirty cups and saucers, the counter stained and unwashed and the assistant wearing grubby clothes with dirt under his fingernails, you would be unlikely to stay. On the other hand, if the café was clean and airy, tables were laid out with freshly ironed tablecloths, sandwiches and cakes were in an hygienic display cabinet and the assistant wore a clean, tidy uniform, you would not think twice about ordering your drink! An office environment is very similar to this. You notice and grumble when it is dirty or untidy, but when it is right, you take it for granted.

Offices have to be functional. You must be able to carry out the day-to-day business of the firm efficiently. There has to be adequate space to allow you to use equipment, such as a word processor. There must be storage space for documents and files so that they can be kept safely and easily found when needed again. There has to be space to allow you to move from one part of the office to another without interfering or distracting others from their work. There must be adequate lighting so that you can see what you are doing especially if you are using a computer. And there has to be sufficient ventilation and heating to make the room comfortable to work in.

Today, most offices meet these requirements. It is in the interests of firms to provide good working conditions and a comfortable environment for their workers. If they do not, employees will become dissatisfied and less inclined to work hard. If workers are uncomfortable, they will soon look for another job where the employer treats them better.

External office location

The position of the office within a town or an industrial area can be important to workers for a number of reasons. When choosing an office site employers should consider the following factors:

- How near is it to public transport, such as buses and trains? Some workers may not have their own transport and lengthy journey times add to the working day.
- What are the parking arrangements? Is there a car park nearby, and if so, is it free or do you have to pay? If the firm has its own car park, who is allowed to use it?
- How near are the local shops, banks and other facilities? Many working people have to shop during their lunch break or immediately at the end of their working day and do not have time to get into the centre of town.
- What local eating facilities are there that would be suitable for lunch? Does the firm have a staff canteen and if so how much does a meal or a snack cost?
- Are there crèche facilities or child minders nearby for those workers who have small children? Very few businesses provide these for their staff despite the considerable increase in recent years of both partners working.

It should be noted that whilst the factors above are important, many firms are faced with financial restrictions which prevent them from taking all or any of them into consideration when locating their business. Many businesses develop from small units which initially employ only two or three people and where expansion is a financial risk which has to be minimised. As the business grows, it may take over more accommodation in the existing building even though the external factors are not ideal for the workforce. The cost of moving to another, more suitable part of town may be too high.

Internal office location

Once the external site of the office has been decided, consideration can be given to the internal layout. The position of various offices within premises depends primarily on their purpose. Careful consideration must be given to the following:

- The number of outside callers may determine that the reception area is placed close to the main entrance.
- The delivery of materials may require a production or storage area to have ground floor access.
- Heavy machinery such as photocopiers and printing equipment may need to be located in an area with specially strengthened floors.
- The central services of a firm such as the post room, reprographics or cloakroom facilities and toilets may need to be positioned to allow easy access by all workers.
- Access for the disabled may prevent the use of stepped areas or require proximity to wheelchair ramps and lifts.

Some companies, especially small businesses which have to share premises with other firms, may not have any choice in the areas that can be used for certain purposes, because the geography of the premises is not large enough to give them any choice. So, again finance needs to be taken into consideration when determining internal office location and may prevent the optimum layout being achieved.

Exercises

1. Carefully explain the difference between external and internal office location. (2)
2. Make a list of six factors you should take into account when considering a new external office location. (3)
3. Write a short paragraph explaining how a business' finances can affect the location of its premises. (3)

4 List three advantages and three disadvantages of expanding a firm's accommodation on the existing site, rather than moving to new purpose-built premises. (6)

5 When deciding where to locate the different departments of a business in new premises, there are many factors to be taken into account. List five. (3)

6 How could the Disabilities Act affect the layout of an office? (3)

Imagine you are working in an office 500 metres down the road from your school or college. Using the list of factors which can affect external office location, word process a brief report on the availability of public transport, parking, local shops, lunch facilities and child minding facilities. Is this a good location for your office? What additional facilities are required to make the area ideally suited?

Using Yellow Pages/Thomson Directory or any other suitable publication, make a list of all child minding/crèche facilities which are available in your local area. On a map of the area indicate where they are situated. Also indicate on the map the location of suitable car parking for up to 100 cars, the route of the local bus and train services and the location of local shopping areas. From the information you have obtained decide on a suitable location for a new office employing 150 staff. Are there any drawbacks to the site you have chosen?

Extension material

Your school or college has asked you to provide a new design for their administrative office environment. You need to consider and include the following:

-  the reception area
-  the office environment for the office staff
-  cloakroom and toilets
-  computer facilities for the school/college administration system
-  reprographics
-  the library and resources centre
-  rest room facilities

Use your word processing system or a desktop publishing package to prepare an outline plan of the new reception area. Try and base it on the existing outline shape of the school/college building if possible.

The office environment: office layout

Once the site of the office has been chosen and the plan of the internal design made, the layout of each office needs to be considered. Offices can be set out in any of the three ways described in this unit.

Cellular office

This is usually for one person and is a small to medium sized room with a door and windows (where the room contains an outside wall). It is called a 'cellular' office because it is one of a number of 'cells' or units within the building. There are a number of advantages to this type of office layout:

- They provide privacy for those who may need to discuss confidential issues with others.
- They can be locked, providing security for documents or money when the office is not staffed.
- They provide a quiet working environment where there are few distractions from other workers.
- They can confer status on the occupant as they are usually occupied by management.

There are also however, disadvantages which need to be considered:

- It is more difficult to supervise staff when they cannot easily be seen.
- They take up more space in a building as each office unit has to be partitioned with doors and windows.
- Junior staff find it more difficult to approach senior staff who occupy cellular offices because of the 'barriers' created by the partitioning.
- Separate offices require individual lighting and heating, which is more expensive to provide and operate than in a larger open office environment.

- It is less easy to talk to colleagues when they are in separate offices, which can slow down communication within an organisation.

Open plan office

Many organisations today make use of the open plan office layout where a large working area is broken down into smaller areas, each of which can accommodate small groups of workers, through the use of shoulder height screens or filing and storage cabinets. This type of office layout will normally accommodate several different grades of employee, and managers may work alongside their secretarial support and administrative assistants. The popularity of this style of layout lies in the advantages it brings:

- Staff supervision becomes easier and more subtle, as it is possible to see who is doing what in this open environment.
- Communication between different workers, different departments and management and subordinates is made easier because there are fewer artificial barriers to overcome.
- The layout of the office can be altered with relative ease by moving partitions or filing cabinets should it become necessary to increase or decrease the size of one or more working areas.
- Work flow between individuals and departments tends to be faster and more straightforward as workers can see and talk to each other with ease.
- In larger organisations, the open plan layout makes it easier to organise centralised services such as reprographics and wages departments.

Despite these points in favour of this form of office layout, some disadvantages still remain which need to be considered carefully:

- The open plan environment is often noisier to work in and there are often more distractions.
- There is less security as there are no lockable doors between working areas, although filing cabinets and cupboards that are often used as partitions can provide some secure means of storage.
- Lighting, ventilation and heating cannot be regulated to suit individual tastes as they can in a cellular office.
- Managers may resent not having their own office with the privacy that they may feel their position and status deserve.

Centralised offices

Some large firms will use an office layout which allows them to 'centralise' some of the facilities which are common to all departments or individuals. These services may include reprographics, the post room, the accounts department and the wages office. The reasons for using this layout may include the following:

- Staff with specialised skills can be grouped together to provide a more efficient service and to enable them to spread the service they offer to all departments. For example, reprographics and post room services.
- Bulky and noisy equipment, which may disturb the quiet working of an office, can be housed in one area to reduce any disruption it may cause.
- There is no need to provide expensive equipment such as photocopiers in all areas, when one or two centrally placed can provide for all departments and workers.

Again, disadvantages can also occur with this type of layout:

- Staff may not achieve the same level of personal contact when working in a centralised office area, which may slow down communications and reduce efficiency.
- Centralised services may not be immediately available to staff. These delays can lead to an increase in bureaucracy, which again reduces efficiency. Eg request slips may have to be completed to get photocopying done, rather than being able to do it yourself.

Very often firms will use a combination of all three types of office layout. Senior managers and directors may have cellular offices. Middle management and different grades of office staff may work together efficiently in an open plan office and be supported by centralised services for word processing, computer support, mailing and reprographics.

Exercises

1 Explain what is meant by the term *cellular office*. (2)

2 Give two examples of members of staff who would use a cellular office. (4)

3 What are the benefits of an open plan office? (4)

4 Name three different services which could be provided in a centralised office. (3)

5 Name two disadvantages of using a centralised office for these services. (2)

6 What are the disadvantages of a cellular office? How might a firm overcome these disadvantages? (5)

Using your word processor, prepare a table of advantages and disadvantages of each of the three types of office layout. Set your work out in two columns and make use of a border or boxed display so it is easier to see the distinction between the positive and negative points. Make sure you spell-check and proof-read your work carefully before printing a copy of the table for your notes.

You have been asked by your teacher to replan the classroom in which you are currently working so as to make it a more attractive and comfortable place to work in, and so as to accommodate fifteen computer work stations. Draw an outline plan of the room on your word processor or desktop publishing system and design an open plan layout. Remember to include storage facilities such as filing cabinets, book cases and cupboards and a supervisor's table or desk. You may move any radiators, heaters or other fixtures you wish, to accommodate work benches and desks, etc.

Extension material

You work for Aardvark Engineering plc who employ 1,500 people in their workshops manufacturing luxury bathroom and kitchen fittings. The firm is moving from an old cellular office block into new purpose-built accommodation beside the factory, which consists of two large rectangular office areas, on separate floors of the new building. Most of the office staff have been used to working in small offices with no more than one or two colleagues. You have been asked to suggest ways in which the new accommodation can best be used to create a modern, efficient working environment that will encourage fast and effective communication. You have been given a free hand to partition off any part of the new accommodation to create offices if you wish. The new office must accommodate the following:

- The Managing Director and her personal assistant
- 30 sales staff, three area sales managers and the Marketing Director
- 12 purchasing clerks and a purchasing supervisor
- 16 accounts clerks, three wages clerks, an accountant and the Financial Director
- Eight word processing operators, three receptionists/telephonists and an office manager
- Six reprographics technicians
- Two maintenance staff
- Two office cleaners

Prepare your suggested layout in the form of a word processed report supported by a simple outline plan of the two office areas showing how you intend to set them out.

Ergonomics

The word 'ergonomics' comes from the Greek 'erg', which means 'a unit of work', and is the study of work and the environment in which we work.

Over the years it has become apparent that a well designed and comfortable working environment can be a strong motivating factor for workers. Due to this, much attention has been given recently to the design of office layouts and the equipment and furniture in them. Designers are not just concerned with creating a pleasing effect for people to look at; they devote time to the development of offices and office equipment which are both functional and comfortable to use. This unit describes the key factors that contribute to the overall working environment.

Decoration

An office needs to be decorated in a pleasant manner. Bold, striking colours are avoided and neutral or pastel shades often used, such as cream, pale pink or blue, to try to give a warm and welcoming appearance. Carpets are more comfortable than vinyl floor covering or tiles and have the advantage of absorbing sound, so reducing noise levels. Care must be taken to select the correct type of industrial carpet that does not create dust, as this may affect electronic equipment like word processors.

Placing some pictures on walls will also enhance the office, however, it is good to allow staff to select these or provide their own to personalise their working space, especially in open plan offices.

Furniture

Wooden furniture has a softer look, but in the event of fire, steel furniture is less of a risk. Steel cabinets are also more fire resistant and this may help protect documents should a fire occur. Plastic and other man-made furniture products, which can also be used, may give off toxic fumes should they catch fire.

Chairs are also important for comfort especially if you spend much of the day sitting down. For keyboard operators, an adjustable swivel chair with good back support and a foot rest is essential. This will help prevent back and shoulder aches and by adjusting the height correctly it can also reduce the possibility of developing repetitive strain injury.

Where a computer terminal is in use, desks need to be large enough to have room for the computer and still provide adequate working space for documents and other work. Many office furniture manufacturers now provide a range of designs to cope with this, some L-shaped, others curved, allowing the keyboard operator to turn from one area of the desk to another using a swivel chair with the minimum of effort.

Fixtures and fittings

These are the permanent features of an office and include lighting, ventilation, heating and toilet facilities. Lighting in the office must be sufficient to allow all employees to see their work adequately. If visual display units are being used, the lighting should not cause reflections on the screen. It should also meet the minimum requirements for office lighting set out in the 1992 Health and Safety (Display Screen Equipment Regulations).

Ventilation in the office should allow a regular change of air, but not be too draughty or uncomfortable to work in. An increasing number of modern offices provide air-conditioned accommodation which maintains a constant temperature and humidity all year round. Heating must also be regulated according to the Offices, Shops and Railway Premises Act where minimum and maximum office temperatures are specified.

Using ergonomics to help create and design a comfortable and efficient working environment has a number of advantages:

- Staff are happier with pleasant, comfortable working conditions and will be motivated to work harder.
- Staff are less likely to be dissatisfied with their working environment and seek alternative employment.
- Recruitment is easier and a greater variety of applicants are likely to apply for a job where the working conditions are known to be good.
- Less time is lost through illness or other forms of absenteeism.
- Better working relationships are created as employees feel they are being treated with more consideration by employers.

Against these benefits must be set the drawback that providing these pleasant working conditions can be more costly. However, the increase in productivity which comfortable conditions usually brings will outweigh this.

Exercises

1. What does the word *ergonomics* mean? (2)
2. Which Act of Parliament has established legal requirements for
   a) lighting in computer rooms
   b) minimum and maximum office temperatures? (2)
3. What factors should be taken into account when designing an office or office furniture? (3)
4. Explain why bright colour schemes should not be used in office décor. (4)
5. Outline the benefits of carpeting a computer room. (3)

6 List the benefits of planning the office design using ergonomics for both the business and the employees. (6)

You work as a receptionist for Brennan Windows Ltd. who manufacture UPVC doors and windows. Your company is moving into a new purpose-built factory with offices and a reception area on the first floor. You have been asked to prepare a design for the reception area. You have been given the outline plan of the reception area (shown below) on which to prepare your design.

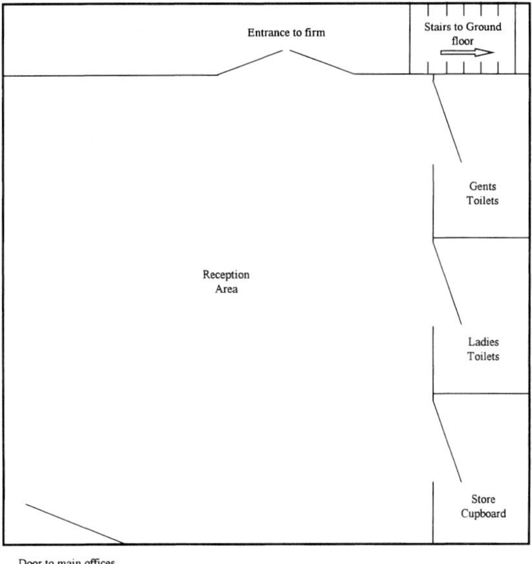

Word process a memorandum to your employer enclosing your plan created in Task One and explaining why you have set out the new reception area in the way you have.

Extension material

Try and obtain a recent catalogue from a company supplying office furniture and equipment. Make a list of the items in the plan of your reception area. Using the catalogue, work out the cost of equipping the new area. If you are including items such as plants and pictures you may need to find an additional source of costs for these. You may also find it easier to present your costings using a spreadsheet.

Health and Safety at work

It is important for all workers to feel safe in their place of employment. Many years ago, this was not always the case and there were many accidents at work caused, for example, by poorly maintained equipment, dangerous chemicals being used and a lack of training for the workforce. Today things are very different as employers have a duty of care for the health and safety of their employees under common law, and there have also been a number of Acts of Parliament passed to strengthen the employee's position.

Organisations now look very carefully at the way in which a building is designed or how a working area is set out, to ensure it is a safe and healthy place to work in. For example, buildings used by the general public such as shops and libraries will contain a whole range of safety features: good lighting; non-slip floors; smoke detectors; fire alarms; fire extinguishers; fireproof furnishings; safety rails and clear notices indicating emergency exits.

Employees also are entitled to be safe whilst they are at work and for many years the government, trade unions and employers have sought to ensure that workers are able to carry out their jobs in conditions which provide a safe and healthy place to work in. Workers also have to take on some responsibility for this and are expected to take reasonable care at all times to ensure they avoid any harm whilst at work and co-operate over health and safety regulations with their employers.

The advantages of a safe working environment are considerable and include the following:

- Fewer accidents occur in the work place, which keeps employees safe from accident or injury.
- Workers remain healthier and so less time is lost through sickness or injury.
- Employees are provided with adequate facilities such as toilets and rest rooms.

- Workers can appoint representatives to raise issues of concern about health and safety with management.
- Workers are happier whilst at work and so tend to be more efficient.

However, there are disadvantages associated with an unsafe and unhealthy environment:

- A loss of production, as workers are more likely to be unfit because of an unhealthy working environment or are likely to be injured on machinery without an adequate guard.
- It is more difficult to recruit labour as people do not want to work in dirty or potentially dangerous conditions.

Ensuring a safe working environment is more expensive for employers. For example, all machinery has to be checked regularly and staff have to be properly trained in its use. These costs may be passed on to customers through increasing the prices of finished goods.

Health and Safety Acts of Parliament

Several important Acts of Parliament have been passed to protect people at work. The most important of these are detailed below.

The Factories Act 1961

This act sets out the minimum basic standards in which people can be employed. It states the minimum space required for each employee to work within, the minimum and maximum working temperatures, the lighting and ventilation requirements, the need to provide protective clothing and the provision of first aid facilities. This applies to all premises where two or more people are employed in manual or factory work.

The Offices, Shops and Railway Premises Act 1963

This Act made the working environment for all employees healthier and safer by extending the requirements of the Factories Act to cover all premises where people are employed. Any employer failing to provide the minimum safety standards set down in this, or the Factories Act is liable to be prosecuted.

The Fire Precautions Act 1971

This further legislation made it law for all premises being used as a place of work to have a fire safety certificate. Certificates can only be obtained if the premises meet the requirements of the local fire authority and pass a safety inspection by a fully qualified fire officer. This has helped significantly to improve the safety of premises and make sure employees have adequate time and escape routes to leave a building in the event of fire.

The Health and Safety at Work Act 1974

This Act represented a new departure in safety legislation and has become the mainstay of health and safety in industry since then. Under the Act, the responsibility of ensuring the health, safety and welfare of employees is placed firmly with employers, as far as is reasonably practical. Employers are required under this Act to provide a safe working environment. This is done in three ways.

Premises

The provision and maintenance of premises that are safe to work in and that meet the standards of cleanliness and hygiene without risk to health.

Equipment

The provision and maintenance of equipment that is safe to use, and adequate arrangements made to ensure the safe use, handling and storage of any hazardous substances.

Training

The provision of all information, training and supervision necessary to ensure the health and safety of workers.

This, and the other laws relating to health and safety, are enforced by inspectors who work for the Health and Safety Executive. Inspectors have the legal right to enter and inspect premises and can issue improvement notices which instruct the employer to carry out any necessary improvements to achieve the required standard of health and safety. Failure to carry out any improvements within a reasonable time can result in the business premises being closed down as unfit places in which to work.

Exercises

1 List the four main Acts of Parliament which seek to protect people at work. (2)

2 What are the advantages to a business of a safer working environment? (4)

3 What are the advantages to an employee of a safer working environment? (4)

4 How does The Health and Safety at Work Act ensure employers provide a safe working environment? (4)

5 Why might an employer not want to conform to the Health and Safety Act? (3)

6 Outline the role of the Health and Safety Executive Inspectorate. (3)

Task One

Study the picture of an imaginary office below.

What can you see that is wrong with this office? Word process a list of all the problems which are likely to be hazardous from a health and safety point of view.

Using your word processor or desktop publishing system draw an outline plan of the room in which you are currently working. Try to draw the room to scale. Then, carefully look around the room and indicate on your plan any potential health and safety hazards. Make sure you check the following: power points; chairs; table and benches; equipment (both electrical and mechanical); trailing leads; floor covering; lighting; ventilation; fire alarms; fire extinguishers, etc. Describe any problems you encounter and suggest ways in which these can be eliminated or improved.

Extension material

Health and Safety legislation applies both to the internal and external aspects of a building. Conduct a survey similar to the one carried out in your teaching room on the site of your school or college. Look for all potential hazards: broken or loose paving slabs; damaged steps; broken fences; access to hazardous substances; ease of access to boiler rooms; gas bottles; electrical switch equipment; poor or broken light fittings, etc.

Draw up a simple outline plan of the site and mark on it the potential hazards you have identified using a key. Word process a list of the hazards giving each a reference which ties in with the key on your outline plan of the site.

Working with visual display units

The increasing use of computers in both business and at home has led to a rise in the number of illnesses which have been attributed to their use. In particular, eye strain from the use of screens for long periods of time and repetitive strain injury (RSI) manifesting itself as inflamed muscles and joints and caused by carrying out repetitive tasks such as keying in data.

The best way of reducing the possibility of suffering from these injuries is through the correct use of the equipment. It is important to have a work station which is comfortable to use and is designed to enhance your work. In this, employees must play an active role to ensure they use their equipment properly.

Posture

Posture is very important whilst using a computer terminal. You should always sit on an adjustable chair which gives good support to your back and allows you to place your feet firmly on the floor. There should be sufficient leg room under the desk

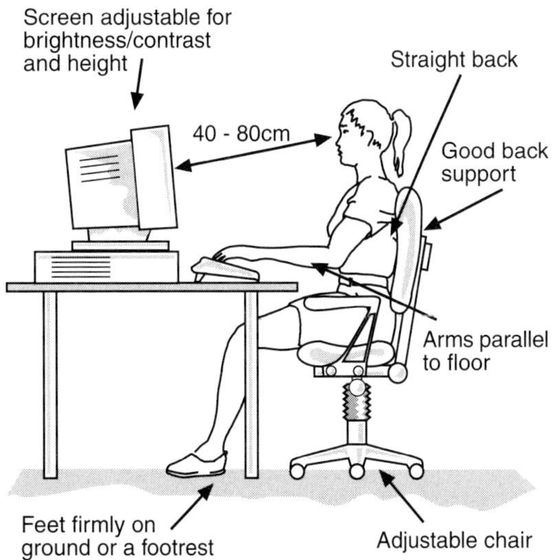

Figure 9 The correct posture for a keyboard operator

to allow you to sit comfortably and the height of the desk should let you use your keyboard with your forearms parallel to the floor or tilted slightly up. The mouse should be within easy reach of the keyboard and on the same height.

The computer screen should be positioned so that bright lights do not reflect onto it, and you should not be facing windows or other sources of strong light. Adjust curtains and blinds to prevent unwanted light and/or install a non-reflective screen on your computer. The VDU should be adjusted so that the top of the screen is at eye level without tilting your head down. When sitting upright your eyes should be at least 40 centimetres and no more than 80 centimetres from the screen.

Health and safety regulations

In 1992, the government introduced regulations on the use of visual display units – the Health and Safety (Display Screen Equipment) Regulations. These did not provide a detailed technical specification of what is required, but set out clear objectives that related to good practice to which employers must adhere. The onus was placed on the employer to provide safe working conditions for all employees using computer equipment and display screens. The regulations set out the following objectives.

Inspections

The employer has the responsibility to assess each work station to ensure that the environment and all equipment is safe. Any risks or problems identified must then be put right by the employer.

Adjustments

All screens should be adjustable. They should have brightness and contrast controls to allow the user to find a comfortable level for their eyes to help reduce strain. They should also have a height adjustment to ensure the correct position for good vision.

Breaks

Work should be planned so that the operator can take breaks from using their screen. Short frequent breaks are better than longer, less frequent ones and the operator should have the option of taking their breaks at their own discretion.

Training

All employees must be trained in the correct use of all aspects of their work station equipment and know how to avoid possible health problems, for example through the use of non-reflective VDU screens or adjustable chairs.

Eye tests

Employers are required to pay for eye and eyesight tests on a regular basis for all employees who use screens as part of their duties. In certain cases the employer may also have to pay for the supply of spectacles if they are needed.

Lighting

Lighting must now be of the appropriate European Union standard in offices and rooms where VDUs are being used.

Basic rules for those using VDUs

The following basic rules apply:

- Adjust your chair to find the most suitable position for you to work. A footrest will help prevent backache.
- Ensure there is sufficient space under the desk to allow you to move your legs freely.
- Do not sit in the same position for long periods of time. Change your posture regularly.
- Adjust your screen and keyboard to give a good viewing and keying-in position.
- Develop a good keying technique by keeping a

light touch on the keyboard and not over-stretching your fingers.

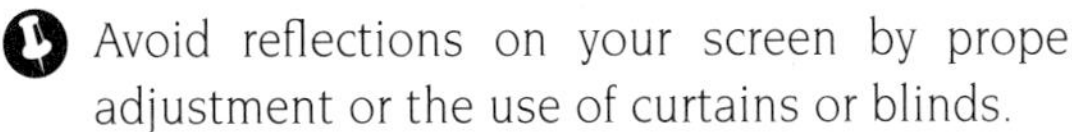

Avoid reflections on your screen by proper adjustment or the use of curtains or blinds.

Exercises

1 What is meant by the term RSI? (2)

2 List the six Health and Safety (Display Screen Equipment) regulations established by the Government in 1997. (3)

3 Explain why posture is important when using a computer terminal. (3)

4 Draw a copy of the diagram in Figure 9 (page 63) taking care to label it correctly. (4)

5 Outline the basic rules you should adhere to when using a VDU. (4)

6 Write a paragraph to explain to a new employee how to ensure prevention of unnecessary strain or injury. (4)

Use your word processor or desktop publishing system and key in a copy of the previous list of basic rules on a sheet of A4 paper. Prepare it for display as a notice to all VDU operators in your office.

Look at the diagram showing the correct posture for a computer operator in this unit. Identify one health problem which could occur when working for long periods of time at a computer work station. Design a Health and Safety poster which highlights that problem and possible ways in which it could be avoided. If possible include colour in your design to give your poster more impact.

Extension material

You have been asked by your line manager to inspect the room in which you are currently working to ensure it meets the Health and Safety requirements for display screen equipment. Following your inspection you are required to prepare a word processed report indicating your findings and making any suitable suggestions to improve those areas which require further attention (if any).

Produce your report in the form of a memorandum using an acceptable format on A4 paper. Make sure you spell-check and proofread your report before printing a hard copy and submitting it for consideration.

Security

Security takes many forms. You will have seen the security vans which collect and deliver cash to banks, building societies and shops in your local town. You will have noticed the security guards in large supermarkets, department stores and shopping malls. And, if you have a bank account, you will have your own PIN (personal identification number) which enables you to obtain cash or details of your account from an automatic banking machine. If you use a computer network at school or college, you will have your own personal password. These are all forms of security.

Businesses frequently require information to be kept secure. Details of a new product must not be disclosed to a competitor. Cash received for goods or to be paid out in wages must be kept safe until paid into a bank or to workers. Personal information about employees must be kept secure from those who have no need to know.

Probably the first instance where you will need to keep information secure in a 'working environment' is with the computer files you create for this course. You could do this by storing them on a floppy disk and not allowing others to use it. Alternatively you may be using a network terminal, in which case you will have your personal identity to log into the system and also a password which only you should know. As soon as you let someone else use your floppy disk or let them know your password, your work is no longer secure, as someone else has access to it.

In any business, three forms of security must be given consideration: personal security, financial security and security of information.

Personal security

This covers the personal belongings of the workforce. For those who are required to wear a uniform, for example supermarket employees or police, or for those who are required to wear protective clothing, such as garage mechanics or those handling food products, secure lockers need to be provided where these workers can leave their personal belongings, including money. Their belongings should then be safe from possible theft or damage. Large shops frequently have a policy which does not permit employees to carry any personal cash with them whilst working. If found with money on their person during working hours they may be suspected of pilfering and face possible dismissal.

Many firms now require workers to wear security badges which contain their photograph, name, job description, and detail the extent of their security clearance. These should be worn in a prominent place as they enable employees to be quickly identified as belonging to the organisation.

Financial security

This relates to the cash which flows into and out of a business. Retail organisations in particular take a considerable amount of cash through the tills which needs to be accounted for and kept safe prior to being banked. Similarly, an organisation which pays some or all of its workers in cash will need to make arrangements for the security of the money used to make up the wages. Many businesses which handle cash have a special room or area set aside for this, which can be locked so as to restrict access to only those who have the authority to be there. Large retail stores either regularly collect and store the cash away from their tills, or have a system which allows cashiers to send money direct to the cash office.

Security of information

Information stored in an office, be it hard copy or on a computer, needs to be safeguarded. Very often, the information is essential to the smooth operation of the business, for example, details of customers' orders, wages and salary records, lists of goods received from suppliers and payments made to them. Manually kept records can be locked away in filing cabinets and cupboards, which prevents unauthorised removal and gives some protection in the event of fire or other disaster.

One relatively cheap method of providing backup on a small network or a personal computer is to download data onto CD using a CD writer. These are now available for most computers and can be quickly and easily installed. Approximately 650 Mb of data can be written onto one compact disk. However, although CD writers can provide a low-cost backup system for a personal computer, it should be remembered that most commercial networks will require considerably more storage space and a large number of CDs will be required. If a backup system is to operate after normal working hours, and they are often timed to start late at night or in the early hours of the morning, an operator will be required to change each CD as they fill with data.

Passwords

When information is stored on a computer it can be protected by a password. Providing the number of people who know the password is limited only to those who have a right to know, data remains secure. Passwords should be changed on a regular basis – each week or each month – depending upon the level of security required. Also, it is important to avoid using a password which can be easily deciphered by someone else. Passwords which are more difficult to crack are at least six characters in length and contain a mixture of alphabetic and numeric symbols. Words to avoid include your own first name or surname, your date of birth, the name of the company, or the word 'password' itself!

A further level of security can be introduced on many computer systems, as individual files can also be password protected. This can give an added measure of security; however, when each file is given an individual password, these have to be remembered. Writing them down could allow others, who are determined enough, to obtain access to the files; but to forget the password could leave the legitimate user unable to recall or use the data.

Passwords provide an excellent means of securing data files, providing the password is not forgotten!

Operators should also remember, that once logged onto a computer system, if they leave their workstation unattended and do not log out, any passing member of staff or the general public can obtain access to the information stored on it without having to know the password.

Copying files

There is often no hard copy of information which is stored on a computer file. Therefore, it is important that copies of the files themselves are made and kept on a regular basis, so that if the computer fails for any reason, the information can be retrieved from the copy. Considerable amounts of data are stored on computer and it would be virtually impossible to recreate it if the system failed unless an adequate backup system is in operation.

To safeguard against loss of data, many businesses make copies of the data files on their computer. One way in which this can be done is to download or copy data to floppy disk. However, because of the speed of the disk drive and the large quantity of information to be processed, this could take several hours and hundreds of disks. To create copies of data files quickly, firms can now make use of digital audio tape (DAT) on which the contents of the computer's data files can be recorded. This is a high density cassette tape on which very large quantities of data can be stored in a compressed format. Using DAT, firms can automatically program their system to 'back up' their data file at the end of each working day so that they have a copy of all data should anything happen to the computer's hard disk. It is important that the copy of the data is stored away from the computer, preferably in another building, to avoid both original and copy being destroyed should there be a fire, or other disaster.

Data must also be kept secure from individuals who have no right to see it, or who might use the information for their own ends. To prevent unauthorised use of personal data held on computer files, the **Data Protection Act** was passed in 1984, and amended in 1998 (see Unit 16).

Exercises

1 When deciding on a password, list five words to avoid. (5)

2 Explain why it is important, when selecting a password, to use a mixture of alphabetic and numeric characters. (2)

3 List, together with an example of each, the three forms of security which any business must consider. (3)

4 Explain why many forms now issue staff with uniforms and identity badges. (3)

5 Why is it important to create back up copies of data stored on computer? (3)

6 What do the initials DAT stand for? Why do computer back up systems use DAT rather than floppy discs? (4)

Word process a list of all the ways in which your school or college provides security. Set out your list under three main headings: Personal security, Financial security and Security of information. At the end of your list compose another paragraph giving ways in which this level of security could be improved.

You work for Meridan Music Supplies, a wholesale company which supplies musical CDs and tapes to retail shops. At present your firm has no security arrangements and a recent stock check has shown that a considerable unexplained loss of stock has occurred. Your employer Jeannette O'Brien has asked you to prepare a report on this problem and suggest methods of security which the company could introduce to prevent this problem happening again. Make sure you spell check and proofread your report before producing a hard copy.

Extension material

Your school or college has decided that all students should wear security identification badges. Devise a suitable design for the badge. It should show the school/college name, the student's name, a photograph and a signature of the user plus anything else that you think is appropriate.

Data protection

Today, most businesses, whatever their size, make use of computers to store and process data about their employees, their customers and their suppliers. The growth in the use of computers to store information has proved to be largely beneficial. Less storage space is required, information can be found more easily and more quickly and fewer employees are needed to keep information up-to-date. As a result we receive prompt and efficient service from just about every business or organisation with which we have contact – banks, mail order companies, the Health Service to name a few.

When information is recalled from a computer we know it is accurate. Or we expect it to be! Unfortunately, information about us held on computer may not always be accurate. Errors can occur in three main ways:

1. Information about us could become mixed up with that of another person with the same or similar name. For example the telephone number of two John Smiths could become transposed.
2. Information can become out of date and affect the way in which we can be treated. For example a previously outstanding bill, now paid, may be recorded as still unpaid because the computer record has not been updated, and a business may refuse to supply us with goods we require.
3. Information can be wrongly entered and stored onto a computer system. For example the year of your birth could be incorrectly entered as 1998 rather than 1989, which would make you 11 years younger than you really are!

The effect of errors such as these can be serious for an individual. You may not be granted credit to purchase a new car, or you may be turned down as unsuitable for a job, or refused a driving licence because you are too young!

The Data Protection Act 1998

The original Data Protection Act, passed in 1984, was replaced by the Act of 1998. This later Act incorporated the European Union directive that 'any person, organisation or business wishing to hold personal information about people, must register with the Office of the Data Protection Commissioner'.

The Act seeks to provide protection as the volume of data held about individuals on computer rapidly increases in this technological age. Under the Act individuals have the right to see a copy of any of the information an organisation is holding on computer files about them. In addition, all users of personal information held on computer are obliged to register with the Data Protection Commissioner and a copy of the companies who have registered is available for anyone to inspect in all major public libraries.

The register shows which companies hold information on data files, the type of information they hold, the purposes they use it for, where the information was obtained and to whom it may be disclosed. The Register does not give a list of individuals about whom data is held. To obtain this information you must write directly to the company listed, requesting your details. When you ask, the company must tell you if they are holding any data about you and provide you with a copy.

Data protection principles

In addition to the rights the Act gives to individuals, it also places controls on those companies holding data about individuals on computer. These controls are outlined in the Data Protection Principles which state that computer users handling personal data must:

- obtain and process the information fairly and lawfully and for specified purposes
- hold only the information which is adequate, relevant and not excessive for the purpose
- hold only accurate information, and where necessary, keep it up-to-date
- not keep the information any longer than necessary
- not use or disclose the information in any way contrary to those purposes
- give individuals access to information about themselves and, where appropriate, correct or erase the information
- take appropriate measures to ensure data is secure against loss, damage and unauthorised and unlawful processing
- not transfer data to countries outside the European Union.

The Data Protection Commissioner will investigate any company believed to have broken these principles.

There are, however, some exceptions to your rights to see data held about you and these include data held for the purpose of:

- preventing or detecting crime and catching or prosecuting criminals
- assessing or collecting taxes
- health, educational and social security work
- household, personal and family affairs.

In addition to the Data Protection Act, two other Acts of Parliament seek to protect individuals and companies from the misuse of electronic data.

The Copyright, Designs and Patents Act, 1989

This Act makes copying or pirating of computer software a criminal offence. This includes making illegal copies of programs and operating purchase software on two or more computers at the same time without the appropriate licences. It is currently estimated that more than fifty per cent of all software currently in use has been illegally copied. The Act allows penalties of up to two years imprisonment and unlimited fines to be imposed should an individual or company be found guilty of software fraud.

The Computer Misuse Act 1990

This Act was introduced to protect against hacking, computer fraud and computer viruses which are all relatively new crimes. Hacking is the process of breaking codes and passwords in order to gain unauthorised access to a computer system. Some people find the challenge of trying to break into a computer system irresistible, but once they have gained entry they may do considerable damage and so businesses need to have some legal protection against them. If you are found guilty of unlawfully hacking into a computer system under this Act you can be fined up to a maximum of £2 000 and be subject to six months imprisonment.

Viruses cause the unauthorised modification of a computer system or the data stored in it with the intention of reducing or impairing its operation. The worldwide effects of the Love Bug virus passed via email in 1999 show just how dangerous and expensive viruses can be to business computer systems. Anyone found guilty of introducing a virus into a computer system is now subject to an unlimited fine and a prison sentence of up to five years.

Similar fines and sentences have also been introduced to help prevent computer fraud. This is where a computer operator uses the computer to his/her own advantage, usually to obtain goods without payment or money. Computer fraud, however, frequently goes undetected or unreported. Many of those who become involved in this type of crime are young and do not have a previous criminal record. They are also often very clever and have carefully thought through the ways in which they can avoid detection. Firms, when they discover computer fraud, often do not want the publicity which will surround their discovery and so do not prosecute those involved, preferring to maintain the company's image and credibility instead.

Exercises

1 List the three Acts which aim to protect individuals and companies holding data on computer. (3)

2 What are the main categories of data which are listed as exceptions in the Data Protection Act? (4)

3 Write a paragraph explaining precisely what is meant by the term *hacking*. (3)

4 Why do companies not always prosecute those who are caught attempting to defraud them through their computer systems? (4)

5 Explain what a computer virus is and how it can be a risk to a business. (3)

6 Explain the difficulties a software company, such as Microsoft, would face if there were no laws to prevent others copying its programs. How can these laws be enforced? (3)

Using your word processor or desk top publishing system, prepare a copy of the Data Protection Principles. Set out your work in the form of a poster which can be displayed in the office to remind staff handling personal data of the principles to which they must adhere.

Prepare a draft letter to a company which you believe to be holding personal data and enquire if there is a fee payable for providing it. Enclose a stamped addressed envelope for their reply. Set your letter out in the blocked style of presentation using open punctuation.

Extension material

Your friend has written asking for your help. She has been refused car insurance by the Norfolk Insurance Co. Ltd on the grounds that she has a serious heart complaint. In fact she is a very healthy individual despite suffering from mild asthma. She suspects that the insurance company's computer records are incorrect but does not know how to challenge them. Write a personal letter to your friend giving her advice on how to resolve this problem.

PART 3

Human Resources and Recruitment

Human resources

Recruitment

Equal opportunities

Letters of application

Application forms

Curriculum Vitae

Interviews

Conducting interviews

Contract of employment

Training and appraisal

Wages and salaries

Methods of Payment

Deductions

Fringe benefits

Human resources

Human resources are the people, or personnel, who work for a company and help it achieve its aims in business. They are essential to its success. A firm which employs people who are unable to carry out their duties because of a lack of ability or training, is unlikely to remain in business.

Personnel

Every business is made up of individuals. Each individual carries out a specific task such as machine operator, lorry driver, computer operator or manager and is often 'grouped' together with others who carry out the same task. Modern industry often encourages workers to work together in 'teams' using their combined skills to complete a given task. For example, building a house requires the individual skills of bricklayers, electricians, plasterers, carpenters, roofers, painters and decorators who all need to work together to complete the job.

It is important to realise that every individual who works for a firm is different. You will have already noticed these differences amongst your school or college friends. These differences can take a number of forms.

Physical

This includes features such as height, weight, colour of eyes and size of shoes.

Intellectual

This can be measured by means of an Intelligent Quotient or IQ test which seeks to show how good you are at solving a series of logic tests. Other tests are frequently used by schools to assess your ability. These include the Edinburgh Reading Test (ERT) or the Cognitive Abilities Test (CAT). These tests give a score from which your ability to reason and understand can be predicted.

Personality

This can be measured through a range of different traits or personal characteristics, for example are you quiet or outgoing, trusting or suspicious, undisciplined or controlled, relaxed or tense?

Knowledge and skills

These include previous experience and technical training necessary for the job, as well as more general skills in communication, literacy and numeracy, Information Technology and problem solving.

Businesses need to evaluate carefully the different characteristics of employees to ensure they place them in a post within the firm where they can be of most use. An employee who does not have the ability or training to cope with a job will not work very effectively and may lose the firm customers. Alternatively, an employee who has abilities and skills which are not being used, is under utilised by the firm and may become frustrated with their work. The firm will then not gain maximum benefit from them.

Job analysis

To help place employees in the right position, businesses can conduct a job analysis. This is a study of what the job actually entails and will include a description of the skills, training and tasks which are required to carry it out successfully. You should remember that different people within a business may have different views of what a job entails and so it is important when carrying out any analysis to talk not only to the person actually doing the job, but also to those who supervise them as well as those they supervise.

This will give a variety of views on what the job involves, some of which may be subjective, and include prejudice or bias. For example, subordinates may be jealous of those above them and perhaps believe they can do a better job. Alternatively, managers may have a prejudice against particular individual employees which could prevent them from recognising their true worth.

Businesses can use job analysis not only to help decide on the right criteria they are looking for in a person for a particular job, but also to help set the correct rate of pay for a job, to establish appropriate training programmes, to select individuals for possible promotion and to help appraise staff in the work that they are doing.

Job specification

Once a job has been analysed, a description of what it entails can be prepared. This job specification is simply a word picture of what the job involves. It should:

- Establish the qualities and skills which a successful candidate will require to do to the job.
- List all the different tasks and activities which make up the job.
- Provide ways for a company to 'measure' how well an employee is doing the job by comparing his or her activities with the job specification.
- Help settle any disputes which may arise about the way an employee is carrying out his or her work by comparing the job specification with the actual work done.

Job specification usually consists of four sections.

General information

This includes the job title, a job summary, which gives the main task or tasks and where the post fits into the company structure.

Duties

This section details the tasks involved and includes the purpose of the work, the methods involved in its completion and any other functions which may be required together with any responsibilities for staff, equipment or finances.

Working conditions

These include the area or building in which you will

work as well as the starting and finishing times, the length of the working day, the number of days holiday to which you are entitled and the period of notice required should you wish to leave or be dismissed.

Performance criteria

This is how your performance in the job will be measured and may be used as a basis for regular appraisal interviews.

A possible job specification for an Office Supervisor is given below:

General	Office Supervisor, responsible to the Administration Manager for providing efficient word processing, reprographics and telephone switchboard services to company personnel.
Duties	Responsible for five staff to be allocated between duties involving word processing, reprographics and the switchboard as required to provide an efficient service for other employees. To ensure proper maintenance and repair of equipment within the department. To order stationery and other materials and maintain an up-to-date record of all stocks. To maintain an accurate and up-to-date record of all departmental costs and to work within the financial budget set. To provide a training programme for all employees within the department and to assist in the selection of new staff when required.
Working Conditions	Normal office hours are 9.00 am to 5.00 pm Monday to Friday and the Office Supervisor will be required to work 35 hours per week and overtime as and when necessary. Holiday entitlement is 25 working days each year increasing to 30 days after five years service. One calendar month's notice in writing is required should either party wish to terminate employment.
Performance Criteria	You will be expected to conduct your duties in an efficient and courteous manner and ensure that all work passed to the department is completed and returned within 24 hours. An annual appraisal interview will be held with the Administration Manager.

Figure 10 Job specification

Exercises

1 List the different personal characteristics each employee may have. (3)

2 Why is it important for a business to match these personal characteristics against a job analysis? (2)

3 Explain what is meant by the term *job analysis* and what benefits a firm may gain from carrying out a job analysis. (4)

4 List the criteria which would be included in a job specification. (4)

5 Carefully explain the difference between a job analysis and a job specification. (4)

6 What criteria would you use to assess performance? (3)

Consider the following occupations:

- airline pilot
- shop assistant
- garage mechanic
- brick layer
- social worker

For each occupation:

1 Make a list of all the tasks that might be needed to carry out each job.

2 List all the skills which an employee doing the job would require.

3 List criteria which could be used to assess good performance in each job.

Study the following advertisement and identify the key elements.

THE GLOBE
Require an
Executive Assistant
Starting salary £10.500

The Globe PLC is the leading publisher of international newspapers world wide.

We are looking for an articulate, dynamic and creative individual who possesses both the determination to succeed and the drive and enthusiasm to achieve their Goals.

Applicants should have a minimum of 5 GCSEs at Grade C or above, or equivalent qualifications.

Good IT and communication skills are an essential requirement of the post.

We can offer excellent career prospects, full on-going training and an excellent benefits package, leading to a company car after 12 months.

Please send your application in writing, together with your CV to:

Wendy Marlow. Personnel Manager
The Globe PLC
Dunhill Industrial Park, Norton Fitzwarren
Yeovil Somerset BA2 6RM

You work in the office of a local garage and have been asked by your employer to use your word processor or desktop publishing system to prepare an advertisement for an experienced and qualified garage mechanic who is capable of working without supervision. The salary offered is £12,500 a year plus productivity bonus and pension scheme. The advertisement is to appear in the local paper. Use the previous advertisement to help create any further details you feel will be of interest to possible applicants.

Extension material

Study the following job advertisement.

SALES MANAGER
for products and systems for the Roofing Industry
Based in the South or South Midlands **Salary £35,000 + bonus + car**

We supply a range of innovative high quality products to customers throughout Southern England. Structured Polycarbonates, other specialist materials and roofing systems are sold to fabricators of conservatories and window systems as well as other related market sectors.

The Sales Manager is responsible to the Managing Director for developing profitable business, identifying and exploiting new opportunities and the introduction of new related products.

We are looking for an enthusiastic, experienced Sales Manager who has achieved considerable success not only through their own personal sales skills but through the management and motivation of a small sales team. Whilst knowledge of the roofing industry is highly desirable, a background in builders merchant or building product sales could provide the right mix of experience.

Please apply in writing with a full CV quoting reference DT/23, to CGJ Roofing Consultants, Old London Road, Winchester, Hampshire, SO21 8RY

Using the information given in the advertisement and the example in Figure 10, page 78, prepare a job description for the post offered.

Recruitment

The objective in recruiting staff is to obtain the best candidate for a particular vacancy. This can prove to be quite difficult, because if the wrong person is recruited they may find the work so easy as to be boring, or alternatively beyond their ability. This can cost the firm money.

A survey by the Chartered Institute of Personnel and Development carried out in 2000 estimates the cost to a firm of recruiting an unskilled worker at £1200, a skilled worker at £3500, and a professional, such as an accountant, or senior manager, at £5200.

The personnel department

In a small firm, the function of recruiting staff may be the responsibility of the manager or owner. Larger firms may have a Personnel Department to assist with the task of recruitment. Personnel Departments employ specialist staff who are skilled at interviewing and assessing people and managing human resources. They evaluate the strengths and weaknesses of individuals and seek to place them in the post most suited to their skills. Often they are faced with the task of turning down possible applicants for a job where their skills or personal qualities do not match the requirements of the job specification. The Personnel Department do not just recruit new staff, they look after all aspects of employees' welfare and their duties will include:

- recruitment and selection of suitable employees
- induction and further training of employees
- promotion prospects and career development of staff
- appraisal and discipline of employees
- pay, wage bargaining and other fringe benefits
- working conditions and conditions of employment.

If a vacancy does exist in a firm, then the Personnel

Department needs to ensure it is filled. This can be done in two main ways. Firstly, by recruiting employees new to the firm – external recruitment – or secondly, by appointing someone who already works for the firm. This is called internal recruitment.

Today's employees are now required to have an increasing level of technological knowledge and skill when they start work. This, coupled with the fact that the number of people leaving school and college and seeking work is less than the number taking retirement, means that employers in this country are facing a more difficult task to find new, suitable workers to fill vacancies. Consequently there is a growing trend to fill vacant posts using internal rather than external methods of recruitment.

Internal recruitment

Many companies such as Marks & Spencer prefer to recruit from within to fill vacancies. They will always advertise vacant posts to their existing employees and seek to find a suitable applicant who can be promoted or transferred to the new post before considering external candidates. This may occur through advertising on a noticeboard, or by producing a circular giving details of the job which can be sent to all eligible staff. Those companies who produce their own newspapers or journals may include a 'vacancies' section where jobs can be advertised.

There are a number of advantages associated with internal recruitment methods:

- It can strengthen employees' commitment to the firm, knowing they will be given opportunities for promotion before new staff.
- It provides the structure for a career development path which employees are aware of and so can motivate them to work harder.
- Existing staff know the business and procedures of the company and so require less induction (see Unit 26) into the new post.
- Those responsible for appointment know more about the strengths, weaknesses and suitability of internal candidates. This can reduce the possibility of appointing the wrong person.
- Internal appointment is often quicker and less expensive than recruiting from outside a firm.

There are, however, still some disadvantages to internal appointments which also need to be considered:

- Applicants for a post are limited to those from within the company when better qualified and more suitable applicants may be available elsewhere.
- The person appointed may be known to others within a department by a reputation which may be poor.
- It can often prove difficult to manage colleagues who, until recently, regarded you as their equal.
- Resentment may exist if others also applied for a vacancy but were unsuccessful.

External recruitment

External recruitment occurs when a new employee is employed from outside the organisation. There are many ways of attracting external candidates, and the method used by a firm will differ depending on the vacancy and the type of employee the firm is seeking. Each method has its own benefits and drawbacks.

Vacancy boards outside premises

This is a very cheap method of advertising a vacancy, which will only be seen by those who pass by the business premises. Professional and more senior posts, such as shift supervisor or manager, would not be advertised in this way.

Advertising in the local paper

This is read by local people seeking employment, but as with the vacancy board, is unlikely to attract many professional people.

Advertising on the Internet

Increasingly, firms are including details of any staff vacancies they may have available on their web sites. With the dramatic increase in access that people now have to the Internet, and its vast wealth of information and resources, this is seen as a natural progression in making information available to a wider audience.

Commercial employment agencies

These agencies specialise in providing temporary workers for businesses, as well as helping firms recruit and select permanent staff. They will advertise a post, sift through the responses and prepare a short list for a company to interview. This service is usually more suited to the employment of secretarial and clerical workers, but it does allow the company to concentrate on running the business, only getting involved in the recruitment process when selecting from a short list of candidates. However, the agency fees for providing this service can be expensive.

Advertising in the national press

This method of advertising will reach a much wider audience and so will attract interest from all over the country. However, it can prove expensive.

Advertising in a technical journal

This will be read by people in the relevant occupation or profession. However most technical journals are published infrequently; some monthly, but many quarterly or at longer intervals.

Recruitment agencies

These can be privately run or operated by the Government. Privately run recruitment agencies tend to concentrate on finding suitable professional and senior management candidates for business. The fees for this service, however, are often quite substantial, with some agencies charging three, or more, months salary to the firm for finding a suitable employee.

The Department for Education and Employment operates a network of job centres which advertise vacancies supplied to them by local companies. As the centres are connected with the registering of those unemployed, often in the same building, vacancies are regularly seen by those actively seeking work.

The Careers Service

This service not only provides careers guidance and advice for young people, it also collects details of local employment opportunities which are then advertised in schools and colleges. The Service has the advantage of receiving many enquiries from young people actively seeking work who are able to take up a post fairly quickly, although they operate on a local rather than a regional or national basis.

Youth Training Schemes

These provide training for all young people not receiving full-time education or who are not in work. Training can be linked to a permanent post or to provide work experience to aid young people in subsequently finding a job. The main advantage of these schemes is that they enable companies to see how well a trainee can work before they are offered a full-time post. Costs are also reduced as all trainees are paid an allowance by the government.

Head-hunting

This is where a successful individual is approached by another company or agency and is encouraged to

change jobs. The advantage of this is that a business can approach someone whom they know has all the attributes they are seeking. The main disadvantages are in the ethics of encouraging staff away from other companies, the cost of enticing people to move and that other equally suitable applicants are excluded from applying for the vacant post.

Many of the advantages and disadvantages of external recruitment vary depending on the way in which staff are recruited. However, some advantages are common, as follows:

- New staff will bring with them new ideas and techniques which may be to the advantage of the company.
- New employees are keen to make a good start and so will work to make the job a success.
- The introduction of new staff may make existing staff work harder to achieve promotion or obtain an increase in salary in the future.

The disadvantages of external recruitment methods include:

- Many of the qualities of the new employee are not known and they may subsequently prove unsuitable for the job.
- The introduction of a new member of staff, especially in a management position, can lead to resentment from more junior existing staff who feel passed over for promotion and undervalued.
- It can take longer for a new member of staff to become an effective worker, as they need time to settle in to the new company and learn the requirements of the job.
- External recruitment is more expensive than an internal appointment and takes longer to complete.

Exercises

1. List the main functions of a human resources department. (3)
2. Explain carefully what is meant by the terms (a) *Internal Recruitment* (b) *External Recruitment*, and (c) *Induction*. (3)
3. Outline the benefits of internally recruiting staff to a management post. (2)
4. Give four ways in which a business could attract new staff, and one benefit for each. (4)
5. What are the disadvantages of headhunting? Why do firms engage in it as a means of recruitment? (4)
6. Describe the disadvantages of internally recruiting new staff. (4)

Word process a table showing the advantages and disadvantages of both internal and external recruitment.

Obtain a copy of your local/regional newspaper. Prepare an analysis of all the vacancies advertised. Include the following points:

- Full-time and part-time.
- The required age of applicants.
- The location of the job.
- Level of qualifications required, for example, GCSE/GNVQ/A level/vocational, etc.
- Experience required/training given.

Extension material

Obtain a copy of a national broadsheet newspaper on the day they publish an appointments supplement. Prepare a similar analysis to that in Task Two. Word process a report outlining the results of your analysis. What comparisons can be drawn between your findings in the two tasks? Can you determine any conclusions from the data?

Equal opportunities

Today it is generally accepted that a man and a woman will receive equal and fair treatment if they apply for the same job. Decisions about who to employ are no longer based on the sex of the applicant, or on them being part of a certain ethnic group, or on their religious beliefs. Today the decision about whom to employ is based on the suitability of the applicant to fulfil the requirements of the job specification rather than any other factors.

Discrimination

It is illegal for firms to discriminate between employees on the grounds of sex, race or religion. Discrimination can also occur with training, promotion and pay. Some discrimination, however, can be considered reasonable and is legal. For example a large department store interviewing two equally qualified school-leavers for a job as a junior shop assistant may prefer to select (or discriminate in favour of) the candidate who has previous experience working Saturdays in a local shop.

Most discrimination stems from generalisations and ideas, which have little or no basis in fact, about certain groups in society. The following are examples:

- Physically handicapped people are often regarded as having lower intelligence and are thought to be unable to cope with anything other than menial tasks.
- Women with children are expected to require more time off work to look after their children when they are ill and during the school holidays.
- Older people are supposedly unable to learn new ideas and processes quickly and so work more slowly than their younger counterparts.

It is important that these views are not allowed to

persist or influence the way in which decisions about selection and promotion take place in businesses. For many years the government has sought to reduce discrimination in industry and several Acts of Parliament have been passed to help with this.

The Disabled Persons (Employment) Acts of 1944 and 1958

These Acts introduced a scheme to encourage the employment of disabled people. Firms are required to employ disabled people as at least 3% of their workforce if they employ 20 or more workers. This is a form of positive discrimination where the law is actively promoting the interests of a minority group within society. It is argued that without this pressure from the government many disabled people would remain out of work today.

Disability Discrimination Act, 1995

This Act clarified and amended the two earlier Acts on the employment of disabled people. It provided a framework to prevent discrimination against any applicant or employee in the recruitment or employment of any individual. The Act also established that all employers have a responsibility to maintain their business premises so they do not discriminate against the employment of any individual. In addition, the Act was widened to include public transport (including taxis, buses and rail) and education. These services must now ensure they can provide an equitable service and not discriminate in any way against one individual.

The Equal Pay Act, 1970

This Act stated that employees of both sexes doing the same or broadly similar work should be paid the same rate for the job. The aim of the Act was to increase women's rates of pay to bring them into line with those of men. Other conditions of employment such as overtime rates and holiday allowances were also covered by the Act. In 1983 the Act was amended to allow women to claim equal pay for work regarded as being of equal value,

including the demands such as the skill level or degree of decision making which the job involved.

The Sex Discrimination Act, 1975

This Act made discrimination against anyone because of their sex or married status illegal. The Act covered all aspects of the recruitment and dismissal of staff. In 1986 it was updated by a further Act to remove any restrictions on the hours which women could work, so making it easier for them to take jobs which involved shift work or flexible working hours. Together, these two Acts ensure that:

- Advertisements must make use of job titles which do not indicate that preference will be given to one particular sex. Terms such as 'salesperson' or 'shop assistant' should be used.
- Job descriptions have to be applicable to both sexes.
- Interviews have to be conducted in such a way that they do not give preference to any one particular candidate and that any prejudices the interviewer may have are eliminated.

The Race Relations Act, 1976

This Act was passed in an attempt to prevent discrimination against any ethnic group, and states that it is illegal for an employer to discriminate against a candidate for a job because of their race. Job advertisements and job descriptions should be worded so that they do not indicate a preference for any one ethnic group. Advice to help employers avoid discrimination is given in the Race Relations Code of Practice which states the following:

- Literature sent to applicants should state clearly that the firm is an equal opportunities employer.
- Suitable applicants with overseas qualifications should be treated equally with those who have qualifications obtained in the UK.
- Advertisements should not be restricted in any way which will limit applicants from a particular ethnic group.

Applicants and employees who feel they have been unfairly discriminated against on the grounds of race can appeal to the Race Relations Board, which will investigate each case on their behalf.

Equal opportunities

Many firms now have equal opportunities policies which seek to eliminate discrimination based on sex, race and religion. These policies actively work to give all employees an equal opportunity to receive training, promotion opportunities and pay. There are a number of advantages to introducing an equal opportunities policy in a business:

- Workers tend to be better motivated if they all believe they stand an equal chance of advancement.
- Training opportunities are available to all employees, which improves the overall quality of the workforce.
- The most suitable person is more likely to be employed, which will lead to better production, supervision and management.

However, the introduction of this type of policy is not without its disadvantages:

- The payment of equal wages for both men and women is likely to increase the total wage bill.
- Additional facilities may be required, such as separate toilets for men and women, crèche facilities for those with young children or ramps and wider doors to allow for wheelchair access.
- Working practices may need to be revised to include job rotation and job sharing. More flexible working hours may have to be introduced to accommodate those with young families.

Despite this, there is still evidence that women continue to be discriminated against in the workforce. Many are employed in low paid, part-time jobs which utilise only a low level of skill.

Exercises

1 What is meant by the term *discrimination*? Why has it been made illegal in the recruitment and employment of staff? (4)

2 Why was it felt necessary to introduce the Disabled Persons (Employment) Acts of 1944 and 1958? (3)

3 What are the main aims of the 1970 Equal Pay Act? Why was it amended in 1983? (4)

4 What do the Sex Discrimination Acts seek to overcome? (2)

5 How can the Race Relations Code of Practice help when advertising for staff? How can those who feel unfairly discriminated against register their concerns? (3)

6 What are the benefits for an employee and a business in introducing an equal opportunities policy? (4)

Your employer has left you the following note asking you to word process an advertisement for a new clerical assistant for insertion in the local paper. Read through the information carefully and identify as many reasons as you can for why it cannot be used in the advertisement.

> *We are looking for a new clerical assistant to work in the main office. As most of the other assistants are female I would like to advertise for a woman. I do not want to upgrade our toilet facilities to provide for a male employee in the main office. Make sure she is between 35 and 50 so that she is unlikely to have small children not yet at school – in fact it would be better to have someone without children. If she is married, so much the better, because if we have to dismiss her because the extra work we currently have in the office does not continue, she'll be OK because her husband can support her. She will have to work one Sunday morning each month so cannot have any strong religious beliefs which prevent that. Pay will be £4.00 per hour which is 75p less than the permanent staff.*

Word process a memorandum to your employer outlining the problems in her note and explain why it cannot be used.

Use your word processor or desktop publishing system to prepare the advertisement for a new office assistant using the information in Task One which will meet the requirements of the law and will be accepted by the local paper.

Extension material

Obtain a copy of the jobs section of your local/regional newspaper. Study all the advertisements carefully and make a list of all those which you think might infringe some aspect of equal opportunities. Explain what you think the problem is with each advertisement you have identified and provide a way in which it could be corrected.

Letters of application

When a vacancy occurs in a business it is important that the firm selects a person who will suit their needs. They must have the right qualities, not only to be able to carry out the demands of the job, but also to be able to fit into the organisation with the minimum disruption to existing staff. One way in which firms can select new staff is to make all applicants for the vacant post apply for it in writing.

Very often a prospective applicant will be asked to write a letter of application. The letter should state the following points:

- Why you want the job (e.g. you have always been interested in this type of work or you are hoping to make a career in this occupation).
- What qualities you can bring to the job (qualifications, punctuality, hard-working, relevant skills).
- Your ideas about the job (e.g. the first step in your career or fulfilling a long-held desire).

An outline of the type of letter which you could write when applying for a job or a college place is given in Figure 11. This is not the only way in which such a letter can be written. However, all letters of application must be neat, accurate, precise, relevant and free of spelling and typographical mistakes. This example is displayed in the blocked style which is more straightforward to produce on a word processor.

The letter of application may often be only a part of your application for a particular job. You may be asked to submit a Curriculum Vitae (see Unit 22) and also complete an application form (see Unit 21).

14 Old Church Road
Exeter
Devon
EX14 3RT

21 April 2001

Mrs R J Roundtree
Manager
Cadbury Cleaners Ltd
Barnside Avenue
Exeter
Devon
EX5 2DJ

Dear Mrs Roundtree

I would like to apply for the post of office junior advertised in the Exeter Evening News on Monday 14 April 2001.

I am 16 years old and currently attend Ashdown Community School. I will be leaving school at the end of June and am hoping to follow a career in office work. I enjoy word processing at school and have passed my RSA stage 1 word processing certificate.

I will be taking my GCSE examinations in May and June and expect to achieve the following grades:

English Language grade C
Double Science grades CC
History grade D
Mathematics grade C
Business and Communications systems grade B
Sociology grade D
Religious Education grade D

I am enclosing a copy of my curriculum vitae with this letter for your consideration. I will be pleased to attend for interview at any convenient time. I look forward to hearing from you.

Yours sincerely

Ann Other

Figure 11 Sample letter of application

Exercises

1 When preparing a letter of application on a Word Processing system why would you use the fully blocked style of presentation? (2)

2 Explain why a business might ask prospective employees to write a letter of application when applying for a particular vacancy. (4)

3 What are the advantages to the candidate in being asked to provide a letter of application? (4)

4 Explain why a firm may have difficulty in short-listing suitable candidates for a job from letters of application. (2)

5 Why is it important to ensure there are no errors in a letter of application? (3)

6 Make a list of as many characteristics as you can which you would not be able to consider when shortlisting candidates for a job using the information on their application forms. (4)

The following is a letter of application for a job as an Accounts Clerk with Wright's Garages Ltd which has been received by the company's personnel department. Study it carefully, and then answer the questions which follow.

15 Orchard Street
Redland
Bristol
BS6 5TY

15 May 2001

Ms Anne Gordon
Personal Manager
Wright's Garages Ltd
Bedminster
Bristol
BS3 3DG

Dear Ms Gorden

I would like to apply for the vacancy of accounts clark, which was advertised in the bristol Evening Post yesterday.

I am 16 years old and will be leaving school at the end of June after I have taken my GCSE exams. I shall be taking exams in English, Maths, Science, French, History, Art & Design, Business Communications and Systems and Sociology.

I have resently completed a week's work experiance at British Home Stores and also work on Saturdays as a part-time as a waitress at Fortes Cafe in Redland.

I will be pleased to come fro interview at any time convenient to yourself.

Yours Sincerly

1. Make a list of all the errors you can find in the letter below.
2. Give two reasons why you think it is important for a letter of application to be relevant, accurate and free from errors.
3. What other relevant information could have been included in this letter?

Word process a corrected version of the letter in Task One on plain A4 paper and in the fully blocked style. Ensure you correct all the errors you have identified in question one and make use of any additional information which you have identified in question three to improve the overall quality of the letter.

Extension material

Read the following advertisement for a junior receptionist. Then, using the previous letter as a guide, compose and type a letter of application on A4 paper.

Scene Magazines
require a
RECEPTIONIST
to work in our Bristol offices

Duties will include dealing with enquiries from the public both by telephone and in person, processing advertisements and payments together with general administration duties. Keyboarding skills are essential as is experience in using computers.

Salary £8,500 to £9,500 subject to experience
plus annual bonus payment

25 days paid holiday

Please send a full letter of application to:
Mike Sansum
Office Manager
Scene Magazines
PO Box 235
Bristol
BS3 3DG

Closing date for applications – 10 June 2001

Application forms

When recruiting staff, many firms like applicants to fill in an application form. These provide the Personnel Department with similar details about each applicant in a standard format. Due to this the process of sorting applications and selecting a short list of candidates for interview is made much easier.

The information on the application form can also be used as the basis for discussions at interview. It is important, therefore, that when you complete an application form you do so with care. It may also be useful to keep a photocopy of your completed form to remember what information you gave and to help you prepare for an interview if you are short listed. For example, if you give reading as one of your interests, you may be asked at the interview which books you have read recently and what you enjoyed about them; or who is your favourite author and what do you like about him or her.

Application forms differ from company to company in the way they are set out and the information which may be included. However, the main items in most forms are as follows:

- Your personal details such as name, address, age, sex and nationality.
- Details of any educational and vocational qualifications you have obtained.
- Details of the previous jobs you have done including any part-time work.
- The reasons why you want the job for which you are applying.
- How you spend your spare time – the hobbies and interests.
- Details of at least two referees who can be contacted to provide references for you.

However the application form is designed, its main purpose is to allow you to present information about yourself in such a way that those responsible for recruitment can decide quickly whether or not you will be suitable for the vacant post. They can do so by matching your details with those required in the person specification.

Completing an application form

When filling out an application form it is important to remember that you may not get a second chance. You need to be particularly careful not to make mistakes and to ensure the information you give is clear, concise and accurate. The following guidelines may help:

- Always take care to keep the form clean and tidy. Keep it in the envelope in which it arrived until you are ready to fill it in.
- Always read through the form first, before writing anything, and check what information you need and how the form is to be completed. For example, should you write in block capitals or use black ink?
- Ensure you have all the information you need before you start, such as your examination grades or the dates when you started previous employment.
- Take a photocopy if you can, and practise completing the form in pencil. This will make sure you can fit what you want to say in the spaces provided and give you something to copy from.
- Make sure you write neatly and clearly. Remember, your handwriting will give an impression of you to those reading the form who make the decision whether or not to include you on the short list for the post.
- Avoid leaving any blank spaces. If you have nothing to put under a particular heading, put the abbreviation N/A which stands for 'Not Applicable'. This shows that you have read the question and decided it is not relevant and not simply forgotten to complete that section.
- If you have to write out a paragraph, for example on why you want the job, practise beforehand to make sure it will fit into the space provided on the form.
- Check everything carefully once you have completed the form. Then, and only then, should you sign and date it.

If you are successful at interview, the information given on your application form will provide the basis of your personnel record. This will be stored by the Personnel Department in a secure environment such as a computer system with password control or a lockable filing cabinet.

Company personnel records should be kept up-to-date and you should notify the Personnel Department of any change in your personal circumstances, such as a change of address or your marital status.

Exercises

1 List the main categories of information usually included on an application form. (3)

2 How might applicants completing an application form help the Personnel Department in drawing up a short list? (3)

3 Why might it be a good idea to make a photocopy of an application form before starting to complete it? (2)

4 Why do prospective employers frequently ask you to give details of your hobbies and interests? (4)

5 Most application forms require you to give two referees. Why? (4)

6 Why is it important to ensure you keep your employer informed of any changes to your personal details? (4)

The following advertisement has appeared in your local paper. You have decided to apply for the post and have telephoned for an application form. Using your own personal details and the information given in the advertisement, complete a copy of the application form given in the Teachers' Book.

Six Way Sports Products

require an

OFFICE ASSISTANT

to work in their Manchester Offices

Must be numerate and literate with good communication skills
Excellent keyboard skills are essential
Would suit a school leaver
Starting salary from £6,500 per year with 4 weeks paid holiday

Telephone for an application form on 0161 899 9001
to be completed and returned to
Six Way Sports Products, PO Box 44,
Manchester, M16 5FG

Using your word processor or a desktop publishing system, design an application form suitable for use with a large clothing manufacturer which employs skilled machinists to work on a two shift system. The shifts run from either 6.00 am to 2.00 pm or 2.00 pm to 10.00 pm. Use the information given in this section and the specimen application form used in Task One to help you.

Extension material

Cadbury Printers Ltd is run by John and Frances Kay and currently employs a staff of ten. They are planning to expand their business having recently obtained several new customers who require colour printing work. They are seeking to employ someone with design layout skills and experience of running a four-colour printing press and have placed an advertisement in the local paper. They have received more than 40 enquiries about the job and have sent out applications forms. However, two weeks later they have received only three completed application forms and after reading through them only one of the candidates seems suitable.

1 Make a list of all the sections which should appear on the application form and indicate which of these are general and which are specific to the job.

2 What problems do you think Cadbury Printers Ltd. may have with the application forms they have sent out to prospective employees?

3 Suggest ways in which Cadbury Printers Ltd. could improve the design of their application form.

4 Using your answers, prepare a new application form for the company which will help them overcome the problems you have identified in your answer to questions (2) and (3).

Curriculum Vitae

A Curriculum Vitae or CV is a personal work history. Today, many firms ask applicants applying for jobs to include a CV with their letter of application or application form. They are best prepared on a word processor so that they can be updated whenever a change to your personal circumstances occurs. This also allows you to tailor each CV to the demands of each particular job you apply for and then print fresh copies as required.

It is important to put as much relevant information as possible into your CV as the person who is looking at it will probably never have met you. Think of it as a piece of advertising where you are trying to sell yourself to someone else! Although the layout of a CV may vary slightly from individual to individual, the main elements you would include are given in Figure 12, together with an explanation of the

CURRICULUM VITAE	
Name	Give this in full with your surname in capitals.
Address	Full present address where you can be contacted during the day. Include your postcode.
Date of Birth	Day, month and year of birth in full.
Status	Whether you are married or single.
Education	Give details of secondary schools you have attended together with the dates. It is not necessary to give details of your primary education.
Qualifications	Present information about examinations you have taken/will take and the grades or levels obtained or that you expect to obtain.
Employment	Write about all the part-time jobs you have had. Include the name and address of the company, your job title, the dates you worked there and the duties you carried out. If necessary give details of how you progressed from one job to another within the same firm. Start with your most recent job and work backwards.
Work Experience	Give details of your work experience placements. Include the reasons why you decided to go to each firm, what you did and what you gained from the placement.
Hobbies/Interests	Try and give as much information as possible. For example - reading science fiction not just reading. Try to give details which may be useful in the job for which you are applying. For example - I enjoy working on my computer.
Personal Qualities	Do not be afraid to point out personal characteristics which will be useful in your work. Be brief and honest giving reasons to support what you say.
Any other Information	There may be things you would like to say which do not fall into any of the above categories. For example - charity work or a special activity you have been involved with at school.

Figure 12 Curriculum Vitae

information which should be included in each section.

Although it can take a long time to prepare, a Curriculum Vitae can provide you with an opportunity of 'selling' yourself to a potential employer in a way that a letter of application or an application form may not allow you to.

Advantages of using a Curriculum Vitae

These include the following:

- Candidates can include other information which may not be requested on an application form.
- A Curriculum Vitae can be prepared in advance, ready to be used as and when a vacancy arises.
- CVs provide an insight into how candidates see themselves to be suitable for a particular job.
- Applicants can tailor their CV to suit the requirements of a particular job.
- They can save a firm the cost of producing application forms.

Disadvantages of using a Curriculum Vitae

These include the following:

- Each applicant may set information out in a different way, so making it more difficult for employers to compare them.
- A previously prepared CV may not provide all the details an employer would require when they are using them to help select a short list of candidates.
- Applicants may deliberately omit information which does not present them in a good light.

Despite these drawbacks, many firms now ask for applicants to submit CVs with their letters of application for a post, and they are used as one of the main criteria on which the short list of applicants who will be called for interview is drawn up.

Exercises

1 What is a Curriculum Vitae or CV? (2)

2 Why is it a good idea to word process your Curriculum Vitae? (2)

3 List the main information headings you would include on a CV. (3)

4 What advantages does a CV have for a prospective employee rather than completing an application form? (3)

5 Why is it important to spell check and proof-read your CV before sending it out? (4)

6 What are the drawbacks of a CV to (a) an applicant and (b) a potential employer? (6)

Using the example Curriculum Vitae given previously, word process a copy of your own CV. Save it for future use. Make sure you take care to spell check and proof-read your work.

Your friend has recently left school and has word processed a Curriculum Vitae which she intends to use when applying for a job at a local branch of Boots the Chemist. She has asked you to check it for accuracy. She has also asked you to suggest any other alterations she could make or anything else that she could include.

Curriculum Vitae

Name	Carley Anne Bush
Address	10 Tickenham Road, Bedminster, Bristol BS3 1JL
Date of Birth	13 Jan 1984
Status	Single
Education	Eastleigh Primary School, Bedminster, Bristol BS3 4JR Ashton Park Community School, Ashton Park Drive, Bedminster, Bristol BS3 2RP
Examinations	GCSEs in Geography grade B English Language grade C Media Studies grade E Design Technology grade E Home Economics grade C Mathematics grade C Double Science grade C PE Studies grade B
Employment	I have been working on Saturdays at Pullens, the Bakers in North Street, Bedminster for the past 10 months. I serve customers, handle money and stock shelves. I enjoy the work and have got on well without too many problems.
Work Experience	I spent two weeks at the vets helping with operations and looking after the animals. I like animals and have 2 cats, a dog and 3 gerbils which I look after in a cage in my bedroom.
Personal Qualities	I am neat and tidy and enjoy working as part of a group. I am fairly outgoing and enjoy meeting new people. In the past year I have occasionally been late for school, but can get up on time when I want to.
Other Interests	I enjoy socialising with my friends at the weekend, although my dad says I go out too much and stay out too late. I am a member of Ashton Gymnastics Club and play hockey for Bedminster Ladies each week.
Referees	Ashton Park Community School, Ashton Park Drive, Bedminster, Bristol BS3 2RP Jenny Jay, The Manager, Pullens Bakery, North Street, Bedminster, Bristol BS3 1JL

Write or word process a list of ways in which you can help Carley improve her Curriculum Vitae. Give brief reasons to support each of your suggestions.

Extension material

Word process a copy of a Curriculum Vitae for Carley, including any of the alterations and amendments you have suggested in Task Two.

Interviews

The most common way of deciding on who is the most appropriate person for a particular job is to meet them face to face, to interview them, to ask questions and judge their responses. An interview is, however, a two-way process and it is just as important for the potential employer to gauge the worth of the candidates as it is for the candidates to use the interview to decide whether or not they wish to work for that particular company.

Interviews can range from the informal, where a candidate may meet their prospective employer for a chat, which enables both to find out more about each other and the job, to the formal interview. A formal interview is likely to be conducted by a panel of two or more interviewers and will follow a more structured approach.

No matter how confident you are, very few people look forward to an interview because it is seen as a test of abilities. If you are not offered the job you feel rejected and inferior to the person who has been successful. Despite the concerns the applicant may feel about interviews, there are a number of advantages to employers in interviewing prospective employees.

These include:

- Interviews allow you to meet and see the applicants face to face.
- They provide an opportunity to judge how an individual responds under the pressure of a formal situation.
- They enable you to gauge how an individual thinks and if they are able to answer questions sensibly without preparation.
- They enable you to get to know the personality of the candidate which may not be apparent on paper, for example do they have a sense of humour?

There are also some drawbacks to interviews, which must be taken into consideration when using this as a means of judging people's suitability for a particular job:

- Some people suffer from nerves and therefore cannot perform well at interview although they may be extremely capable of doing the job.
- They rely on the interviewer being able to judge the character and ability of the applicants in a relatively short space of time.
- Some people are able to disguise their shortcomings, and in doing so cause the interviewer to misjudge their ability.

Some people are naturally good at interviews, although they may not necessarily be good at the job. Most interviewers however, are trained to ask those questions which will enable them to assess the applicant's personality and ability to do a particular job.

Interview preparation

The key to success at interview is preparation. Make sure you know where the firm is and how to get there. Allow yourself sufficient time to ensure you arrive on time for your interview. Remember, to arrive thirty minutes too early is as bad as arriving five minutes late. First impressions count. Check your appearance and make sure you are dressed appropriately. Do not wear your best disco outfit for an interview for a clerical job! As a guide, think what you will be expected to wear to work each day. Try and also think what questions you might be asked and prepare suitable answers for them. It is easier to plan your answers in advance than to rely on thinking up a suitable response off the cuff.

Interview technique

Do not forget that the interview also gives you an opportunity to find out more about the job and the company you may be working for. Keep your eyes open and look around when you go to a company to see what working conditions are like and to note the tasks which existing employees are undertaking. Do they seem happy in what they are doing?

You will also have an opportunity to ask questions at the end of the interview. These may be factual, such as what is the salary or what is the holiday entitlement? Alternatively, they may be more open-ended, such as what are the opportunities for further training or what prospects does the job offer?

Exercises

1 What is the main purpose of an interview for (i) the applicant, and (ii) the prospective employer? (2)

2 Why do firms prefer to interview candidates for jobs rather than solely using letters of application and CVs? (2)

3 How can you prepare for an interview? (3)

4 What are the drawbacks of interviews as a method of selection? What can the firm do to overcome these drawbacks? (4)

5 What opportunities does an interview provide for applicants of a job? (3)

6 What are the differences between the skills and qualities shown by an applicant for a job? Give two examples of suitable skills and two examples of suitable qualities. (6)

Compose and word process answers to each of the following questions which you may be asked at interview, and which are more than just 'yes' or 'no' answers.

1 Do you have a part-time job?

2 Which subject do you like most at school/college?

3 Which subject do you like least at school/college?

4 Are you computer literate?

5 Can you use a spreadsheet?

6 What was the last book you read?

7 Do you enjoy sports activities?

Draw up a list of skills and qualities an interviewer would be seeking from applicants for the following job:

Bristol's leading hairdresser

ROBERT JAMES

requires an

experienced hairdresser with qualifications

to work as part of a well-motivated team

Outgoing personality

Sense of humour

The successful candidate will be required to

cover staff holiday and other absences

in our shops in the Bristol area

Own transport essential

35 hours per week including

some evening work

Salary £7,500 plus tips

telephone Sara for further details 0117 942 6030

Extension material

Obtain a copy of the jobs section from your local/regional newspaper. Select a particular job which appeals to you and for which you think you would be qualified.

Word process a memorandum to the Assistant Office Manager setting out the requirements you feel are necessary for a suitable place in which to conduct the interview. Also include a paragraph giving details of appropriate clothing for the interviewer to wear. Prepare a list of five questions you would ask each applicant for the job which will encourage them to give more than a 'yes' or 'no' answer. Under each of these explain how you would expect a good candidate to answer the question.

Conducting interviews

To be successful and to give the candidates the best possible opportunity to show what they are capable of, firms should plan their interviews carefully. On arrival at a company for an interview, it is important that candidates are greeted in a courteous and friendly way which will help them feel more relaxed. A suitable, quiet area needs to be set aside where candidates can wait without being in the main area where business is conducted, together with toilet facilities so that they can ensure they are comfortable and look presentable.

Sometimes candidates are all called for interview at the same time and meet together to be 'briefed' at the start of the day and possibly shown around the company. They are then interviewed individually in an agreed order. At other times, the interviewees may be given specific times to attend for interview and do not meet any other candidates.

Depending on the nature of the vacancy, interviews may be conducted by an individual or by a panel of several people. Applicants for senior posts are more likely to be interviewed by a panel who will then discuss each candidate in turn and reach a consensus of opinion. Applicants for junior office posts are likely to be interviewed by one person – perhaps the Office Manager – who will make the decision.

Whenever possible, the interview itself should be conducted in private, free from any industrial noises and without interruption from other staff or telephone calls. The surroundings in which the interviews take place should allow the candidate to relax and to concentrate on the questions being asked. It is very difficult for both applicant and interviewer to concentrate when there are frequent interruptions or a great deal of noise in the background.

A good interviewer will consider the following when setting up an interview:

1. Adopt a suitably friendly manner, showing respect to all candidates.

- Ensure that all questions meet the legal requirements to give every applicant a fair and equal opportunity to succeed.
- Conduct the interview at an unhurried pace ensuring there are no interruptions.
- Ensure candidates are encouraged to answer questions as fully as possible and give them time to do so.
- Try to get the candidates to discuss areas which they have not fully explained in their application forms or Curriculum Vitae.

Interview structure

To meet the requirements of equal opportunities legislation, all applicants should be asked the same questions at interview. This will help ensure that each interviewee receives the same opportunity to demonstrate their knowledge, understanding and skills during their interview and no one candidate will be favoured over another. The responses to these questions are used to assess an applicant's ability and suitability for the vacancy. The average interview lasts about thirty minutes and will be broken down into three main parts.

The introduction, which is designed to relax the candidate and dispel any nerves, will last no more than four to five minutes. Here the members of the panel and the candidate will be introduced and the nature of the vacancy explained. This may include why the vacancy has occurred, details of the job description and some indication of the attributes of the successful candidate.

The main part of the interview may last for 20 minutes or more and the candidates will be asked questions by the interviewer or members of the interviewing panel in turn. This part of the interview needs to be sufficiently flexible to allow the interviewers to develop any areas of interest which may come up in the discussion.

Finally, candidates should be given the opportunity to ask any questions they may have or raise any other relevant issues. They should also be informed of when they may hear whether or not they have been successful in their application.

Assessment and selection

Once the interview has ended, time should be spent immediately on writing up notes about the candidate and how they performed. A great deal of information will have been obtained during the interview and the interviewers will need to record this in order to help them decide which candidate is the most suitable. This information may be obtained in a number of ways:

- Physical appearance, such as dress and mannerisms.
- Qualifications, both academic and vocational.
- Experience.
- Intelligence, assessed in the way candidates respond to open ended questions.
- Motivation, judged by enthusiasm and interest expressed.
- Interests and hobbies, which show how people make use of their spare time.

The decision as to who is successful will be based on the interviewer's appreciation of all of the above as well as their personal impression of each candidate. The key factor in this will be their impression of how well the successful applicant will be able to meet the requirements of the job specification and whether the candidate will be able to fit in with existing employees. Inevitably there is some subjective judgement involved on the part of the interviewer.

Most firms appoint for a trial period of time, often called a 'probationary period', to ensure the successful candidate is indeed able to meet the requirements of the job specification and settle in to his or her new post. During this period the candidate will be monitored and assessed to see how well they are able to do the job, to assess their attitude towards it, and to see how they get on with colleagues. Candidates are only likely to be appointed as a permanent member of staff if they successfully complete this probationary period.

Exercises

1 How can you prepare for a job interview? (3)

2 List the requirements a firm should consider when organising a job interview. (3)

3 Why are most interviews broken down into three main parts? Explain the purpose of each part. (4)

4 When you start a new job, what is meant by the term probationary period? (2)

5 Why are applicants for more senior posts likely to be interviewed by a panel of interviewers, rather than an individual? (4)

6 During an interview, how would an interviewer be able to judge a candidate's intelligence and possible motivation for a job? (4)

You are the Office Manager for a medium size company selling china and glassware to restaurants and cafés. You would like to employ a new Office Junior and have drawn up a shortlist of five possible candidates from all the applicants. The duties of the Office Junior will include the following:

- Some word processing.
- Talking to customers and potential customers on the telephone.
- Taking responsibility for all office filing.
- Making tea and coffee for the other office staff.
- Standing in for the receptionist during her lunch break.
- Running occasional messages between the office and the warehouse.

Prepare a list of criteria you would be looking for in each of the applicants and state the minimum requirements which would satisfy you for each of the criteria.

The afternoon before the interviews take place you have asked your assistant to prepare the interview room for the following day. Complete either of the following tasks:

1 Draw up a detailed list of requirements you need to ensure the interviews go off smoothly and give each candidate the best chance of doing well.

2 Draw up a plan of the interview room and waiting area indicating what you would require in each of them and why.

Extension material

You are the secretary to the Office Manager and she has asked you to draw up a list of five or six questions to ask each applicant for the Office Junior's job. Once you have devised your list of questions, set them out on a sheet of A4 paper to include sufficient space after each question for your employer to make notes during the interview. Remember to include a heading at the top of the sheet for the candidate's name and any other information you think is relevant.

Contract of employment

Under the Employment Protection Act, 1978, once a person is offered a job by a firm they are entitled to a Contract of Employment within thirteen weeks of starting work. This contract should show the main terms and conditions of the employment. In addition it will also give details of any grievance procedures which can be invoked either by the employer should the employee prove to be an unsatisfactory worker, or by the employee should he or she feel unfairly treated by the firm.

Information in a contract of employment is set out in four main sections, although other conditions relating to individual companies may often be included. The four main sections include:

1 Details of the company, the employee, the job title and the date on which employment commenced.
2 Details of the normal hours of work including meal breaks and the rates of pay together with the frequency and the method of payment. It also details holiday entitlement and holiday pay and the length of notice required by employee and employer should either wish to terminate the employment. The period of notice may be waived should the employee be dismissed for professional misconduct. Details of this will be given in the fourth section.
3 Any terms and conditions related to involuntary absence through sickness or industrial injury. It also gives details of the terms and conditions of any pension provision and, where applicable, any conditions which may relate to trade union membership.
4 Information on disciplinary or grievance procedures for both employee and employer and the arrangements for dealing with them.

The contract of employment will be signed by both employee and employer to show their acceptance of the conditions and a copy issued to the employee for them to keep.

An example of a contract of employment is shown on page 110.

Freshco Supermarkets Limited
Freshco House, Market Street, Bristol, BS2 3DG

TERMS AND CONDITIONS OF EMPLOYMENT

This statement sets out the terms and conditions of employment between Freshco Supermarkets Limited and:

Title: Ms
Forenames: Rebecca Louise
Surname: Courtney
Employee number: 01234/56

Date of Employment

Your continuous employment began on 25 September 1999. If you subsequently rejoin the company following a career break, your separate periods of service will be linked together to calculate your total cumulative service.

Job Title

Your job title is: Customer Service Assistant
Your job code is: CSA91
You will also be required to carry out other duties that may be reasonably required of you in any other department.

Location

You will be based at: Branch 231, Broadmead, Bristol
but you may be required to work from an alternative location within reasonable travelling distance of this location. You may be required to go to other locations for staff training purposes.

Hours

Your normal paid working hours will be: 37 hours per week
The days to be worked, together with starting and finishing times will be those agreed with your immediate superior. You will be expected to work additional hours if necessary. If you work less than 37 hours per week you will be expected to cooperate in extending your normal working week, at short notice, in special circumstances. If you are contracted to work on Sunday as well as other days in the week you will be paid double the standard hourly rate.

Pay

Your hourly rate of pay will be: £4.10 and your total weekly pay will be: £151.70
Details of the individual elements making up your total pay will be given in your itemised payslip.

You will be paid monthly on the last working day of each month in arrears by credit transfer. The company reserves the right to recover any overpayment of earnings.

The company operated an Inland Revenue approved Profit Related Pay scheme (PRP) details of which can be obtained from your store Personnel Manager.

Sickness

Details of absence due to sickness or injury, and entitlements to sick pay, can be found in your Staff Handbook.

Holidays

You will be entitled to four weeks paid holiday for each twelve months service you complete. You are also entitled to time off in lieu should you have to work any of the statutory Bank Holidays.

Pension Scheme

Details of the Company's pension scheme and how to join it are given in your Staff Handbook. Unless you complete a form, available only from the Pensions Department, stating that you do not wish to join, pension contributions will be deducted automatically from your pay.

Notice

A minimum of four weeks notice is required from either party should you or the Company wish to terminate your employment. Employees with more than two years service will be entitled to redundancy should their post no longer be required.

Disciplinary Procedures

Full details of the disciplinary procedure which may be used if your conduct or performance falls below the required standard are available from your store Personnel Manager or can be found on the Staff Notice Board.

Grievances

If you wish to raise a grievance about a job related issue, you need to complete a Grievance Registration Form and return it to your store Personnel Manager who will arrange for your grievance to be heard. If you subsequently wish to take the matter further, you should follow the procedure set out in the Company's disciplinary procedure, a copy of which can be obtained from your store Personnel Manager or can be found on the Staff Notice Board.

Changes

Any changes to the details provided in this document will be communicated to you in writing within one month of the change. Should your individual Contract of Employment need to be changed you will be consulted for a minimum of four weeks prior to being given notice of the change taking place.

I understand and accept the terms and conditions of employment outlined above.

Employee's signature .... Date::........................

Employer's signature .... Date:::........................

Figure 13 Contract of employment

Termination of Employment

The contract of employment will include a period of notice which either the employee or the employer must give if they wish to terminate the employment. The most frequent way in which employment is terminated is with mutual agreement by both parties, possibly when an employee retires or when they obtain another job and hand in their notice and resign. In the normal course of events the employee then continues to work for the agreed period of notice in the contract of employment after which they move on to retirement or their new job. However, there are times when the employer will wish to end the contract of employment. For example, if the employer is dissatisfied with the employee in any way – they may be unpunctual, or incompetent, or have acted in an inappropriate way – then they may be dismissed once the correct disciplinary procedures have been followed. Alternatively, if the business is faced with a shortage of work or orders, then the employee may be made redundant. In this case, employment is terminated and, depending on how long the employee has worked for the company, they may receive compensation in the form of redundancy pay based on the number of years of service with the firm.

Exercises

1 How soon after starting work must an employee receive a Contract of Employment? (1)

2 Explain what you would expect to find in the four main sections of a Contract of Employment. (4)

3 What is meant by the term *period of notice*? (1)

4 When would the period of notice be waived? (1)

5 Who signs the Contract of Employment? Why do you think this is? (2)

6 Which Act of Parliament regulates the terms and conditions of employment? (1)

Word process a list of the four sections which a contract of employment should contain. Give each section an appropriate title and set your work out using marginal or side headings on a sheet of A4 paper. Include a suitable main heading and centre your work vertically on the page.

Using the job details in the previous section for an Office Junior and the sample given in the text, prepare a contract of employment for the successful applicant to sign. Use the details given and insert any other relevant information necessary to complete the contract.

Extension material

Try to obtain a contract of employment from a member of your family or a close friend. Compare it with the contract given in the text. Check carefully for any similarities and differences between the two contracts. Then word process a list of the differences you have found. What, if anything, would you add to either contract to make them more complete?

Training and appraisal

If the workforce in a company is to be kept up-to-date with new technology and developments in the industry, they will require training. Training is essential to ensure employees learn new skills and improve those they already have. This can have a number of benefits for both the employee and the business:

- Trained workers are able to produce more which makes them more profitable to employ.
- Trained workers can improve efficiency in a number of ways. They may be more confident dealing with customers as they know what they are doing; they may be trained in health and safety procedures so are less likely to suffer industrial accidents.
- Workers who are trained to do several tasks are described as 'multi-skilled'. This makes them more flexible as they can do a number of different jobs within a business. Unexpected vacancies due to illness can be covered quickly and easily by those workers who have the necessary skills. Supermarkets frequently train all their staff to work on the checkouts, so they can call them from the shop floor to operate extra tills when the store is busy.
- Training can also help to motivate employees and encourage promotion. Once they have spent money training them firms will want to retain workers so their job becomes more secure. In addition, those employees who gain qualifications will find it easier to obtain work elsewhere if they decide to move on.

Despite the advantages training brings, it is expensive and can often tie up employees in work, which at the time, is not contributing directly to production. Training must therefore be effective. By the end of any training session workers should be better educated and more skilled to enable them to work more quickly with fewer errors, thus making them more productive.

There are five types of training methods detailed in this unit: induction; on-the-job; off-the-job; in-house and Government training schemes.

Induction

This is the training which introduces new employees to a business. It is often about the way in which the business works rather than about the job the new employee may have been hired to do. An induction training programme would usually include instruction on:

- The history and management structure of the firm.
- The terms of employment as set out in the contract of employment.
- Facilities, benefits and services available to the employee, such as a subsidised staff canteen or a pension scheme.
- Any rules, regulations and safety procedures.
- An introduction to other workers including any supervisory staff in the area the new employee is to be working.

On-the-job training

This type of training involves workers being trained as they continue to do their jobs. There are several ways in which this form of training takes place:

'At their elbow'

This is the most common form of on-the-job training, and is where the new employee works with or next to an experienced worker and learns the job 'at their elbow'. Whilst this method of training is relatively inexpensive and less likely to disrupt the productive flow of work, new employees can often learn bad habits or develop poor work practices from the established employee who may not be an accredited trainer. The quality of this form of training is also dependent on the degree to which existing workers are willing to involve themselves in the process.

Mentoring

Many office and professional workers use a scheme of mentoring. This system enables a new employee to work on their own initiative whilst being paired with a more experienced member of staff who is able to offer them advice and help, as well as discussing any problems which they may experience. New workers are given more freedom and are able to use their initiative but still have the 'safety net' of being able to refer possible problems to more experienced staff.

Coaching

Less popular than mentoring is the system of coaching where a senior employee can guide the development of a junior by continuously watching them at work, offering advice and help when required and assessing their overall progress. Whilst the management may feel the work is being carried out to their satisfaction, new employees can feel they are being continuously watched by their immediate superior, which may not engender good working relationships and could lead to possible resentment.

Job rotation

Some firms use a system of job rotation, where new employees work for a short period of time in each of the different departments in a company. This system has been used successfully in the retail trade where supermarkets train their future managers by making each of them work for a period of six months in every department in the store. In this way they learn how each section of the store functions on a daily basis. This helps them develop a working knowledge of all aspects of the business.

Off-the-job training

This training occurs where employees receive their training away from their work station or place of work. As with on-the-job training, it can take several forms, ranging from companies organising their own training to courses being run by local colleges or national training organisations.

Businesses often pay to send employees on courses which will provide them with additional skills and knowledge. Some employees, however, may embark on courses to improve their working skills in their own time and at their own expense. Evening classes, particularly those which provide computer related skills, are currently very popular.

In-house training

Many companies organise their own, or in-house training. Induction training is often handled in this way, as new recruits are introduced to the working practices of a business. This form of training tends to be popular with many companies as it takes place in the employee's normal place of work, is related directly to the company's requirements and is relatively quick and inexpensive to organise. The level of training, however, is dependent upon the skills and expertise of those doing the training. If they have poor communication skills or lack the expertise to demonstrate procedures correctly, bad working practices may be taught.

Some larger organisations, such as banks, building societies and insurance companies endeavour to overcome these problems by employing their own specialist trainers to deliver the training needs of all the company's staff. This may take place in a specialist training unit within the organisation or at a central training centre. One day, weekend and weekly courses can be offered and accommodation provided where necessary. The armed forces, police and fire brigade, who often require specialist equipment, provide training in this way. The use of specialist trainers also means that the courses offered are more likely to be of a high quality and will include the latest ideas, new techniques and processes. Consequently, the training will be up-to-date and so more highly valued by those who receive it.

During the 1990's the Government, in consultation with employers, employees, trades unions and trainers, set up the Employment Department of National Education and Training Targets which has led to the introduction of National Vocational Qualifications, or NVQs, in most industries. These are courses which provide employees with training in the skills and levels of competence directly related to the industry in which they work. Those who achieve the required standard are awarded appropriate qualifications by examination boards such as AQA and Edexcel.

Government training schemes

In addition to NVQs, the Government also promotes training schemes for young people through the Department of Employment. These include the **Youth Training** scheme (YT) which ensures that all sixteen year old school leavers going into employment receive both on-the-job and off-the-job training, which will in turn lead to nationally recognised qualifications. The **Modern Apprenticeship Scheme** has also been established to provide apprenticeships for young people, ensuring they receive full and proper training in the trade or profession in which they are working.

Recently, the Government has launched the adult training scheme **Employment Training** (ET) which aims to provide off-the-job training for those registered as long-term unemployed. Initially the scheme is offering 300,000 training places in an attempt to improve the skills of this section of the workforce to make them more attractive to potential employers.

Appraisal

Appraisal occurs when an employee's performance and value to the company is assessed. It is supposed to be a non-threatening process, not judging an individual, but seeking to establish how well they are carrying out their duties in comparison with their job description. The results of an appraisal can help management to determine future training needs of their employees and can also help in assessing future human resource planning requirements.

An increasing number of employers are now appraising their employees regularly, usually on an annual basis. This enables them to evaluate the usefulness of the employee to the organisation. Once this has been established, the firm is then able to set objectives to improve performance and productivity and to identify the training requirements needed to achieve them. Employees' motivation comes from the possibility of increased pay through productivity bonuses or possible promotion. However, appraisal is usually carried out by a superior or line manager which makes it difficult for them to remain impartial. Consequently workers very often feel threatened by the process.

Appraisal can take place in several ways:

- By line managers who have the advantage of knowing the employee's working practices and habits, and so are able to make a more informed assessment. However, as has already been mentioned, this can be intimidating for the worker who often sees their superior as a potential threat.
- By a work colleague of equal standing who has a full understanding of the demands of the job and so can measure the real worth of the employee. This form of appraisal, however, is unpopular amongst workers who are often unprepared to appraise each other and see it as a means of informing on colleagues.
- Self appraisal, where the employee assesses their own performance. This is often regarded as the most accurate but still needs to be linked to some form of validation by the employee's line manager. Many workers, however, are reluctant to 'blow their own trumpet' and results can often undervalue the worth of the employee.

Appraisal schemes are important if employers are to be able to provide relevant and up-to-date training for their workers. To be successful everyone involved in an appraisal scheme must understand clearly its purpose and method. It must be an 'open' process, where each individual has access to any assessment which results from the scheme. The criteria on which the appraisal is based must be related to the job and not the individual, and must be seen by the worker to be fair and unbiased. Finally, the appraisal must have some constructive purpose that is apparent to those involved in it. Workers are unlikely to co-operate in an appraisal system which provides them with little or no personal benefit.

Exercises

1 Explain the benefits to (a) the employee and (b) the firm of providing training opportunities for employees. (4)

2 What are the benefits of training employees so they are multiskilled? (2)

3 Why do businesses operate induction programmes for new staff even though they cost money to run? (3)

4 Describe the methods which can be used to provide on the job training, giving an advantage and a disadvantage of each. (4)

5 Why does the Government provide training schemes? Give two examples of schemes offered. (3)

6 What is the purpose of an appraisal? Explain the benefits it can bring to (a) an individual employee and (b) the business. (4)

Your employer has asked you to develop a training programme to improve the skills of those working in the office of your company. Prepare a written report on one side of A4 paper to show the benefits of using an in-house training scheme rather than bringing in an external organisation to arrange courses.

Following your report, your employer has decided to carry out training using the firm's in-house facilities. Compare the advantages and disadvantages of on-the-job rather than off-the-job training. Word process a memorandum to your employer showing your findings. Prepare a final paragraph in which you outline your recommendation as to which of these two methods of training would be more suitable.

Extension material

You have been asked to introduce a new student to your school or college. She is taking the same subjects as you are. Devise the draft outline of the information you would include in an induction programme so that she will be able to fit into the school/college and her programme of study easily and comfortably. Prepare the outline in four sections:

1 Personal information, such as the structure of the working day, the geography of the buildings, food and toilet facilities, etc.

2 Course information, such as staff members, rooms, topics previously covered, etc.

3 Training requirements, such as use of computers, logging on to the network, etc.

4 Appraisal. What form of appraisal will you use to ensure she has settled in to her courses, etc?

Wages and salaries

What is the difference between wages and salaries? Wages are paid weekly, often in cash, and salaries are paid monthly, usually directly into an employee's bank account. However, some firms, for example Tesco, pay their employees' salaries on a four-weekly basis, so they receive thirteen pay days each year.

The one thing everyone looks forward to when they are working, is the day they get paid! Many of you will already have done some paid work. It could be a paper round, Saturday work in a local shop or café, or possibly baby-sitting for a friend or relative.

There are two main ways in which the reward for the work we do is calculated: piece rates and time rates.

In the examples given in this unit, whether you are paid using piece rates or time rates, you earn the same amount of money, but which method of payment is best for you? Both have their advantages and disadvantages.

Piece rates

In this method you are paid for the number of 'pieces' or 'units' of work you complete or sell. For example, you might work for a local gardening company planting trees and get paid £2.00 for each tree you plant. If you planted 12 trees you would earn (12 × £2.00 per tree) £24.00.

The advantages of being paid by piece rates include:

- The faster you work, the more money you can earn.
- You can pace yourself to earn what you wish and not have to work flat out all day.
- You are paid according to your ability to do the job, as the rewards are better for faster, more efficient workers.

There are, however, disadvantages:

- Speed to complete more work can lead to shoddy, poor quality work.
- Rates of pay can be set too low, so the work is regarded as 'slave labour' and workers are seen to be exploited.
- Pay-based employment often ignores other factors which motivate people, such as helping people, as in the case of nursing.

Time rates

In this method you are paid for each period of time you are at work. If it took you six hours to plant the 12 trees and you were paid £4.00 per hour, you would earn (6 × £4.00 per hour) £24.00.

The advantages of being paid by time rates include:

- You are paid for the hours you are at work even though you may not work all the time.
- Everyone receives the same rate for the same job.
- Overtime rates can be calculated to compensate you for the loss of your leisure time if you have to work longer hours.

The disadvantages include:

- Your employer has to pay you regardless of the output you produce.
- Those able to produce more may be less motivated to do so as they get paid the same rate as those who produce less.
- There is little financial incentive to work hard.

Overtime

As the name implies, overtime is paid to an employee when they work extra hours, or 'over the time', for which they would normally expect to be paid. It is usually calculated as an additional fraction added to the basic hourly rate. For example, time and a quarter. For each extra hour worked, the employee is paid the normal hourly rate plus a quarter of that rate as compensation for having to work longer than normal. If an employee's usual rate of pay is £5.00 per hour, if they are being paid overtime at time and a quarter, they would receive £5.00 plus a quarter of £5.00 (£5.00 + £1.25) ie £6.25 per hour for each extra hour worked.

The advantages of overtime include:

- employees are rewarded for working over and above their normal working week
- it can act as an incentive to those employees who wish to, or may have to work longer hours
- regular overtime can increase an employee's weekly earnings and so improve his or her disposable income and standard of living
- it may encourage employees to work during unsociable hours (eg evenings, weekends and bank holidays) when it may otherwise be difficult to obtain employees willing to work for the normal hourly rate. This is particularly true in the retail trade since the introduction by many supermarkets of 24-hour opening.

The disadvantages of overtime include:

- some employees may work slowly during the day to 'create' work which has to be completed in overtime
- it increases the firm's wage bill and the payment of labour is often one of the highest costs in a business
- some employees may not be willing to work overtime, even though they are offered extra money for doing so, which may make it difficult for a business to provide the required number of staff or meet production deadlines.

In recent years, as we have become more conscious of the need to protect workers from exploitation, there has been a move away from paying workers using a piece rate formula. Most people are now paid on a time rate basis. This ensures that unscrupulous employers do not take advantage of workers by making them work very long hours in order to obtain a reasonable income on which to live. Recent Government legislation has introduced a minimum wage for those aged 18 years or over. This is based on a time rate which is currently set at £3.70 per hour for those workers aged 22 years or over.

Exercises

1 Explain the difference between wages and salary. Give an example of an occupation which is paid using both methods. (3)

2 What are the benefits to the employee of being paid using a time rate formula? (3)

3 What are the benefits to a business of paying its employees on a piece rate system? (3)

4 Why has there been a move by firms towards time rate schemes in recent years? (4)

5 Explain how workers could be exploited by unscrupulous employers if they are being paid on piece rates. (4)

6 Explain the meaning of the term *national minimum wage*. At what rate is the national minimum wage currently set? (3)

1 Will Courtney runs a newsagents and employs five part-time staff. He currently pays them £4.35 per hour. Use a spreadsheet and the following information to calculate his total wage bill. Ensure the third and fourth columns are set up in currency format.

Employee	Hours worked	Rate	Weekly wage
Lisa Granville	15	£4.35	
Matt Hickey	20	£4.35	
Karen O'Brien	24	£4.35	
Raj Singh	18	£4.35	
Zac Wootton	12	£4.35	

Table 10 Wages bills

2 Lisa and Raj have now worked for Will for more than two years and take charge of the shop when he is not there. He would like to pay them an extra 70 pence per hour. Use the spreadsheet you have created to calculate the increase in Will's weekly wage costs.

3 Karen has been able to obtain a full-time job in the Greengrocer's shop next door. Delete her record. Will has employed two new staff to replace her. These are Jane Thorogood who will work 16 hours a week and Janet Barrett who will work the remainder of the hours previously worked by Karen. He has agreed to pay them £3.70 per hour for the first two months whilst they are learning the job. Amend the spreadsheet to show the total Will now has to pay in wages.

When he left school at 16 years of age Edwin Burston worked for an engineering firm helping to assemble water pumps. After four years of this, he believed he had gained sufficient experience and knowledge to set himself up in business assembling pumps. He obtained a bank loan and rented premises and equipment. He decided to pay each of his six workers 65 pence per assembled unit. They assembled the following number of pumps in the first week:

Employee	Water pumps Assembled
Simon Bryant	256
Gemma Banks	310
Owen Richards	209
Carly Suchecka	265
Oliver Topham	301
Melanie Woodward	287

Table 11 Pumps assembled

1 Calculate each worker's weekly pay and the total paid to the whole workforce.

2 Unfortunately Edwin found that a number of the assembled units did not work properly. An investigation showed that each employee had produced the following number of faulty pumps:

Simon	10	Carly	12
Gemma	23	Oliver	15
Owen	2	Melanie	23

Table 12 Faulty pumps

Edwin decided not to pay his employees for the faulty units and to deduct them from the total each had produced. Enter the appropriate additional columns in your work to show the number of faulty units produced by each employee and the number on which Edwin will now calculate each worker's pay. What is the new total wage bill?

Extension material

Shelina Ali runs a small factory producing sunglasses for a large high street retail chain store. She has always paid her workers £2.05 for each pair of glasses produced. Recently, however, the quality of workmanship has declined. To encourage her workers to take more care, Shelina is planning to introduce a revised payment scheme. The new scheme is based on a basic payment of £100 per week for each worker, plus £1.45 for each completed pair of sunglasses.

Calculate the difference this will make to Shelina's weekly wage costs.

Shelina has also decided to make an allowance for rejected work of 10% of each employee's output. Re-calculate the costs for both methods of payment to include this reject rate.

Philippa Frost produces 162 pairs
Claire Rostron produces 167 pairs

Fiona Moncrieff produces 146 pairs
Wendy Smith produces 124 pairs

Methods of payment

Whether you are paid weekly or monthly, in cash or directly into your bank account, most people receive a notification of their gross and net pay and the deductions which they have paid. In a small company these may be prepared by the company accountant or a trusted member of the clerical staff. In larger companies these pay slips are usually prepared by the wages department. A typical pay slip is shown in Figure 14 with the main items indicated.

HOLDSWORTH ENGINEERING LTD
Pay and Deductions for the month ending August 2001

Gross Pay		Pay and Deductions to date	
Basic Monthly Pay	£625.25	Taxable Pay this year	£3078.75
Overtime 10 hrs @ £5.00	£50.00	Tax deducted this year	£499.80
Total Pay	£675.25	Nat Insurance this year	£223.62
		Superannuation this year	£187.60
Deductions			
PAYE Income Tax	£91.50		
National Insurance	£42.78		
Superannuation	£37.52		
Union Subscriptions	£5.50	EMPLOYEE NAME	TAX CODE
Total Deductions	£177.30	**Shuheb Khan**	**238L**
NET PAY TO 31.8.01	**£497.95**	NATIONAL INSURANCE NO	PAY REF
		YZ 296972 A	5432/2B

Figure 14 Sample pay slip

The left hand side contains details of how the gross pay has been made up ie basic pay and overtime. Below that are listed the deductions (see unit 29) which are taken from the total gross pay to give the net pay, or pay actually received by the employee.

On the right hand side of the pay slip the cumulative figures for pay and deductions are shown for the current tax year. In addition, personal details, such as National Insurance number and the code on which the amount of tax to be paid is calculated.

At the end of every month, the total Income Tax and National Insurance Contributions collected from all employees in the firm are totalled and payment sent to the Inland Revenue.

At the end of the tax year (5 April) an end of year return is prepared for each employee showing details of gross pay they have been paid, any statutory sick pay received, income tax and national insurance deducted and the net amount paid to them. This statement is prepared on a form called a **P60**.

Methods of payment

In addition to preparing the pay slips, the wages clerk will also obtain any money needed for those employees paid in cash and inform the bank of the amounts to be transferred into the accounts of those employees whose payment is made directly into their bank accounts. This is done using BACS the Bankers Automated Clearing System. This computerised system operated by the banks allows money to be transferred from one account to another without having to draw out any cash.

Payment in cash

Some employees prefer to be paid in cash. The advantages of this include:

- Employees receive their pay immediately.
- They can spend it in any way they like as cash is universally accepted.
- They can see exactly how much is left as they spend their money.

Disadvantages of being paid in cash include:

- Mistakes can be made in counting out large sums of money.
- Cash can easily be lost or stolen.
- Moving large sums of money for payrolls from the bank to the company requires special security measures which can be costly.
- Employees in the wages department can be put at risk through potential robbery or possibly be tempted to steal.

Payment through BACS

Advantages of being paid through BACS include the following:

- There is no risk of robbery as there is no cash!
- The whole payroll operation is much quicker and therefore more efficient.

Disadvantages of being paid through BACS include:

- Those workers who prefer to be paid in cash will now have to go to the bank to obtain it.
- Adjustments and amendments to wages cannot be rectified as quickly.

Exercises

1 Why do firms issue pay slips to employees with their wages or salaries? (3)

2 Carefully explain the differences between Gross pay and Net pay. What happens to the various deductions taken? (4)

3 What is the purpose of the Inland Revenue form P60? (2)

4 A firm pays its employees in cash. Explain
a) the advantages of this to an employee
b) the disadvantages of this to the firm. (4)

5 Why are more and more businesses using the BACS system to pay their employees? (3)

6 What are the drawbacks of paying employees through the banking system? (4)

You work as a wages clerk for a small company that manufactures components that are used in the assembly of washing machines and tumble dryers. You employ 26 workers who are currently paid weekly in cash. You would like to change the method of payment to a system where everyone is paid directly into their bank account. Prepare a memorandum to be sent to the Accountant outlining your ideas and the advantages it would bring to the business.

1 Several employees at your company have heard a rumour that the method of payment is to be changed, so they will no longer receive their wages in cash each week. Prepare a notice to go on the staff noticeboard which gives details of the change, explains the disadvantages of cash payments and the advantages to the employees of having their earnings paid directly into their bank account.

2 You have heard that four of your employees have not got bank accounts. Write a personal memo to these employees to explain the benefits of the change and offer them help to set up personal bank accounts.

Extension material

Copy the pay advice note given in the text (Figure 14), using your word processor or desktop publishing package so that it will fit onto an A6 size page. Place your copy in the centre on an A4 sheet and using pull-out boxes, label the different parts of the payslip to show personal details, gross pay, deductions, net pay and the method of payment.

Deductions

Unfortunately, you are not always able to take home all the money you earn. Everyone is allowed to earn a certain amount of money before they have to pay income tax and National Insurance contributions. The full amount we earn, before anything is deducted, is known as gross pay. This is then reduced by certain payments which we are required to make (statutory deductions) or which we can agree to make (voluntary deductions). Once these deductions have been made, what remains is net pay, sometimes called 'take home pay' – the amount which you actually receive.

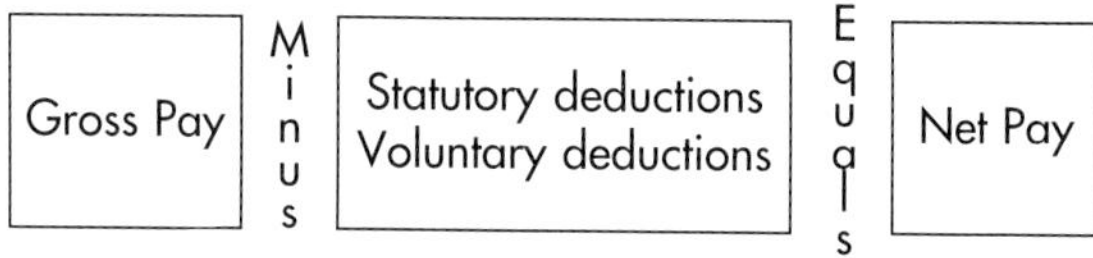

Figure 15 From gross to net pay

Statutory deductions

These are deductions which you are required to pay by law and it is against the law to try to avoid paying them.

Income tax

This is a tax on the amount you earn. It is calculated on your gross pay using a tax code, based on your personal circumstances, supplied by the Inland Revenue. The more money you earn, however, the greater the proportion you will have to pay in tax, although you are allowed to earn a certain amount each week or month before you have to start paying any tax. This is known as your 'tax free allowance'. Income tax is deducted from your wage or salary by your employer before you receive your earnings. Your employer then pays the money deducted to the Inland Revenue on your behalf.

National Insurance

This is another tax which is deducted from your earnings before you receive them. Money taken in National Insurance contributions is used to help finance the National Health Service. Employers are also required to pay an amount equal to or greater than that which each employee pays. The amount you pay in National Insurance varies according to the amount you earn.

Voluntary deductions

These are deductions which you have agreed to have taken from your wage or salary. They are not compulsory, and may include the following:

Superannuation

In addition to the state retirement pension many people nowadays also pay money each week/month into a company pension fund. This ensures that when they decide to retire they will continue to receive some income from the fund into which they have made their payments. This will enable them to receive more when they retire than the basic state pension. This may be operated by the company or it may be run by another organisation such as an insurance company, for example Prudential Assurance.

Union subscriptions

Many workers join a trade union to protect their interests whilst at work. The subscription they pay can be deducted directly from their wage or salary.

Save As You Earn

As the name implies, this is a saving scheme where you can nominate a regular amount to be taken from your pay before you receive it. The advantage of this is that your savings are taken out of your pay before you receive your pay and placed into a savings account so your savings are 'guaranteed'.

Give as you Earn

It is also possible to donate money to charity directly from your weekly or monthly earnings. The Give as you Earn scheme, which is supported by all the major charities, allows an employee to nominate a regular amount which is then deducted from his or her pay, before they receive it, and paid directly to the charities of the employee's choice. This encourages regular charitable giving, avoids the need to remember to make weekly or monthly donations, and as the money is deducted before net pay is received, is less likely to be 'missed' by the employee.

Exercises

1 Using examples explain the difference between statutory and voluntary deductions. (4)

2 Explain how income tax is calculated. (3)

3 Who is responsible for paying the tax owed to the Inland Revenue? (1)

4 What are National Insurance contributions used for? Who makes them? (4)

5 Explain what is meant by the term *superannuation*. Why is it deducted from pay at source? (4)

6 What are the advantages to an employee of Save as you Earn? (4)

Word process a list of all the statutory and voluntary deductions together with an explanation of each on plain A4 paper. Use marginal paragraph headings to make your notes easier to read.

Use your WP or DTP system to create a copy of the diagram following the first paragraph which shows how your gross pay is reduced to net pay, for your notes. Include examples of Voluntary and Statutory deductions.

Extension material

Using the example of a pay advice slip in the previous unit on page 121, design a pay slip based on an A6 size. This can be either landscape or portrait. When complete, copy and paste the slip onto A4 paper so four copies can be printed on one sheet.

Fringe benefits

Fringe benefits are the additional rewards which employees receive in addition to their weekly or monthly net income. It is a way in which an employer can give additional 'income' to an employee without increasing his or her wage or salary on a permanent basis, and can also be a way of not paying any additional tax. These benefits can be paid in cash, such as an allowance for entertaining clients at home, or in kind, such as a private health insurance scheme.

Benefits in kind

These are the benefits which an employee receives in the form of a product or service such as a car or private health insurance.

Company car

This is the most common fringe benefit in business today. Many employees require a car to carry out their job, such as sales representatives, but are also allowed to use the vehicle for their personal motoring. However, others, such as company directors may not need a car for them to carry out their job but receive one which is paid for by the company as a perk or a benefit which supplements their income.

However, the company car is no longer a 'free' benefit and, depending on the size of the car, employees are now expected to make some payment to the Inland Revenue to cover the income they save by having private use of a car supplied for business use.

Despite this, many people still feel a car is a benefit as they have the prestige of owning a modern, up-to-date vehicle, do not have to pay for servicing or repairs and do not lose money as the car depreciates in value.

Staff discount

Companies, particularly those in the retail trade, will often allow their employees to purchase goods and services at a reduced price. These discounts are often extended to include all the other companies which are part of a group. For example, the Kingfisher Group which controls Woolworth and Comet, amongst others.

Subsidised food and drink

Many companies make food and drinks available to their employees at considerably reduced prices in rest rooms or canteens. This is a particularly useful benefit for those working unsocial hours when cafés and restaurants may be closed. It also ensures workers can obtain a decent meal which provides energy for the second part of the day or shift.

Private health care membership

Employees and their immediate family may receive free private health insurance from a scheme such as BUPA or PPP. This is now often offered as a benefit particularly to those employed in a management position. This benefit allows employees to receive prompt medical attention so ensuring they can get back to work as soon as possible.

Accommodation

Traditionally this is a benefit which has been offered to those working on the land in the form of a tied cottage. Landowners have provided housing for their workers at very low rents, often well below the market price. The term 'tied' indicates that the accommodation is tied to the job and once the employee leaves the job or retires he or she is no longer entitled to the use of the accommodation. Other examples of jobs which can provide living accommodation for those who wish to take advantage of it include the police, school caretakers, the armed services and some hotel workers.

Jobs which include accommodation are sometimes less well paid to take account of the cost to the employer of providing their workers with somewhere to live.

Profit sharing

This is a relatively new form of benefit and, as the title implies, allows employees to share in the success of the firm by receiving part of the profit they have contributed to making. Employees usually receive their payment in the form of company shares, which they can either sell or keep. Many companies, including several major retailers such as Tesco and Marks & Spencer, offer this benefit to their employees.

Benefits in cash

These are the benefits which are paid to the employee in money. This has the advantage that it can be spent on anything the employee wishes, however, any additional income received in this way has the disadvantage of being subject to income tax as additional income.

Bonus payments

This is usually a one-off payment in addition to a wage or salary, which may be paid to an employee for achieving a certain level of performance in their job. The aim of this benefit is to encourage workers to make the effort necessary to achieve the set targets. For example, factory workers may receive a weekly bonus for punctual attendance each day or for producing more than a certain level of output in a given time.

Commission

This is a similar benefit to the bonus payment but the amount paid varies, usually based on a percentage of target sales or output. An example of this could be the commission paid to a salesperson based on the value of sales they achieve in a month.

The main difference between commission and a bonus is that a bonus is based on receiving a fixed amount obtained once a certain target of work has been achieved; whereas a commission payment will vary with the sales or output achieved. The more that is produced, the greater the commission payment is likely to be.

For example, a sales assistant in the perfumery department of a large store has a target of sales to achieve each week of £1,000. She is paid a commission of 5% on all sales in excess of her target. If she sold £1,200 worth of perfume last week she has exceeded her target figure by £200 and would receive commission at 5 per cent on that sum which would amount to an additional payment of £10.

Advantages of fringe benefits

These can include the following:

- They reward the employee for working hard, through for example, bonus and commission payments.
- They allow the employee to share in the success of the firm and so encourage them to work for the future success of the firm, for example profit-sharing schemes.
- They can give a higher social status to the employee, for example receiving a new car each year or an executive model such as Mercedes or Jaguar.
- They avoid having to pay higher incomes to employees, which may be associated with higher taxation rates, by supplying goods they benefit from. For example, accommodation and entertainment allowances.
- The firm can off-set the cost of these benefits against profits and so reduce the amount of tax the company will have to pay.

Disadvantages of fringe benefits

- They are often paid in kind, so the employee has no choice on how the additional earnings can be spent.
- They can disguise actual earnings, for example farm workers are amongst the most poorly paid but often receive reduced cost housing and other produce such as milk and eggs.
- Some benefits lost when the employee leaves a job or retires may cause hardship, for example, housing or a car.
- Schemes related to output or performance will result in fluctuating earnings so making it difficult to be certain of income and to plan expenditure.
- Where earnings are related to success, such as commission payments, less successful employees can become jealous of those who are receiving higher payments. This may in turn, adversely affect working relationships.

Exercises

1 Make a list of possible fringe benefits offered by an employer. (3)

2 Explain why an employee may prefer to have a company car rather than use their own, even though they have to make a contribution to the Inland Revenue. (3)

3 What is the difference between a bonus and a commission payment? Illustrate your answer with a numerical example. (4)

4 What are the benefits of profit sharing to the company? (3)

5 Explain the advantages of awarding fringe benefits to (a) the employee and (b) the business. (4)

6 What are the disadvantages of providing fringe benefits to an employee? (3)

Clinton Pharoh has just obtained a job as a sales representative selling china to retail outlets in the South West. He is expected to travel an average of 1200 miles each month on business. Clinton's new employer, Jenny Schofield, has offered him a new company car, but he will pay the company £30 per month so that he can use the car for his own private motoring. He will also receive a mileage allowance of 10 pence per mile for all business miles to cover the cost of petrol and oil.

Clinton already owns a three year old car which he has paid for. If he uses this car for business he will be paid an allowance of 30 pence per mile for his business mileage.

1 What are the advantages and disadvantages to Clinton Pharoh of running:
 i) the company car, and
 ii) his own car for business purposes?

2 Calculate the monthly payments Clinton would receive when using each car, if he drives:
 i) 1000 miles
 ii) 1200 miles, and
 iii) 1500 miles.

3 Using the information in questions one and two above, select the most appropriate option for Clinton. Compose and word process a memorandum on his behalf to his employer explaining which option he has decided on. Support your decision with both financial and non-financial reasons.

A firm selling carpets employs five sales staff in its high street showroom. It is currently looking at the way in which it can encourage its staff to sell more and has decided on three possible alternatives:

1 Pay all employees on a commission only basis of 5% of everything they sell.

2 Pay all employees a basic weekly wage of £100 and 2.5% commission on everything they sell over £1,000 worth of carpets.

3 Pay all employees a basic weekly wage of £25 and 5% commission on everything they sell over £1,000 worth of carpets.

Set up a spreadsheet to show an employee's gross earnings for each of the three options given if they sell £1,000, £2,000, £3,000, £4,000 and £5,000 worth of carpets in a week.

Extension material

Visit your local supermarket to find out if they have a profit-sharing scheme for their employees? How does this scheme work? How are the profits paid to the employees – in cash, in shares? Do employees keep or sell their shares? If they sell them, what is the procedure?

Compose and word process a report explaining how the scheme works. Include in your report the advantages to the employees and the advantages to the company of the scheme.

PART 4

Communications

- The Process of communication
- Written communication
- Verbal communication
- Electronic communication
- Visual communication
- Business letters
- More on business letters
- Letter composition

The Process of communication

Communication is all about the sending and receiving of information between individuals. In any business there are a number of people who need to share information with each other in order to carry out their jobs successfully. These include workers, managers, directors, shareholders, customers and suppliers. Without clear and effective communications in business, the following problems can arise:

- Products will not be produced on time and to the specification of the customer.
- Supplies of materials will not arrive at the right place, or on time.
- Workers will not know which job they are required to complete first.
- Managers will not know what progress is being made.
- Engineers will not know which machinery requires maintenance and repair.
- Customers will not know when to expect delivery of their orders.

Effective communication is essential to the success of any business organisation.

Communication of messages

Although the process of communication within a business can take many forms, if communication is to take place there are six elements which are common to all messages. These are shown in Figure 16.

The sender

All messages have an originator who sends the message to the receiver and who decides the nature of the message, the channel to be used and the medium by which it is to be sent.

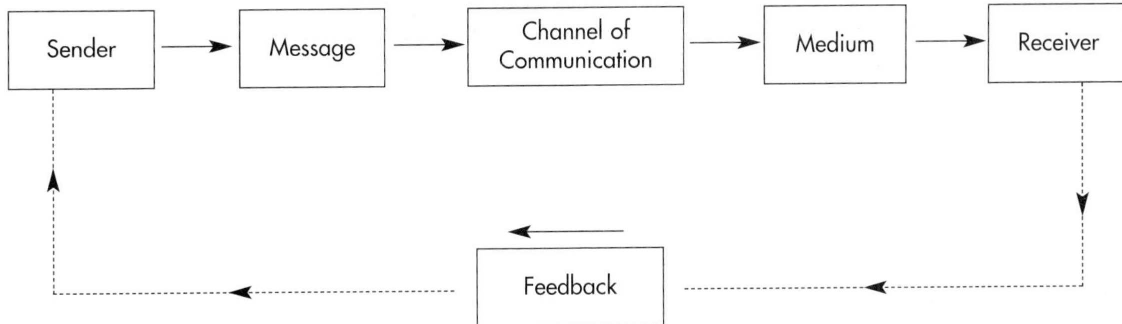

Figure 16 The process of communication

The message

To be effective, the message must be clear and unambiguous. It needs to be correctly understood and may be sent to provide information, for example, an annual report showing the performance of a company; or to give or request instructions, for example, which letters need to be word processed before others; or to persuade or influence people, such as an advertisement or a sales brochure.

The channel of communication

Messages can be sent via a range of channels in a company. Within the hierarchy of an organisation these can be vertical (such as between a manager and his/her junior) or horizontal, such as between two heads of department of equal status. Other channels, both formal or informal, may be used depending on the nature of the message.

The medium

This is the method or medium by which the message is transmitted from sender to receiver. This will vary, depending firstly upon the type of message sent. For example, a resignation notice would be sent as a formal written communication whereas a colleague asking what time the lunch break ends would be verbal. Secondly, it will vary according to the speed with which the message needs to be delivered. For example, urgent messages to a colleague could be by e-mail or telephone, whereas non-urgent messages could be sent in a memorandum. Thirdly, it will depend upon the relationship between sender and receiver. Colleagues working in the same office may talk informally and pass information, whereas management talking to union representatives would meet formally and have minutes of their meeting taken.

The receiver

This is the person who receives the message. The receiver will interpret it not just on its content, but also on the way it has been worded and the medium by which it has been sent. Each element will be used by the receiver to help them interpret the message. For example a final demand for payment of a bill sent by second class mail will be treated as less urgent than one sent by recorded delivery.

Feedback

This is essential to the sender in order to ensure that the receiver has obtained the message and has correctly understood its meaning. Feedback could be in the form of a brief comment such as 'OK' or a written reply to the sender. Only when feedback is received does the sender know that the message has been understood and the communication process is complete.

Channel of communication

Within an individual company there are two main channels of communication: formal and informal. Formal channels of communications are those which employers and employees both recognise and have approved as necessary for the successful

operation of the firm. For example, a wage slip or a warning letter to an employee concerning poor attendance.

Informal channels of communication are those which often operate through rumour and hearsay, and are usually referred to in an organisation as 'the grapevine'. Messages received via the grapevine must be treated with caution as they are not official company policy, unlike formal messages, and do not have the authority of management.

Both channels of communication are necessary for a business to function efficiently and can be used to good effect by those who understand how they operate. For example, informal messages about possible changes in working practices can be rumoured first on the grapevine so that management can judge the reaction of workers before they issue a formal notice. This use of both channels allows workers' feelings and reactions to be taken into account before a final decision is made and ensure that the decision is acceptable to both employees and employer.

Problems with communications

Effective communication occurs only when the message which the sender transmits is fully understood by the receiver. However, there are a number of reasons why this may not always happen.

Skills

Both sender and receiver must have the necessary skills to transmit and receive the message. The sender must be able to write or 'encode' the message correctly so that its meaning is not lost, and the receiver must be able to understand or 'decode' the same message so they receive and interpret the original information in the way the sender intended.

Jargon

This is the use of a word or phrase which has a specialised or technical meaning when used in the context of a particular product or business. For example, a sheep farmer talking about 'ram' would give the word a very different interpretation from a computer engineer.

Within some businesses, eg the engineering industry the use of jargon can ensure that messages have a precise interpretation which is understood by sender and recipient. However it can create problems when one party is not aware of the precise meaning of the jargon used.

The medium

If a message is sent using an unsuitable medium or channel of communication it may not be received in time for it to be effective. For example, a message requesting someone to meet an early morning train the next day, which is sent by post, may not arrive in time for the receiver to do anything about it.

Breakdown of the medium of communication

This prevents the message from being received. For example, if postal workers take industrial action this will slow down or stop the delivery of letters, or a computer failure can prevent the dispatch and receipt of E-mail.

The wrong target

The receiver of the message may be the wrong person and so can do nothing about the message being sent. For example, a company selling stair lifts targets its sales literature at those aged under 30, or if a letter complaining about the quality of components is sent to the wrong supplier. This can also have repercussions on the firm as incorrectly targeted messages are often seen as a lack of efficiency by others and may lead to a loss of confidence in the way the business conducts its operations.

The wording of the message

If the message is not clear or contains too much or too little information, it is unlikely to be understood or remembered. For communication to be accurate the message must be clear and concise so that the person receiving it can understand it and act to ensure it is correctly carried out.

Exercises

1 How can businesses be affected by poor communication? Explain your answers giving examples. (4)

2 Draw and label a diagram to show how the channel of communication in a business can be both horizontal and vertical. Include arrows to show the directions in which information can flow. (4)

3 Why is feedback important in the communication process? (2)

4 Write a paragraph explaining what is meant by informal and formal communication. Why would it be difficult for a company to operate on a day-to-day basis if the management insisted all communication must be formal? (6)

5 Jargon is often used in business communication. What is jargon and what are the advantages and disadvantages of its use? (4)

Use your word processor or desktop publishing system to produce a copy of the diagram showing the Communication Process (see Figure 16) given in this section. Include lines with arrow heads to ensure the direction of the flow of information is clear.

For each of the following messages select a suitable medium of communication to use and explain carefully why you have chosen it:

1 Confirm a business appointment for the next day.

2 Confirm a business appointment for the next month.

3 Send details of a new product to an Australian colleague for a meeting the next day.

4 Notify all office staff of an additional day's holiday at Christmas.

5 Inform the production manager of an increase in faulty goods being produced.

6 Inform an employee of their dismissal for poor timekeeping.

7 Let the Gas Board know of a suspected gas leak in the staff canteen.

Extension material

1 Make a list of all the different forms of communication which are used in your school or college. For example, verbal messages, noticeboards, pupil bulletins. Under each one write a brief paragraph to say how well, or not, you think each one works. Offer a suggestion of how they could be changed to make it more effective.

2 Prepare a report to be submitted to your class teacher, including your list and suggestions.

Written communication

Communication can take many forms in an organisation both internally, between different members of the same company, and externally, between members of a company and those who are outside the firm such as customers, suppliers and shareholders. Both internal and external communication can occur in any one of the following ways, written, verbal, visual or electronic.

The written word is an important method of communication in business and is used extensively for both internal and external messages.

Business letters

These are the most widely used form of external written communication. They can be sent to customers, suppliers and to any other individual or business associated with the firm. They have the clear advantage of providing a written or hard copy of the message for both the sender and the receiver, which can be stored in a filing system. Today, most organisations who word process their business letters will store them electronically. Both methods allow relatively simple retrieval when required.

Business letters are also used as a form of internal communication when writing a formal message to an employee. For example, a newly promoted member of staff will receive a letter appointing them to their new post, or an existing employee may be sent a letter advising them of an increase in salary or a change in their working conditions.

The way in which business letters are set out is also important. A good, well presented letter containing no errors can promote a positive image and inspire confidence in a company. Letter layouts are dealt with in Units 36 and 37.

The memorandum

This is the most commonly used form of written internal communication. A memorandum is less formal than a business letter as it is not usually signed, but it provides a written record of the message sent and received by individuals within the firm. Today many memoranda are sent by email, especially if they are going to other premises within the same company, so combining new and more traditional methods of communication.

The format of a memorandum may vary according to the chosen house style of different companies, but all will contain headings to indicate 'To' whom they are sent, 'From' whom they originate and the 'Date' they were issued. In addition, some firms may also include a 'Reference' and a 'Heading' or title to indicate the main content of the message. Some examples of different memorandum formats are given in Figures 17 and 18.

Notices

These again can be both internal and external. External notices may be placed outside premises, for example, when advertising for staff, or in the press when announcing a shareholders' meeting. Internal notices may have similar purposes but will appear on noticeboards in corridors or rest rooms within the firm. Some larger companies may also use an 'in-house' journal, or company newsletter, in which details of company news and developments, social activities and vacancies may be announced.

MEMORANDUM

To	**Date**
From	**Ref**

MEMORANDUM

To

From

Ref

Date

Figures 17/18 Memoranda layouts

Agenda and minutes

A number of meetings will take place within a company. Sales staff will meet to discuss new products and sales strategies, directors will meet to decide on company policy and heads of departments will meet to ensure they are all working to meet company objectives. Each person attending these meetings will be given a written agenda in advance which informs them of the business to be discussed. A record of what has been decided at the meetings, in the form of minutes, will also be produced and circulated.

Reports

Frequently, a report will be presented and discussed at one of these meetings. Reports are formal written documents prepared by an individual or a committee and can cover any aspect of the business, such as the effectiveness of a training programme, the need to replace ageing equipment or the projected sales figures for the next financial year. Reports provide useful ways of informing a number of interested persons of progress or possible developments in different areas of a company. Each year limited companies must send all their shareholders a copy of their Annual Report and Accounts, which is prepared by the directors for the benefit of those who own the company.

Trading documents

In the course of carrying out its business a firm will issue a number of trading documents such as orders, delivery notes, invoices, statements and receipts. These too are a form of external communication and are essential to the successful running of a business. Most firms use standard forms for these 'messages' to their customers and suppliers, and generate them using computerised accounting systems.

Business cards

Business cards are often used as a form of communication by those who visit another company. By calling on a firm and leaving a card a sales representative allows it to act as a form of introduction and signals that they wish to talk to someone in the company about future business. The card is small (usually measures about 10 cm by 4 cm) and gives the company name, address and telephone number in addition to the name and title of the person who is presenting the card.

Summary

Whichever method is used, there are a number of clear advantages to written communication:

- It provides a copy of the message so there can be no ambiguity between sender and receiver about what is required.
- Confidential or personal messages can be sent in sealed envelopes so they will only be read by the receiver.
- The use of forms, such as memoranda, can speed up the process of passing on routine written communications.
- Written messages allow the recipient time to study them before replying. This may be particularly important when considering a report which recommends two or three alternative courses of action that a business could take.

Figure 19 Example of a business card

Despite its popularity and widespread use in business, written communication does have some disadvantages:

- Written messages can be expensive to produce. For example, they may require a secretary, word processing equipment and office space.
- It may be slow in being prepared and the information may be out-of-date by the time it is ready to be transmitted. For example, the annual report and accounts of a firm are often sent to shareholders well into the company's next financial year.
- Feedback on the message may also take time if the receiver has to prepare a written reply.
- Copies of documents may get lost or perhaps mislaid through poor filing and so cannot be easily found when required.
- Written messages rely on the receiver reading them to learn of the message. In the case of notices pinned to noticeboards, this may not always happen and some messages may get overlooked.

Exercises

1 Explain when a business would use a business letter and when a memorandum would be used. (2)

2 Give three examples when a business would use a formal method of written communication and three examples when informal written communication would be used. (4)

3 Why is it important that all external written communications are sent out free of errors? Give two ways in which an employee can ensure business letters contain no errors. (4)

4 What are the benefits of using email for (a) the employee and (b) the business? (4)

5 What is an in-house journal? Why do companies produce them? (3)

6 Why do many business people have business cards? (3)

Use the examples in the text to help you prepare your own memorandum format. Word process a memorandum on a copy of your form to the Office Supervisor, outlining the disadvantages of using the office noticeboard to inform the staff of all the changes taking place in the office. These changes range from the appointment of a new Administration Manager to a staff social event at a local hotel.

You are on the social committee at your school or college. The committee has decided to hold a Christmas disco for students at a local hotel. Obtain details of a suitable local hotel and prepare a business letter asking if they will be able to accommodate your party on 18 December from 8.00 pm until 1.00 am. You anticipate there will be 200 people attending and you would like to make a provisional booking. Find out how much the cost of hiring the room will be. Prepare your letter on A4 headed paper using a blocked style of presentation.

Extension material

Make a list of the different forms of external and internal written communication which businesses use. List one advantage and one disadvantage against each and print a copy on A4 paper for inclusion in your folder.

Verbal communication

Verbal communication occurs when there is direct, live contact between two or more individuals. This form of communication has taken place between people since they first began to articulate sounds. In business today, a good verbal communicator is essential. A sales representative who can inform and persuade a potential customer to purchase a product or service will obtain more business. A customer service assistant who can explain why a problem has occurred and what is to be done about it will help retain the customer's loyalty. A telephone sales person must get their message across to the person they phone in a clear, friendly and non-threatening manner before the potential customer hangs up!

To be a good verbal communicator you will need the following qualities:

- A clear speaking voice.
- The ability to speak at the right pace – too fast and people cannot take in all you say; too slow and your audience gets bored.
- Confidence to talk to a range of audiences, from one individual to a large gathering of strangers.
- An understanding of how non-verbal gestures can affect and influence an audience's reaction.
- Good listening skills, so as not to talk over someone else or interrupt them, and to be able to listen and take in replies and then respond to them as necessary.
- Variety in your voice to engender interest in the listener.
- Not talking for too long – listeners soon stop listening, even to the most interesting speakers!

Verbal communication can be face to face, where the spoken message is passed between two individuals or groups who are in physical contact with each other, or via a medium such as the telephone, which puts the two parties in voice contact even though they cannot see each other.

Face to face verbal communication

Face to face contact can occur in a formal or an informal manner. Formal contact between two individuals or groups occurs when a meeting is organised, such as a sales meeting between representatives and the Sales Manager to develop more effective practices, a team briefing to inform staff of new product developments, or a company's Annual General Meeting of shareholders (a meeting required by law).

Informal face to face communication occurs when one individual talks to another to pass information. This could happen at any time during the working day and can take the form of a simple exchange of pleasantries, an enquiry about the progress being made on a particular customer's order or a request for information about a new product or service. It is often said that more business is conducted on the golf course than in the office. This gives emphasis to the importance of this form of informal face to face communication.

Face to face communication offers a number of advantages:

- It allows immediate feedback to be received about the message or information being passed and an exchange of opinions to take place.
- It promotes the development of ideas, as discussion can prompt further thoughts on the topic of a message.
- Information can be spread quickly amongst a group of people and they will all be given the same message – even though they may interpret it differently!
- It can encourage greater involvement and co-operation as others in a group may be influenced by their colleagues.

There are also some important disadvantages which need to be considered:

- People attending may be unskilled in the techniques of communication or be unwilling to communicate with others.
- Non-verbal communication, such as body language, may create a barrier to effective communication.
- Not everyone will interpret the message in the same way in group meetings.
- There may be no written record of the communication.

Telephone communication

Since the invention of the telephone by Alexander Graham Bell in 1876, its potential as a means of communication has quickly become apparent. Within two years not only were permanent telephone operators being employed as the network of telephone subscribers increased, but the development of the automatic switchboard ten years later allowed direct dialling to take place.

Today the telephone system is based on state of the art digital technology and it is possible to communicate directly to people in all parts of the world. In the last 100 years the telephone has become an invaluable business aid, allowing messages to be sent and received immediately in every form of business operation. The benefits of telephone communication include:

- The immediate passing of information to another person.
- They are easy to use and universally available, as all businesses are on the telephone network.
- An immediate reply can be obtained which gives feedback to the message being passed.
- The service is relatively cheap. Although long distance calls can be more expensive, different rates for calls at different times of the day can be used to help reduce costs further.
- The recent growth in the use of mobile telephones has made the system more flexible.

Despite its universal use however, the telephone does have several disadvantages.

- The sender of the message cannot see the non-verbal reaction and so the recipient may say one thing but mean or feel another quite different response.
- Recent changes in the numbering system within the UK have cost firms money as they have had to change letterheads and repaint vehicles, etc.
- No formal record of conversations is kept, so it may be difficult to prove who said what at a later date.

Mobile telephones

The development of the mobile telephone in the late 1980s has given the telephone network a renewed life as a means of communication and there are currently more than 30 million users in Britain. These portable, easy to use communications devices have added to the benefits of the telephone. They allow contact with individuals when they are away from the office or their normal place of work and can help facilitate working at home. Recent technology has now produced a mobile telephone which also incorporates a fax machine and can be used to access the Internet.

Mobile phones do, however, have disadvantages.

- They are more expensive to operate than the normal telephone network.
- There are still some areas in the UK which are 'blind' spots and cannot be reached using the mobile telephone transmission network.
- The batteries require frequent recharging to ensure that the unit is capable of receiving and sending calls.
- There can be problems when using them in public places, such as the theatre or cinema, or in cars when driving. Although it is not against the law to use a phone whilst driving, unless a 'hands free' system is used or preferably you stop the vehicle to make or answer calls, it can prove dangerous.

Exercises

1 Why do businesses rely on good verbal communicators? (2)

2 List the ways in which verbal communication can take place, together with an example of when each could be used. (4)

3 What are the benefits of face-to-face communication in business? (3)

4 Why do telephone companies charge higher rates for calls during normal business hours than at other times. (3)

5 Despite its universal use and popularity the telephone system does have some disadvantages. What are they? (4)

6 In what ways has the mobile phone benefited the employee and the business in recent years? What, if any, are the disadvantages of using mobile phones? (4)

Your sales manager is very keen to issue mobile telephones to all his sales representatives and has asked you to prepare a report outlining the advantages and disadvantages of this so that she can present the details to the Marketing Director when she meets him next week. Make sure you show how the telephones will help (or otherwise) both the company and the individual sales representatives to improve their work. If you have access to any costs please make sure you include these in your report.

1 You have been asked to talk to the students in the year group below you to inform them about the course in Business and Communication Systems for which you are currently studying. On a sheet of A4 paper make a list of the qualities you will require to be an effective speaker.

2 Next prepare a four minute talk, which you will have to deliver to the students in the year below. Prepare headings of the main topics you wish to tell the students about. Under each of these topic headings make a list of the points you would like to make. Word process your notes and then try your talk out on another member of your group or a friend. Listen to any comments they may have and then amend your notes accordingly. Now record your talk.

Extension material

Obtain any information you can about mobile telephones from a local supplier or outlet. Use this information to design an advertisement for a mobile phone. Include some of the main benefits which the telephone provides to the user. Remember to show the cost of the telephone equipment and any calls.

Electronic communication

Today, the development of electronic means of communicating data has led to a considerable growth in different methods of sending information, which in turn has revolutionised the way in which communications take place both between businesses and within them.

Viewdata systems

These have been available via television channels for many years. Perhaps they are better known by their trade names such as Teletext or Prestel. Viewdata systems provide an electronic information service by transmitting 'pages' of information that are shown on the television screen a page at a time. Some of these services are free; others are only available to those who have paid the relevant subscription.

There are more than 300,000 pages of information available but by modern standards the system is rather slow in responding to requests to display specific pages of data. Pages are set up by 'information providers' and can include advertisements, information of company shares and timetables for airlines and ferries. Although the information on the pages is updated regularly, the system is not interactive and so provides information but cannot be interrogated by the user.

Facsimile

This is an exact copy of the message. A fax (short for facsimile) machine will allow the transmission of a copy of written and graphical information via the telephone network. It works in a similar way to a photocopier, except the copy is transmitted to a distant machine via the telephone network rather than appearing in the one in which it was originally placed. Faxes are being used increasingly in business today for the following reasons:

- They are cheap to use (the cost of the telephone call) and do not require the installation of any expensive cabling, as they use the existing telephone lines.
- They allow graphical and handwritten information to be transmitted without having to prepare it in a special way.
- They are simple to use and do not require any specialist training.
- They accept written data so there is no need to go to the time or expense of keying in data for transmission.
- Provided the receiving machine is switched on, messages can be received at any time, day or night.

However, using a fax machine has its disadvantages:

- As a form of communication it does not provide the sender with any non-verbal communication signals.
- It can tie up the telephone line, if a dedicated fax number is not used, which may prevent telephone callers from getting through or calls being made.
- There can be no immediate response or feedback from the recipient as there is with a telephone conversation.
- The quality of the transmitted document is often poorer than the original, which may make it an unsuitable medium for sending complex data or technical information.

Electronic mail or e-mail

This is a method of communication which is available to anyone with a telephone and a computer with a modem. The modem connects the computer to the telephone network allowing it to transmit and receive encoded data which can be displayed on the computer. Each E-mail user has a 'mailbox' with a unique address into which messages can be sent ready for the recipient to 'collect' and read. This system has become widely used both between businesses and within organisations as a quick and efficient form of communication. The benefits include:

- It is cheap and easy to use.
- All individuals in an organisation can have their own personal mailboxes, which can be password protected if desired.
- Messages can be prepared in advance, so the transmission time is kept to a minimum. This significantly reduces the cost of sending messages.
- Communications can take place throughout any 24 hour period, therefore allowing international connections to be made even when offices may be closed.
- Only one message needs to be prepared, although it can be sent to any number of mailboxes. This is a useful facility when sending company memoranda to a number of employees.

The disadvantages of using e-mail include:

- Using the system requires both sender and receiver to have a modem and an on-line connection to a computer.
- It relies upon the recipient 'emptying' their mailbox on a regular basis. Messages will only

be received if the recipient opens their mailbox and reads them.

- Hard copies of messages are not always made or kept.

Answering or voice mail systems

These allow messages to be left when there is no one available to receive it in person. As it is attached to the telephone, the machine cuts into a telephone call with a pre-recorded message and gives the caller the option of leaving a message. The benefits of these machines include the following:

- You can leave messages when the recipient is not available to answer the telephone in person, and contact people out of working hours by leaving a message.
- They also allow the user to 'filter' telephone calls by answering only the calls of those to whom they wish to speak.

However, many people are often reluctant to leave a message or find it difficult to talk to a machine, and messages are only received when the calls on the answerphone are played back. Answerphones also change the onus of communicating from the sender to the receiver, as messages very often rely on the recipient calling back.

Pagers

As an alternative to an answer machine, pagers can be used to pass on brief messages. These are inexpensive compared with the cost of other forms of electronic communication but can only receive a very short message – sometimes as few as 40 characters. Pagers are small and can be carried in a pocket or bag or attached to a belt. They normally bleep or vibrate when a message has been sent to them, which can then be read from a liquid crystal display (LCD) panel. They have the advantage of requiring only a telephone to send a message, but they are not interactive and so there is no acknowledgement that the message has been received.

Video conferencing facilities

These are becoming more frequently used, as companies invest in the hardware necessary to establish links with other branches of the same company or with firms who are regular customers. Through the use of computer links and closed-circuit television, they allow people to hear and see each other as they communicate. This can be particularly valuable when talking with people in other parts of the country or other countries, as it eliminates the time and expense of having to travel to meet with colleagues. The televisual link also allows any non-verbal communication between sender and receiver to be assessed. These facilities however, are still relatively expensive to install and ideally require the use of a dedicated telephone link in order to be successful.

In recent years the advent of digital video cameras has significantly reduced the cost of video conferencing. Web cams, which can link computers via the Internet, can be quickly and easily installed to provide a video link between two workstations anywhere in the world. Some businesses, however, may be concerned about the lack of security which this form of video communication can be subject to and prefer to use dedicated telephone lines instead. This will increase the cost of this form of communication.

Exercises

1 What is a viewdata system? What are the disadvantages to a business of using such a system? (3)

2 Write a paragraph discussing the advantages and disadvantages to a business of using fax machines for communication. (4)

3 Explain why email communication has expanded rapidly in recent years. (3)

4 What are the disadvantages to a business of using a voicemail system? (3)

5 How can pagers help businesses operate more efficiently? (3)

6 Why are video conferencing systems becoming more commonly used in business? What are the current disadvantages of using this as a means of communication? (4)

Word process a table to show the advantages and disadvantages of all the main types of electronic communication. Spell check and proofread your work carefully before printing a hard copy for your notes on A4 paper.

You work for a large national company engaged in the production of aircraft engines. The firm has strong links with Italian and French designers and engineers and is currently engaged in a research programme to develop a new engine. Word process a report for your employer advising him of the most appropriate methods of communication he needs to establish to enable you to work more effectively with your European colleagues.

Extension material

You have been contracted to set up the offices of a new company which sells tea and coffee direct to small retail outlets throughout the UK and France. The firm obtains its supplies from tea and coffee plantations in Sri Lanka and Brazil, and these are then imported via Bristol where they are processed and packaged. There is a sales force of 35 representatives who all work from home.

Advise the Board of Directors of the most suitable forms of communication for the company to use to manage their business effectively. Give reasons to support your suggestions.

Visual communication

Data is information which has not yet been converted into a form that can be easily understood. Data has to be stored, retrieved and converted into the most accessible form so that businesses can use it to make decisions. For information to be effective it has to be presented in a way that is easily understood. The means by which it is communicated from one person to another is, therefore, of paramount importance.

Nowadays most data is stored on computer, and it is a relatively easy procedure to convert it into a variety of forms to meet different needs. Most spreadsheet programs are installed with a linked graphics system which enable them to convert selected data into graphs, pie charts or bar charts with ease.

'A picture is worth a thousand words'. This old saying is quite true. Many firms rely on visual materials to communicate information to their employees and customers. Visual communication usually has a specific purpose, and on each occasion it is used it is transmitting a single message. For example, posters on the side of a bus must give an instant message to the recipient or it will be missed as the bus passes and travels out of sight.

Visual communication can take a number of forms including posters, advertisements, charts, graphs, television and computer graphics.

Posters

These can vary from the huge hoardings at the side of the road to the small A5 flyers given out to promote a local activity or event. Whatever the size, posters have several advantages:

- They are cheap to produce.
- Their message is conveyed immediately and a large roadside poster can have a considerable impact.

 They allow blanket coverage – tucked under windscreen wipers in a car park, given away with newspapers or delivered door to door.

However, despite these advantages their use is limited, as the message they impart must be simple and easy to take in otherwise it will be missed as you pass by a hoarding or throw a leaflet away. It is also unselective and is read by anyone who sees it, not necessarily those at whom the product or service is aimed. Small posters or leaflets are also often treated like 'junk mail' and so are not read by the recipient. Whilst the cost of each one may be small, when several thousand are produced costs can rise considerably.

Posters do, however, remain a cheap and often colourful way of communicating information to a mass market.

Advertisements

You will undoubtedly be familiar with advertisements for television, radio, magazines and newspapers. These can be classified into three main ways in which they communicate their message: informative, persuasive and generic advertisements.

Informative advertisements

These provide information about the product or service to potential consumers, enabling them to judge the quality of the item against its competitors or to let them know the specification and uses of the product.

Persuasive advertisements

These attempt to persuade the reader to purchase the product or service rather than give details of its composition, specification and uses. They often rely on such concepts as sexual attraction (perfumes and body sprays), keeping up with the Jones' (cars and fitted kitchens) or promoting affluence (investments and savings) which are aimed at making you feel that you need the product to make your life complete!

Generic advertisements

These promote a common product or service without using any specific trade or company names. For example, 'Buy British Beef', 'Diamonds are Forever' or 'Get the Strength of the Insurance Companies around You'. The message is being transmitted by the industry, not by a particular supplier or manufacturer; and the aim is to promote awareness of what all providers of the service or product make available, rather than a particular brand or manufacturer.

Advertising keeps consumers better informed of what products are available and what those products can do. This leads to more goods being sold and so keeps more people in employment. Adverts also help to pay for newspapers, magazines, television and commercial radio, as the fees charged are used to off-set the costs of production.

By advertising at a specific time on television or radio (for example, during a sporting fixture) certain products can be introduced to those people most likely to purchase them. This applies also to specialist magazines. New developments in computing technology are best advertised in magazines such as Computer Monthly or Computer Active which are read by those who are most interested in them.

However, advertisements can encourage people to purchase unnecessary or unwanted products. It can also be argued that the additional cost incurred in advertising results in prices being higher than they need to be, especially when the purpose of the advertising is to maintain the market share of a product rather than to promote additional sales.

Tables

These can be used to present many different types of information. They provide an easy way of dividing text into categories that would not be apparent if it were provided in the form of a list. Equally, tables can be used to present numerical data, especially where the numbers themselves are the main focus or when calculations have to be carried out on the information given in the table. For example,

A computer company is selling PCs and printers in four regions of the country and has achieved the following sales for the last six months. The information has been presented in a table or tabular form:

Monthly Sales of Computers						
Month	Jan	Feb	Mar	April	May	June
Computer sales	100	150	125	200	250	175

Table 13 Monthly sales of computers

Information in tables needs to be interpreted, therefore it is often left in this basic form when the interpretation needs to be precise or if calculations are to be carried out on the figures. Most data used in business documents is converted into another form, which allows it to be more easily understood by the reader.

Charts and graphs

These often provide an excellent way of presenting numerical information that can be easily understood and provides an excellent way of presenting numerical information. Unit 47 describes how graphs and charts can be produced using the facilities of your spreadsheet program. More difficult to produce but equally effective are histograms and pictograms.

Bar charts

This is one of the simplest methods of displaying data. The data is represented by bars or blocks which can be drawn vertically or horizontally. The length of the bar indicates the value or importance of the data. The bar chart opposite is based on the data given in Table 13.

Advantages

When converted to a bar chart the data has a number of advantages:

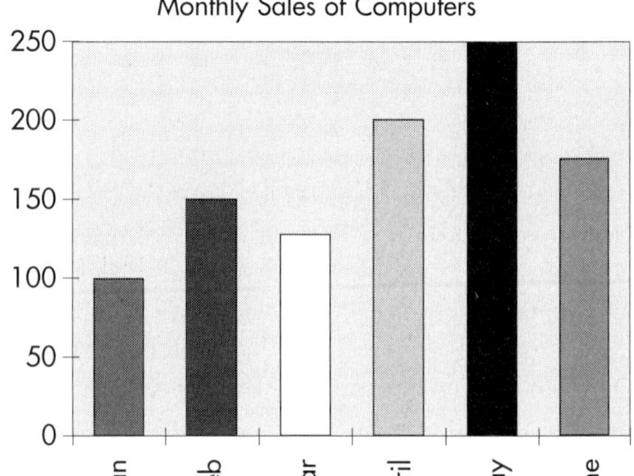

Figure 20 Bar chart showing monthly sales of computers

- It has an immediate visual impact.
- It is easier to understand than in tables of data.
- Trends can be quickly identified over time.

Disadvantages

However, there are also some drawbacks to using simple bar charts as a means of displaying data:

- Bar charts can over-simplify the data.
- Data can be difficult to read with any accuracy.
- Only one set of data can be shown on this chart.

Composite bar charts

To overcome the last drawback of a simple bar chart, a composite bar chart can be used to show more than one set of data. Using the original data, details of printer sales have now been added:

Monthly sales of computers and printers						
Month	**Jan**	**Feb**	**Mar**	**April**	**May**	**June**
Computer sales	100	150	125	200	250	175
Printer sales	75	80	50	100	150	125

Table 14 Composite bar chart data

Both sets of data can be displayed on a composite bar chart, which can take two forms. The first is where two or more sets of data are shown together on one bar:

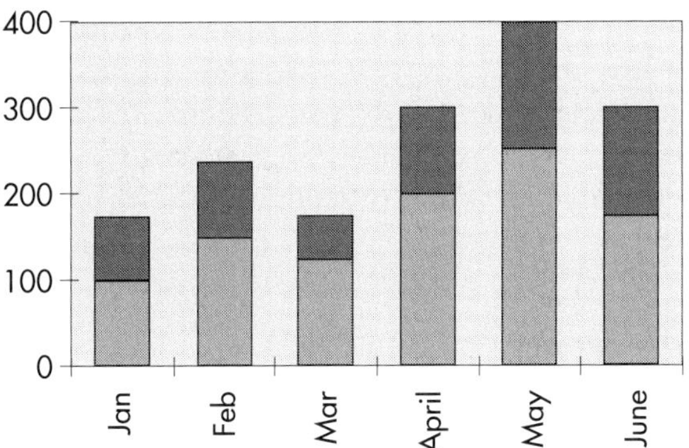

Figure 21 Composite bar chart showing sales of computers and printers

This chart has the advantage of showing more data, however, the total column height relates to sales of both computers and printers and it is also difficult to accurately work out the totals for each of the two sets of data. An alternative form of composite bar chart shows the two sets of data in adjacent columns (see Figure 22).

Although, comparisons between data are easier, the sales totals still cannot be picked out from the chart without some difficulty.

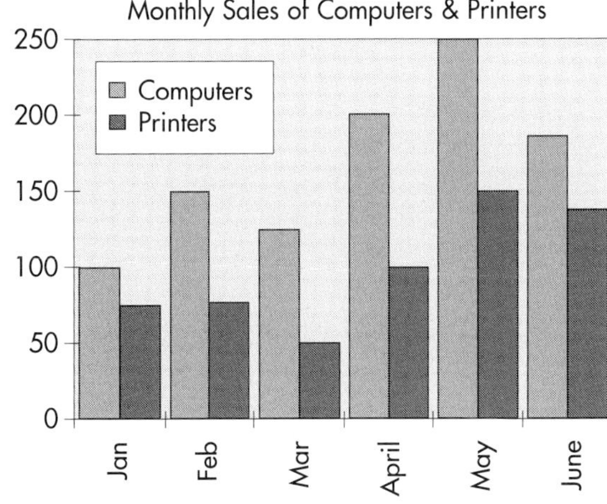

Figure 22 Alternative composite bar chart

Pie Charts

In this method of display, data is represented by a circle and divided into segments. The size of each segment represents the relative importance of the data in relation to the total. Using the original data based on computer sales, this would convert into the following pie chart:

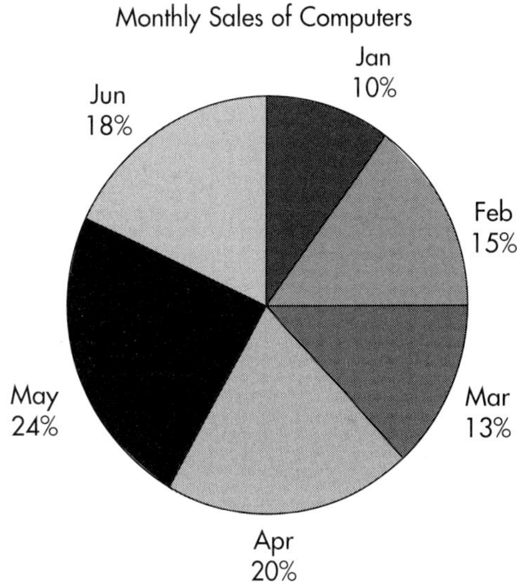

Figure 23 Pie chart showing monthly computer sales

Advantages

Pie charts are useful as they give the reader an immediate impression of the importance of the relative segments and can be used to show comparisons between different time periods by comparing two charts.

Disadvantages

Pie charts do have a number of drawbacks:

- It is difficult to read the data with any degree of accuracy, so comparison between segments is often judgmental.
- If there are a large number of segments it becomes difficult to analyse the data.
- When comparing two pie charts for different time periods, if the totall value of the data

changes this can only be shown by an increase or decrease of the overall area of the chart.

Despite these problems of interpretation, pie charts provide an immediate visual image and are commonly used in business reports and other documents.

Line Graphs

These are often less attractive and do not have the immediate impact of bar and pie charts. They can be read more accurately and allow the comparison of two or more sets of data on the one chart. However, care should be taken to ensure that the scales used on the axes are common. The data for computer and printer sales can be show as a line graph as shown in Figure 24.

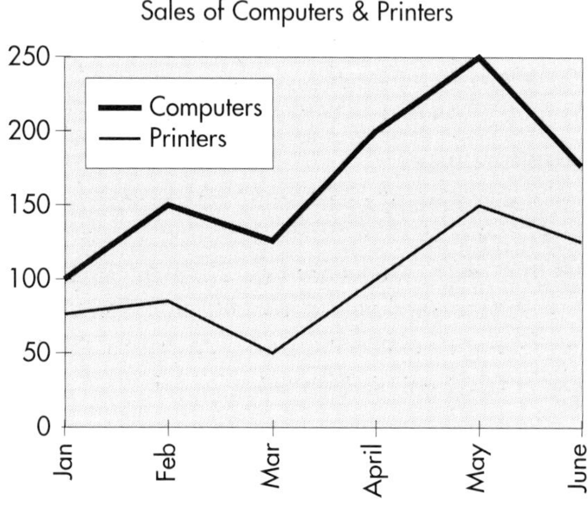

Figure 24 Line graph showing computer and printer sales

Line graphs have the advantage of showing the relationship of the data over a period of time and, when two series of data are shown on the same graph, of drawing a direct comparison between them. It is also easier to take measurements from the graph rather than interpret the figures given in tabular form.

Histograms

A histogram is similar to a bar chart, except that the area shown by the bars represents the frequency against which an item has been recorded. For example, if data is being collected on the ages at which people started to learn to play a musical instrument, the figures may look like this:

Age		**Number**	
	0–14		200
	15–29		300
	30–44		150
	45–89		100

The height of each column shows the number of people who started to play in each 15 year time

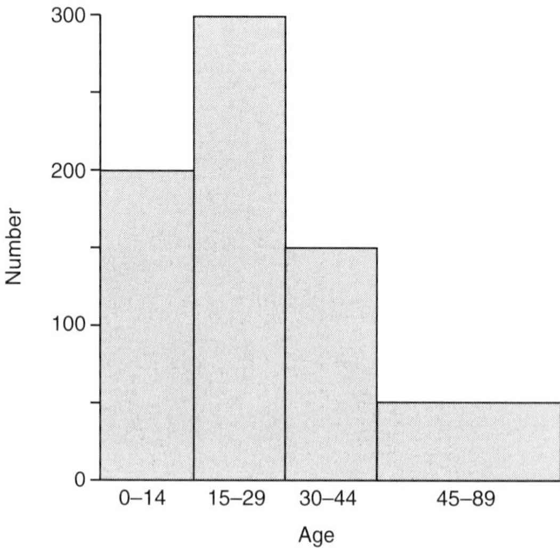

Figure 25 Histogram

period. However, the last age category covers twice the age range (i.e. 30 years) of the other three. In a histogram, this column will be twice the width of the others, but the number will be halved to average the number between the two 15 year time periods covered by the data. This form of presentation is useful when data occurs over a range of values such as age, weight or length. See Figure 25.

Pictograms

These are used to present information on a chart in a similar way to a bar chart, except the bar is replaced by pictorial images which represent the quantity in each column. For example, examine the following table of computer sales:

Year	Computers sold	Year	Computers sold
1994	2000	1997	5500
1995	2500	1998	3600
1996	4000	1999	2800

Table 15 Computer sales

This table could be converted into a pictogram (see Figure 26).

Although this form of display of information is easy to visualise because of the graphics used, it is not easy to read the data with any degree of accuracy. If part of a computer is shown, for example, in the column for 1998, precisely how many sales it represents cannot easily be gauged.

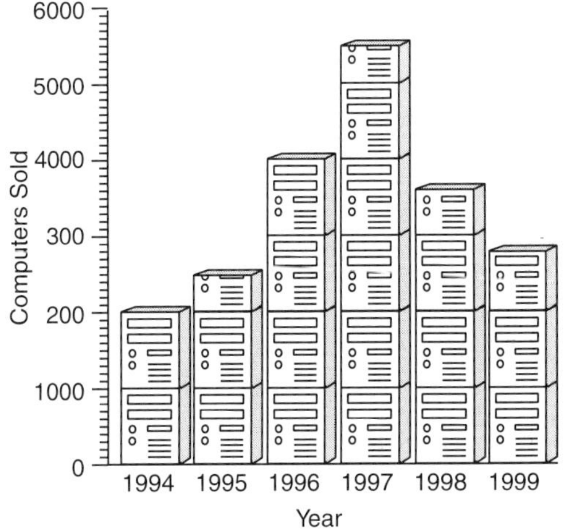

Figure 26 Pictogram

Computer graphics

These are being used increasingly to provide a simulation of an activity or event. They have been used on television for a number of years, but as the technology becomes easier and cheaper to use many more organisations are now using computer graphics as a form of communication. Sales presentations can be enhanced through the use of a moving display, created using a presentation program such as Powerpoint and then either run through a PC onto the VDU or projected onto a larger screen for larger audiences. The cost of these presentations is still however considerably higher than that of other methods of transmitting information, particularly in the time they take to prepare.

Exercises

1 Explain the difference between data and information. (2)

2 Why do some businesses advertise their products on roadside hoardings? Give two examples of products you have seen advertised in this way. (3)

3 Why is some data presented in table form? What are the disadvantages of this? (4)

4 Explain carefully the differences between a bar chart, a histogram and a composite bar chart. Give an example of when each would be used. (4)

5 List the advantages and disadvantages of using line graphs to present data. (4)

6 What type of data would be displayed in a pie chart? Despite being one of the most common methods of displaying information, pie charts have a number of disadvantages. Why? (3)

1 Enter the following data into your spreadsheet and prepare a pie chart from it. Make sure you include the heading 'July Car Sales'. Include either a legend against each segment or a key to identify them.

Sales of Cars in July					
Jaguar	145	Ford	468	Vauxhall	580
Mercedes	201	Renault	338	Volvo	55

2 Dixons, the High Street retailers, has been promoting the sale of its range of cameras and films last month. Sales figures for the Eastern branches are as follows:

Branch	Cameras	Films (100s)
Colchester	23	18
Norwich	67	107
Kings Lynn	34	55
Norfolk	45	91
Cambridge	60	45
Gt Yarmouth	48	120

a) You have been asked to prepare a composite bar chart to show these figures more clearly to the Sales Director. Make sure you label your chart clearly.

b) Word process a paragraph to draw the Sales Director's attention to any shortcomings in presenting the information which this way may have. Prepare an alternative way of displaying the information to illustrate your points.

1 Compile a survey of thirty different television advertisements. Draw up a chart incorporating the following headings:

name of product   time shown
length of advert   type of advert

The length of each advertisement should be recorded in seconds. The type of advertisement will be informative, persuasive or generic.
Analyse your findings using the three different types of advertisement and present your findings in graphical form. What conclusions can you draw from your analysis?

2 Try and categorise the types of product advertised, for example, foodstuffs, luxury products, clothing, vehicles etc. Present your findings graphically. What conclusions can you draw from this analysis?

3 Design a poster to advertise a new brand of margarine that spreads straight from the fridge. You will have to create a product name, which reflects what the product can do as well as what it is. Make sure your poster is designed to attract immediate attention and draw the reader's eye to the new product. Make your poster persuasive and include no more than ten words in it to get your message across.

Extension material

You work for Sandford Textiles Ltd, which has experienced considerable changes in its company structure in the last two years. A decline in overseas markets has resulted in a change in European sales and they now sell 30% to France, 16% to Germany, 37% to Belgium and the remainder in the UK. The size of the workforce has also been reduced from 3,050 to 2,500. The marketing department has expanded from 400 to 750 employees, however the factory labour force has declined from 2,200 to 1,400. The number of administrative workers has also fallen from 300 to 160 and the finance department has seen an increase of 40 to a new total of 190 employees.

Choose appropriate charts or graphs to illustrate these changes. Give reasons for your choice of presentation in each case.

Business letters

The most common type of formal written communication used by businesses is the letter. It has a number of advantages:

- It ensures that a clear and accurate message is sent.
- It provides a permanent visual record which can be stored if required.
- It can be cheaper than telephoning, particularly over long distances or abroad.
- It gives time for the recipient to read and consider a response to the message in the letter.

However, despite its popularity, the business letter does have a number of disadvantages:

- It is time-consuming when compared with telephone/fax.
- There is no immediate feedback.
- A letter tends to be less personal as there is no direct contact between sender and receiver.
- A letter may not reach the addressee, as correspondence may be dealt with by junior staff/secretaries.
- The storage of letters and other correspondence can take up a lot of valuable office space.

Parts of a business letter

Business letters follow a prescribed pattern and have a number of standard parts or sections which are shown in Figure 27.

Preprinted headings

These vary from business to business. What does your school or college letter headed paper look like? Some examples of different letter headings are given in Figure 28.

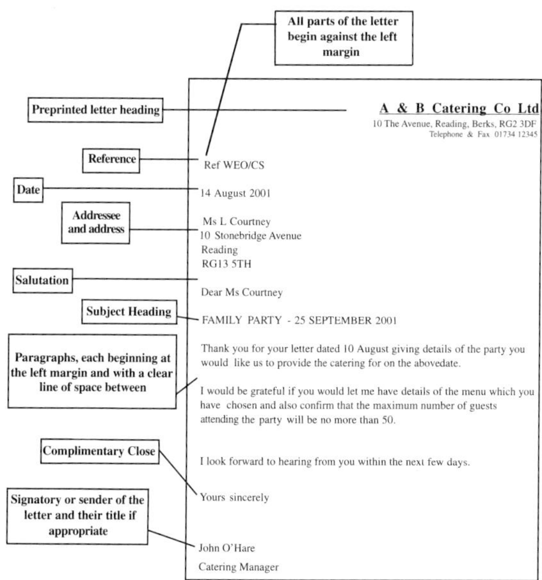

Figure 27 Parts of a business letter

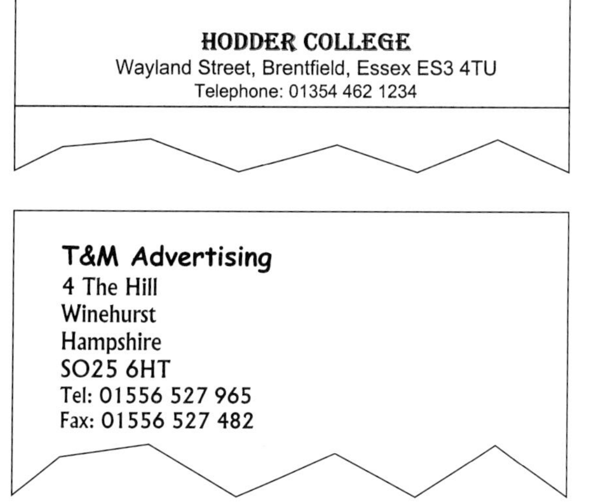

Figure 28 Sample letter headings

Reference

Most business letters include a reference which enables the company sending the letter to identify who originated it and/or what it is about. A simple reference would include the author's initials and those of the person who word processed the letter. An example is given above in Figure 29.

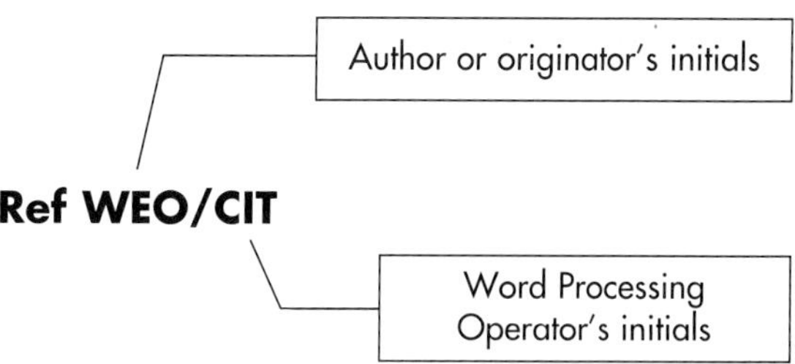

Figure 29 Sample letter reference

Companies design their references to suit their needs. An insurance company may reference their letters with a policy number or a claim number. Banks and Building Societies may use an account number and travel agents a holiday reference.

Date

This is the date on which the letter was written. There are several formats in which the date can be word processed but the most commonly used is the day, month and year, for example: 28 August 2001.

Some businesses like to include the superscript after the day (i.e. $21^{st}/22^{nd}/23^{rd}/24^{th}$) but this convention is declining in use. The month and year are usually given in full. Other acceptable date formats are:

- 28th August 2001
- 28 August 01
- 28 August '01

Dates given in an all figure format (for example, 28.8.01 or 28/08/01) are not generally regarded as being in an acceptable format for a business letter.

Addressee and address

This is the name and address of the person or company to whom the letter is being written. It is usually keyed in an 'open punctuation' format, i.e. without any full stops or commas after initials or at the end of lines. It is no longer thought necessary to key in the postal town in capitals, but the postcode should always be the last line of the address.

Salutation

This is the greeting. If the person you are writing to is unknown, you would begin the letter 'Dear Sir', or even 'Dear Madam'. It is not good practice to use both on the one salutation, i.e. 'Dear Sir or Madam'. If you know the person you are writing to you would use their name, for example, 'Dear Mr Rashid' or 'Dear Ms Roberts'. If you are on first name terms you may be informal and use, for example 'Dear Tracey' or 'Dear Bob'.

Subject heading

Not all letters have or require a heading, but when they are used they aim to give a flavour of the letter's main subject. Headings should always be given some emphasis so that they stand out from the rest of the letter. Capitals may be used or perhaps a bold type face.

Paragraphs

These break up the content of the letter into separate sections. Business letters should make use of at least two paragraphs. A new paragraph is indicated on the page by leaving a clear line of space between it and the previous paragraph. Each new paragraph should begin against the left margin. They should not be indented as this is inconsistent with the fully-blocked style of the letter.

Complimentary close

This is the concluding phrase of the letter which precedes the signature. If the letter is formal and begins with the salutation 'Dear Sir' or 'Dear Madam', then 'Yours faithfully' should be used. Less formal salutations, such as 'Dear Mr Smith', require the complimentary close 'Yours sincerely'.

Signatory

The name of the author of the letter should be keyed in underneath a space of five or six clear lines. This prevents any confusion about the identity of the signatory. If appropriate, the author's job title should also be included. Occasionally the author may not be available to sign the letter once it has been prepared. In this case, a subordinate may sign the letter on behalf of the author. If they do this they should include the initials 'pp' for 'per pro', which stands for 'on behalf of,' before their signature.

Enclosures

Frequently, a business letter will also have some other documentation enclosed with it. When this occurs, it is good business practice to include the term 'Enc', which is an abbreviation for 'enclosure', after the name of the signatory and his or her title. This indicates to the recipient of the letter that additional information has been sent to them with it. If more than one enclosure is sent 'Enc' may appear in the plural – 'Encs'.

Exercises

1. Business letters are still the most commonly used form of communication. Why? (3)
2. Make a list of the main parts of a business letter in the order in which they should appear. (4)
3. Explain the purposes of (a) the reference and (b) the date in a business letter. (2)
4. Explain what is meant by the following terms: *salutation*, *addressee* and *open punctuation*. (3)
5. Why do business letters usually show the name and title of the signatory below the space for signature? (2)
6. Explain how the reference and the subject heading in a letter may help a company identify who sent and who should receive a business letter. (3)

Key in a copy of the following letter using open punctuation and a fully-blocked format. Follow the layout given and insert a single clear line of space between each different part of the letter as shown.

Ref BT/12346

(insert today's date)

Mrs L J Collier
25 Riverside Road
Exeter
EX23 4HH

Dear Mrs Collier

It is now 11 months since you purchased your Panasonic P2030 midi hifi system from us and we hope you have enjoyed using it and that it has given you excellent service.

As you will be aware the original one-year manufacturer's guarantee will expire next month and we recommend you consider taking out an extended policy to cover any mechanical breakdown on your machine for a further two years. Full details of this extended cover are given in the enclosed leaflet.

Should you wish to take up this valuable offer, please contact me, or any member of the sales staff at the store.

Yours sincerely

Jean Ritchie (Mrs)
Retail Sales Manager

en

Key in a copy of the following letter in fully-blocked format using an appropriate business format. Why not create an appropriate letter heading using the techniques given on page 161. Remember to spell check and proofread your work before printing.

> Ref GHL/TPH
>
> (insert today's date)
>
> James Robertson
> 141 Station Road
> Taunton
> Somerset
> TN3 4JH
>
> Dear James
>
> VACANCY FOR A RETAIL SALES ASSISTANT
>
> Thank you for your interest in the post of retail sales assistant recently advertised in the Somerset Gazette. I read your application form and curriculum vitae with interest and was pleased to see that you have previous retail sales experience working part-time in a local greengrocer's shop.
>
> I would like to discuss your application in more detail and would be pleased if you could attend an interview at 2.00 pm next Monday at our head office in Balmoral Street, Taunton.
>
> Would you please telephone my assistant, Ken Bagley, on Taunton 34567, extension 36, to confirm that you will be able to attend at this time.
>
> I look forward to meeting you next week.
>
> Yours sincerely
>
> Ginnette Laycock
> Personnel Manager

Extension material

Prepare a business letter heading for a branch of Clifton Bridge Building Society using an address local to you. Set out the following text in a business letter using the fully-blocked format and open punctuation. Include today's date and insert paragraphs at appropriate points. Remember to spell check and proof-read your work before printing.

> Ref JKL/2356 Stainers & Smythe, Solicitors, Church Road, Swindon, Wilts, SN2 3GH. Dear Sir Court Case 234/2356 Following receipt of the case details by my colleague last Tuesday I have now arranged a further meeting with the defendant's solicitor. At this meeting we will be told more about the defence's strategy. This should give us a good idea of how to tackle the preliminary court hearing later this month. With your agreement I would like to hire a barrister to represent us in court. Whilst this will be more expensive, I believe the expertise they will be able to bring to the case from their previous experience will help us considerably as the case progresses. I would appreciate your comments on this. Yours faithfully, Carmen Giovanni, Solicitor.

More on business letters

Although the blocked style of business letter is now the accepted norm, another frequently used method of presentation is the indented style. It copies the formal, hand-written style used in the days before the use of typewriters.

The indented style of layout

An alternative form of layout, which is less commonly used as it is more difficult and time-consuming to prepare using a word processor, is the indented style of letter. The main difference between this style and the fully blocked style is the positioning of some of the parts of the letter.

Compare the letter in Figure 30 with that given in Unit 36 and identify the differences.

Some parts of the letter – the heading, the compli-

A & B Catering Co Ltd
10 The Avenue, Reading, Berks, RG2 3DF
Telephone & Fax 01734 12345

Ref WEO/CS

14 August 2001

Ms L Courtney
10 Stonebridge Avenue
Reading
RG13 5TH

Dear Ms Courtney

FAMILY PARTY – 25 SEPTEMBER 2001

Thank you for your letter dated 10 August giving details of the party you would like us to provide the catering for on the above date.

I would be grateful if you would let me have details of the menus which you have chosen and also confirm that the maximum number of guests attending the party will be no more than 50.

I look forward to hearing from you within the next few days.

Yours sincerely

John O'Hare
Catering Manager

Figure 30 The indented style of layout

mentary close, the signatory and his/her title – are centred. The first line of each paragraph is indented by 1cm. The date may also appear on the right, under the pre-printed heading if desired.

Exercises

1 Explain the primary difference between the blocked style and the indented style of letter layout. (2)

2 Why is the blocked style of letter layout easier to prepare when using a word processor? (2)

3 Explain what is meant by the following terms: *signatory*, *subject heading* and *complimentary close*. (3)

4 Why is accuracy when keying in data regarded as important when preparing business letters? (2)

5 Many offices no longer keep hard copies of business letters, but store them on a central computer system. Why? (2)

6 Explain how you would set up a central computer storage system of folders for business letters. (4)

1 Using the indented style of letter layout shown below, prepare a copy of the following letter and print a copy on A4 paper. Remember to spell check and proofread your work before printing.

Ref SC/rtw

(insert today's date)

Ms Jenny Salisbury
100 Walton Road
Cowley
Oxford
OX21 3RT

Dear Ms Salisbury

Many thanks for your letter dated (insert last Monday's date) asking about our new range of windows, doors and conservatories.

I have pleasure in enclosing a copy of our new catalogue and price list. I would like to draw your attention to the latest addition to our product range, the Excelsior conservatory. This comes complete with lockable window catches and slim-line Venetian blinds for all windows. Full details of the conservatory can be found on page 25 of the brochure.

Should you be interested in purchasing an Excelsior conservatory, and would be prepared to allow us to show prospective buyers around your conservatory, only by appointment, we would be able to offer you a 20 per cent discount on the price listed.

I will contact you again within the next few days to see if we can come to some mutually convenient arrangement.

Yours sincerely
Angular Windows plc

Rokib Ali
Sales Director

Enc

2 Prepare a business letter heading for the branch of a local estate agents. Key in a copy of the following business letter in an indented style using today's date and the reference AS/223. Make sure you paragraph the letter at suitable points.

Jones, Roberts & Jones Ltd, Painters and Decorators, 44 Kelly Street, Weston-super-Mare, Somerset, BS23 4DD. Dear Sirs 29 Edward Road, Worle, Somerset, BS24 2GH

Thank you for your recent quotation to decorate three bedrooms and the bathroom of the above property. I have now spoken to our clients who would like you to commence the work as soon as possible. I understand from the owners that there is no-one living in the house at present and that Mr & Mrs Brian Stout, who live next door at number 27 Edward Road, will provide you with a key. This should be returned to them at the end of each day's work. Please write and advise me at the above address when work will commence. Our client will be returning to England at the beginning of next month and would like to reoccupy the property on their arrival. Yours faithfully, (include the name of the Estate Agency as the signatory).

The ability to prepare accurate and well presented business letters requires practice. The following exercises are designed to give you just that. Before starting, study the sample layout given in Figure 27 and Figure 30.

Remember, accuracy in keying in data is important. Typographical errors and poor proofreading reflect badly on an organisation, and modern technology makes it so easy to avoid them. Prepare your own business letter headed paper suitable for each task before you start keying in.

1 Prepare a copy of the following letter on A4 headed paper in blocked style using open punctuation. The letter is to be addressed to RJB Building Contractors Ltd., Norton Wood Lane, Cardiff, CF3 6GH. Insert paragraphs where appropriate. Spell check and proofread your work before printing a copy. Save your work using an appropriate file name.

Ref FR/2316 Dear Mr Preston A short while ago you enquired about the prospects for developing the plot of land situated close to the south lane of the M4 motorway just off junction 34. Your letter did not make it clear whether this was to be a residential or an industrial development. Recent changes in planning conditions have now made it possible to develop this land, but only for residential purposes. I would be grateful if you would telephone my secretary to arrange an appointment to discuss this matter further if you are still interested in pursuing it. Unfortunately I shall be out of the office for the next few days on business but expect to return no later than next Friday. At present no other building companies have expressed interest in this plot of land but once it becomes generally known that it is available for development I would expect that to change. Undoubtedly this will affect the final price should the plot be auctioned later this year. Yours sincerely F R Trainer, Building Supervisor.

2 Key in a copy of the following letter to Purcell, Purcell & Bowen, Estate Agents, The Avenue, Preston PR3 8DG. Use open punctuation and the blocked style of presentation. Insert today's date. Sign the letter on behalf of your employer E R Dolling, Senior partner. Print a copy of your work and save it using a suitable file name.

> Ref ERD/FK Dear Sir. We acknowledge receipt of your letter reference PPB/345 dated yesterday. We are particularly concerned to hear that you found the documents concerning the sale of 14 and 15 Maple Avenue did not show the changes agreed at our previous meeting. Unfortunately Mr Kapour was not at that meeting and has subsequently objected to the request to re-wire the properties prior to the sale. After some discussion, however, he has agreed to a reduction in price of £500 to pay, in part, for the work to be carried out once the agreement of sale has been signed. We trust your clients will find this revised agreement satisfactory and look forward to hearing from you in the coming week. Should you have any further queries, please contact either Mr John Purcell or Ms Angela Purcell on the above telephone number. Yours faithfully.

Recall the two letters you have saved in (1) and (2). Amend them to the indented style of presentation and print a copy of each.

Extension material

1 The following letter should be keyed in using the blocked style of presentation and open punctuation. Date the letter for today. The letter will be signed by A G Rattle, Director, and should be addressed to Mrs Farnden, 429 Lower Bristol Road, Manchester, M15 6TG.

> Ref FG/23 (your initials) today's date Dear Mr Farnden I am in receipt of your letter dated last Friday which alleges that poor workmanship and materials were used in the construction of the external fire escape which we recently built following the loft conversion we carried out on your property last month. We are quite sure that these allegations are not correct as we always check the quality of our materials before they are used on any of our projects and have not had any previous complaints about materials used. With regard to your statement that the gap between the vertical bars of the handrail is too wide, these have been made in accordance with the normal building regulations and have been checked by the local authority building inspector. However, I would be grateful if you would telephone my secretary during normal office hours to give her a convenient time when I can call to discuss these matters with you.

2 Set out the following information as an indented style of business letter. Design a suitable letter heading based on information about a local photographic shop which can be found in Yellow Pages, Thomsons or a similar directory. Address the letter to Mrs Jayne Roberts, 46 Exmouth Road, Countess Weir, Exeter, EX14 3RD and date the letter for today.

> Ref Kk/234A Dear Mrs Roberts I was very sorry to hear that when you collected your films from our Exeter shop last week you found that the packets contained your prints but the negatives were from a different film. To date, no other customer has been in contact to say they have been given the wrong negatives. My assistant has checked all other packets of developed films remaining in the shop but has not yet found the missing negatives. Whilst I appreciate your concern I would be grateful if you would allow me a further period of two weeks to re-check the stock in our Exeter store and also to check the developed films in our Bristol, Cardiff and Swansea branches just in case your negatives have become mixed with stock from these shops. Please find enclosed a voucher to cover the cost of developing your film and accept my sincere apologies for any inconvenience caused. Please be assured that I will telephone you as soon as I have completed my investigations, or I find your negatives. Yours sincerely Adrian Dyke, Regional Manager.

Letter composition

So far, the text of the business letters you have prepared has been provided for you. Very often in a work place, a junior employee may be asked to carry out straightforward letter writing tasks by a more senior colleague. For example, you may be asked to make a hotel reservation, confirm a restaurant booking for lunch or reply to a customer enquiry requesting product information or a price list.

The composition and preparation of business letters is extremely important as a business is often judged by its customers on the quality and clarity of the letters they receive. A badly prepared letter which contains spelling errors and poor English will not encourage a potential customer to spend money with a company. You may not be asked to write complex letters, but when you do prepare letters you must be as accurate as possible.

Preparation and writing

Before starting to word process a letter that you are composing, the following steps should be noted:

- Establish the purpose of the letter: make sure

you clearly understand *why* you are writing the letter.

- Obtain the information you need to prepare the letter before you start: can you complete all the 'parts', for example, addressee, full name of signatory? Can you answer all the queries/questions?
- Work in a logical sequence of events: for example, if making a hotel booking, think of the order in which things should occur. Who is the booking for? What is the name of the hotel? What date is the booking for? What time will the person arrive at the hotel? For how many nights will they stay? What type of room is required? Which meals will they require? Are there any special requirements?
- Keep sentences short and to the point: do not over complicate your sentences. Follow the general rule and use one sentence for each point you wish to make.
- Break your letter up by using paragraphs: use an opening sentence or short paragraph; each new topic should prompt a new paragraph; use a concluding sentence to politely round off your letter.
- Check the quality of your English: check your grammar by reading through your finished letter; avoid using colloquial expressions, such as boss instead of employer, mate instead of colleague; ensure you have included the correct punctuation; avoid using abbreviations whenever possible.
- Spell-check and proofread your work: remember, the spell-checker does not pick up every error. If possible, ask someone else to check your work for you before you print.
- Finally, before printing a document, always re-read your composition slowly and carefully. Ensure that it makes sense to you and that it says what it is required to. If you are happy that it does, then you can print it out.

Exercises

1 Explain why it is important to write letters which are correctly spelt and grammatically correct. (2)

2 What is the logical sequence to adopt when composing the main contents of a business letter? (2)

3 Explain why it is good practice to keep short sentences when composing a business letter. (2)

4 List three different types of error a computer spell-checking system will not identify. (3)

5 Write a short paragraph to explain to an inexperienced operator how to make use of the spell-check facility of your word processor. (4)

6 Why should you always proof-read every document before printing a copy? (2)

You will need an up-to-date copy of Yellow Pages or a similar directory. Compose and word process letters in reply to the following:

1 Obtain the address of your local leisure centre or country club and then write to them requesting an application form for family membership. Make sure the application form is sent to your home address.

2 Write to your local Careers Advisory Service office requesting an appointment to discuss future career opportunities. Include in your letter some ideas on the types of work or careers you may be interested in.

3 Send a letter to your local travel agent asking them to provide you with details of possible package holidays for yourself and three friends, for when you have completed your GCSEs. Suggest some possible destinations and dates. Include a maximum cost per person.

1 You have been asked to confirm a hotel booking for your tutor at the Ambassador Hotel, Lower Heath Road, Birmingham, B3 5JR for 2 nights on 23rd and 24th of this month. He/she requires an en-suite room, and will not be arriving at the hotel until 9.00 pm on the 23rd. Compose a letter to the hotel for your tutor to sign.

2 You have purchased a Sony portable mini-disk player which has developed a fault when recording. Write a letter of complaint to the local Sony dealer (obtain the address from Yellow Pages) who supplied the system. Inform the supplier that you require a replacement player, rather than having yours sent away for repair.

Extension material

Compose and word process responses to each of the following. Design suitable letter headings on which to print your work.

1 Write to your local bank or building society manager (find out their name first) and ask for a statement of your account up to the end of last week (give the date), to be sent to you at your home address as soon as possible.

2 Your aunt, who is visiting from America, has asked you to book her and her 15 year old daughter into a suitable local hotel for five nights from the first Monday of next month (find out the date) – twin rooms, en-suite facilities, continental breakfast and car parking. Your aunt would like to know how much it will cost her per night so that she can budget for the visit.

Design and Text Processing

Page and report layout

Text processing

Abbreviations and text processing errors

Rearranging material

Search and replace

Moving and merging text

Common correction symbols

Bullet points and special characters

Graphics

Clipart

Using lines and geometric shapes

Précis

Page and report layout

Have you considered how we take for granted the way that newspapers and magazines present to us the information we read? The first impression of a piece of word processed or printed work can have a strong influence on whether we are prepared to read it. Well displayed work which is presented in a variety of different shapes and sizes attracts our attention, whereas poorly set out work with little white space around it and only limited variations in the print size may not.

Newspaper page design

Tabloid newspaper editors are past masters at presenting information to attract a reader's attention. Sales of the newspapers depend upon their success in creating effective and attractive page designs.

The newspaper page has a plain white border measuring 25 mm around it. The newspaper title is included in a coloured block of text which spans about one quarter of the page. The block also includes the date and price of the paper, but most importantly is used to promote features, which encourages potential readers to look inside. The remaining three quarters of the page is divided into four or five columns of text. Headlines and pictures may cross these rather artificial divisions.

Pictures and articles are often 'boxed' to make them stand out and to separate them from the other items on the page. The main headline is set in a large point size – sometimes as large as 120 point – so that it dominates the whole page. Sub-headings in a smaller point size are used to further explain the main story, and the lead paragraph crosses two or more columns in a point size of 12 or 14 point, with the text rendered in bold.

If a secondary story is carried on the front page, this will usually be in one column, headed by a small picture. A typical example of such a page design is shown in Figure 31.

Figure 31 Sample page design

Display techniques

The effect on the reader of a page such as in Figure 31, is created by the way it is set out rather than the content of the stories and pictures included on it. There are several factors contributing to the display of a page which should be considered.

White space

The use of blank spaces, called 'white space', is very important as it creates the illusion of separation between stories and other items on the page. The page itself is surrounded by clear and uncluttered margins which isolate the whole content from everything else around it. Pictures and photographs, when mounted, use the same technique. The plain mount focuses attention on the centre of the frame rather than on its surroundings.

Font sizes

Obviously, the main headline is set in a very large point size and so it stands out. Tabloid newspapers frequently use sizes in excess of 100 point. What is less obvious is the variety of font sizes and styles used in other parts of the story. The first paragraph of the lead story will be in a point size slightly larger than that of the rest of the text. It may also be in bold type. The secondary story will be in a different font. The fonts will not differ drastically, but perhaps one story will use a font with serifs and the other without. These differences are subtle enough to create interest visually but will not detract the reader from the story or make it difficult to read.

Columns

All newspapers and journals use columns to help break up the page. However, these columns are not adhered to rigidly, and it is common for the first paragraph of a story to spread across more than one. This gives the appearance of substance to the start of the story, before it continues in more narrow columns. It also provides horizontal space for the inclusion of a heading to the text when required. Text in columns is frequently right justified to give it a clean and tidy appearance.

Paragraphing

The style of newspaper paragraphs has remained traditional, the reason being largely to save space. Most newspapers continue to use indented paragraphs without a clear line of space between. Although this reduces white space on the page, the clear line between each paragraph can increase the size of the story which will be printed on what can be a very expensive page!

Borders

These are used to great effect to link together text, headings and pictures that are all part of one story. Borders provide a clear limit for the reader's eye as to what is and is not part of each story. They can, however, limit the amount of text which can be placed within them and so care must be taken to ensure that text is correctly edited or précised and that the sense is not lost. The thickness of the line used in borders can also be varied, although it is important not to use too heavy a line around a particular item as this will draw the eye directly to it as the main feature on the page, rather than the main headline.

Variety

This occurs naturally through the use of pictures, columns, slightly different font styles, various point sizes and the use of bold as a form of emphasis. It is, however, important that the variety of display features is used with discretion. For example, justifying a main heading is likely to place too much space between the letters in single words; or the selection of an **Old English** font certainly creates interest, but is very tiring on the reader after a short space of time.

Colour

This is always good for creating emphasis, but like most other forms of display, colour needs to be used sparingly to be most effective. Take a front page of a tabloid newspaper, for example. Colour, usually red, will certainly be used to emphasise the name of the paper. A different, more subtle colour, such as dark blue may also be used to give emphasis to features within the paper. This may also be used within the text to create contrast. Other colour features are very few and far between. If you are fortunate enough to have access to colour printing facilities, it is often best to limit their use, as the professional would do, for greater effect.

There is no real way in which artistic display techniques can be taught in a book such as this. All the features described in this unit are available to you when designing pages. Make use of them to enhance your work but always remember you can have too much of a good thing!

Report Writing

One of the ways in which information is passed on in business is through the writing of reports. A report is a document that presents information about a particular item or project to a specific audience. A Sales Manager may write a report to the Marketing Director about the success (or otherwise) of a marketing campaign, or a member of the Research and Development team may write a report to the Production Director about the viability of a new product.

Most reports follow a set format. The title page or heading should state the purpose of the report and to whom it is addressed. The report itself should be broken down into at least three main sections: an introduction, which outlines the purpose of the report; the main body of the report, which may be broken up using sub-headings, and a conclusion in which the recommendations or findings of the report are clearly set out. All reports should include the name of the author and the date they were written.

Page Numbering

When word processing a report, it is not unusual for it to print out onto more than one page. To help the reader and to ensure the report remains in the correct order, the pages can be numbered. Most word processing systems will allow the operator to insert an automatic page numbering feature in any multi-page document. This will place a consecutive number on each page of the report. The format of the number can be varied (eg 1, 2, 3 .../a, b, c .../i, ii, iii ...), as can the position on the page where it will appear (on the left, the right or in the centre, at the top or the foot of the page).

Headers and Footers

These allow the author of a report to include a common phrase or description in the margin at the top or the bottom of each page of the document. They are frequently used in longer reports where there may be several sections to the document and by 'labelling' each in the header or footer, it helps the reader find their way around the document. This textbook uses a header in which the title of the book is given above the text on each of the left hand pages and the title of the particular section is given above the text on the right. You may have been taught to label your work using the headers or footers by your teacher. Inserting your name and other relevant details (such as your tutor group or the number of the task) will ensure your work, when printed, is always correctly labelled with your name.

Exercises

1 Explain why white space and a variety of fonts are important when presenting information on the page. (3)

2 Colour is an effective way of helping to display information. Why then do national newspapers publish their daily papers largely in black and white? (2)

3 Why do businesses tend to use fonts such as **arial** or **times new roman** rather than more elaborate and informal fonts when preparing word processed documents? (2)

4 Outline the effectiveness of columns as a means of keeping a reader's interest in a printed story. (2)

5 Explain what is meant by the following terms: *sub-heading*, *banner title*, and *secondary story*. (3)

6 Why can too many varieties of font size and style sometimes have a negative effect when displaying a piece of work? (3)

You have been asked to prepare an outline front page for the company's new monthly staff magazine. The front page is to be prepared on a sheet of A4 portrait-style paper but will be enlarged to A3 when printed. Use your word processor or desktop publishing system to prepare the outline. You do not need to include any text in your draft – boxes and lines can be used to indicate the position of the title bar, any photographs, graphs and charts, the main and sub-headings, columns of text, etc. You are advised to draw a rough draft of your page plan before you start to create it on your computer.

You work for an advertising agency which has just obtained a new contract for a large department store. You have decided to place a double page feature advertisement in the centre pages of the local weekly paper. Using your word processor or desktop publishing system, prepare an outline plan of this feature on A4 landscape paper. Do not include any detailed text on the feature – indicate where pictures, headings and text will appear using frames and boxes where appropriate.

Extension material

Obtain a copy of the television channel listings as published in Radio Times, TV Times, TV Quick, etc. Use this as a guide to prepare your own television guide for an evening's viewing, based around a theme. For example, a science fiction evening, an evening of soaps, great sporting achievements or a music theme.

Present your work in a similar way to the guide and use at least two columns on the page for your text. Leave appropriate spaces for the inclusion of any pictures. Try and include a variety of programmes – documentaries, plays, feature films, comedies, etc. Each listing will need a title, a description of its content and a cast list. Set up areas on the page to give film reviews or a description of choice viewing.

Text processing

Text processing is the task of taking information, altering or amending it and then presenting it in its changed form. For example, you may be required to word process a business letter for your employer from hand written notes that he or she has prepared. After reading the notes you would key the letter content into your word processor and set it out in the style required by your employer. This process consists of three stages, as shown below in Figure 32.

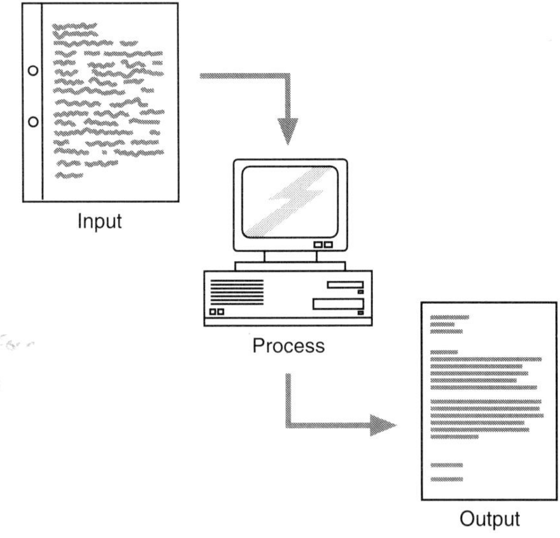

Figure 32 The stages of text processing

The stages of text processing

Input

Input to this process can be in a variety of forms. It may be any of the following:

- Handwritten material.
- A previously word processed draft which contains amendments.
- Recorded on audio dictation equipment.
- In shorthand note form.
- Dictated directly to the person keying it in.

Processing

The information is then processed. This may include the following processes:

- Keying the information into a word processing system.
- Ensuring it is displayed in a consistently acceptable style.
- Reading through and checking for spelling and grammatical accuracy.
- Editing the text and making any calculations which may be required.

Output

Output is usually in printed form, called a 'hard copy'. Alternatively, it may be produced in a 'soft copy' format, such as being left displayed on the screen for your employer to check; saved onto a floppy disk or the computer's hard disk drive for further amendment at a later time, or transmitted to the final user by electronic mail.

Posture and lighting

To be effective as a text processing operator, it is important that when using a word processor you organise yourself so that you can work comfortably and efficiently. Your desk should be the correct height and size for the equipment and there should be a clear space underneath to allow you ample leg room. Lighting should be adequate and not reflect on the screen, or alternatively, an anti-glare screen should be used. There should be sufficient space beside the word processing station so that files, notebooks and any other equipment you may require (such as pens, rulers, etc.) do not get in the way of work.

Your chair should be adjustable with a firm back support. It is very important that you adopt the correct posture for operating your word processor. This will reduce the possibility of aches and strain. Remember, screens and keyboards can be moved, as well as chairs, and can be adjusted to give you the most comfortable working position.

Exercises

1 What precisely is meant by the term *text processing*? (2)

2 List at least six different forms in which an operator could expect to obtain data to input into their word processor. (3)

3 Explain the difference between hard and soft copy. (2)

4 Explain carefully the correct posture to adopt when keying in data. (3)

5 How can the reflections on a computer screen be reduced? Why is it important to try and do this? (3)

6 List the Acts of Parliament that set out the requirements for word processing operators. (2)

Key in a copy of the following passage in double line spacing. Set left and right margins of at least 25 mm and right justify the text. Compose an appropriate heading and then print one copy on plain A4 paper.

On a cold April night in 1912, the magnificent new liner, flagship of the White Star Line, the RMS Titanic struck an iceberg and sank in the icy waters of the North Atlantic. The following day the newspaper headline 'Titanic Lost' shocked the world.

The loss of the Titanic is undoubtedly the most well-known of nine tragic stories of maritime loss which the latest book by Nigel Trevellian, 'Shipwreck!', re-opens and examines. The book, the result of several years investigation by the author, claims to have discovered new evidence on each of the shipwrecks and provides the reader with previously unconsidered explanations of these ship losses.

Adapted from a SEG Examination Question, 1989

Key in a copy of the following text on plain A4 paper in one and a half line spacing. Leave margins of at least 25 mm and compose an appropriate heading for the passage.

Jane Harding is a full-time secretary and personal assistant to the Marketing Director of a local manufacturing company. Dimitri Andreas works as a Business Studies lecturer at the local college of further education. Last year they decided to form a partnership and go into business.

Last September they started their secretarial school which they decided to call the 'First Class Secretarial School'. In the first year, they both kept working at their day jobs and offered a range of classes in the evenings.

Their evening secretarial school was very successful. Not only did they fill all their classes, the results their students attained were excellent.

Jane and Dimitri have now decided to operate their school as a full-time business and raise the necessary finances to rent their own premises and purchase equipment. Dimitri has savings of £8,000 and Jane intends to use the £7,500 she was left by an aunt who died last year. They have made an appointment to discuss their plans with their local bank manager.

Adapted from a SEG Examination Question, 1991

Extension material

Key in a copy of the following passage, which contains some errors that you will need to correct. Set a left margin of at least 30 mm and right justify the text. Insert a suitable heading. Spell check and proofread your work before printing a copy on plain A4 paper.

> The Dorsetshire Steam Railway is planning too social events during the summer. Both will be held at the Red Lion Hotel in Dorchester and admission will be buy ticket only.
>
> The first event is a Barn Dance on Sat 11 July starting at 8.00 pm. Dancing will be to the local band The Turnip Eaters and the Caller will be our very own Jed Fooley. Tickets are available now from the local station office and the Hotel. The cost is £8.50 which includes a ploughman's super.
>
> Three weaks later on Friday 1 august their will be a grand firework display and barbecue in the field by the old signal box. The barbecue will start at 8.00 pm and the firework display will commence at 10.30 p.m. Everyone are welcome to attend. There will be no admission charge, but if anyone wood like to make a donation, these will be gratefully received. The Red Lion Hotel will run a beer tent which will be open from 6.30 pm until midnight. See you there!

Adapted from a SEG Examination Question, 1992

Abbreviations and text processing errors

'A good keyboard operator does not abbreviate.'

Word processing operators very often have to interpret and make sense of handwritten (manuscript) source material from managers and others. As this material is often written quickly, using abbreviations to speed up the process, a word processor operator is expected to spot abbreviations and correctly extend them. It helps if both the word processor operator and the manager use the same abbreviations for the same words! Many of them are straightforward and well known, for example, Mon for Monday and Rd for Road. Others are less obvious, such as ffly for faithfully, sig for signature and wl for will.

Some abbreviations have become an accepted part of the English language such as temp., approx., advert and CD. Whilst these are now generally accepted it is important that a word processor operator is still able to recognise them and extend them correctly if required.

Other abbreviations can have more than one meaning. For example, ref can stand either for reference or referee, exp can be extended into expense or experience. It is important, therefore, to read the

sense of the sentence in which the abbreviated word occurs to ensure the correct extension is used. Take, for example, the abbreviation ref in the following sentence:

The ref awarded a penalty because of the foul on the defender.

In this example the meaning is self-evident and the correct extension for ref is referee.

But what about this sentence?

The young woman obtained the job because she had an excellent ref.

There the meaning is less obvious and either referee or reference could be used to provide a correct extension.

Whereas in the sentence:

The library was unable to find the ref book on horses.

In this example the correct extension can only be reference.

List of common abbreviations

The most commonly used abbreviations together with their extensions are given in the list below:

accom	accommodation	Mon	Monday
a/c(s)	account(s)	necy	necessary
ack	acknowledge	Nov	November
advert(s)	advertisement(s)	Oct	October
appt(s)	appointment(s)	opp(s)	opportunity/ies
approx	approximately	rec(s)	receipt(s)
Apr	April	rec	receive
attn	attention	recd	received
Aug	August	recom	recommend
Ave	Avenue	ref(s)	reference(s)
bel	believe	refd	referred
bus	business	resp	responsible
cat(s)	catalogue(s)	Rd	Road
cttee(s)	committee(s)	Sat	Saturday
co(s)	company/ies	sec(s)	secretary/ies
Cres	Crescent	sep	separate
Dec	December	Sept	September
def	definite/ly	sig(s)	signature(s)
dev	develop	sinc	sincerely

Dr	Drive	St	Street
ex	exercise	suff	sufficient
exp(s)	expense(s)	Sun	Sunday
exp	experience	temp	temporary
Feb	February	thro	through
ffly	faithfully	Thurs	Thursday
Fri	Friday	Tues	Tuesday
gov(s)	government(s)	sh	shall
gntee(s)	guarantee(s)	shd	should
immed	immediate/ly	Wed	Wednesday
incon	inconvenient/ence	wh	which
Jan	January	wd	would
Jul	July	w	with
Jun	June	wl	will
mfr(s)	manufacturer(s)	yr(s)	years
misc	miscellaneous	yr(s)	yours

Text processing errors

As with abbreviations, a good word processing operator must be able to identify and correct all types of errors which may occur in a person's work, to ensure that it is correct. A firm sending out a letter or report which contains errors of spelling, punctuation or grammar, or which contains incorrect words, does not convey the right image to its customers and may lose business. Many customers belief that if the firm does not pay attention to its business correspondence, then it will not pay any better attention when preparing its product or service.

Spell checking

The use of spell checkers has helped to eliminate many of the typographical errors which can occur in business documents, and it is good practice to ensure this facility of your word processor or desktop publisher is used whenever possible. With most word processing systems, the spell checker can be accessed with the click of the mouse on the appropriate icon. Once started, when the system reaches a word it cannot identify from its built in dictionary (which can contain upwards of 70,000 words) it will stop and highlight the apparent error. A list of words which could be likely substitutes are then offered from which the operator can choose an alternative. Spell checkers will also stop when they identify two identical words following each other and will offer the opportunity of deleting one of them.

Most spell checkers allow the operator to build up a personalised dictionary of commonly used words that are not in the main dictionary. This prevents the spell checker from stopping unnecessarily. A personalised dictionary can include words such as proper nouns (for example, your surname or the name of your school or college) as well as technical words that relate to a particular business or an individual operator.

There are, however, a number of errors which spell checkers cannot identify. These can only be picked up and corrected by careful proofreading. The most common groups are discussed here.

Omitted words

The spell checker only checks words that have been keyed into the text. It cannot identify words which have been missed out by the keyboard operator. It is only by careful proofreading and comparing the word processed document with the original, that this type of error can be identified and corrected.

Excess words

If additional words are included in a passage and if they are correctly spelt, then the spell checker will accept them even though the passage may not make sense. The only exception is if two identical words appear in the text consecutively.

Incorrect words

Where individual words are correctly spelt but are incorrect for the sense of the text, the spell checker will still accept them. Common examples include the use of 'there' instead of 'their' or 'buy' instead of 'by'. As all these words are in the spell checker they will not be identified as incorrect. Errors of grammar can also fall into this category. For example, 'we is all going to the cinema' would be accepted by the spell checker as each individual word is correct, although it is apparent that it should read 'we are all going to the cinema'. Again, careful proofreading is the answer.

Misrendered words

There are many words in the English language which differ in only one or two characters. A word processing operator working at speed may transpose letters in a word and inadvertently create another legitimate word. For example, 'from' could be rendered as 'form' and 'them' could be rendered as 'then'.

Punctuation errors

It is easy to render a full stop instead of a comma, but as the computer does not make sense of what has been keyed in, the spell checker will not register this as an error. Similarly, if a question mark is omitted at the end of a question and a full stop is used, this will not be identified.

The only way in which these errors can be identified is through proofreading. A careful comparison of the source document and the work you have prepared is essential to ensure your text is accurate.

Exercises

1. Explain what is meant by the term *manuscript*. (1)
2. Why is it important for a word processing operator to extend abbreviations when keying in data? (2)
3. Make a list of ten words which are abbreviated and where the abbreviation has become an accepted part of the English language. E.g. *fab* for fabulous. (3)
4. List and explain the different types of error which a spell-checker will not always identify as incorrect. (4)
5. How can a word processing operator ensure that words are not omitted from a passage when keying in text? (2)
6. Many word processing systems also have grammar checkers. Explain what they are and how they can help the word processing operator when creating text. (3)

1 Word process a copy of the following passage correctly, extending any abbreviations.

> It was on the first Tues in Dec that the young girl arrived and began looking for accom in the village. She had recd a postcard from one of her old college friends, to which she had replied immed, informing her that there was an advert in the local shop offering a small cottage for rent in Starling Dr, a quiet road at the northern end of the village.
>
> However, when Shalina arrived she discovered that an American couple had already moved in to the cottage on a temp basis at the end of Nov. She was quite concerned about the exp she had incurred coming to the village and did not know if she would now have suff. money in her bank a/c to allow her to stay until the end of the yr. It was an exp Shalina would def not forget in a hurry.

2 Word process the list of common abbreviations given previously on plain A4 paper and include it in your folder. Present your work in two columns. Make sure you proof-read your work carefully to ensure all extended words are correctly spelt and that there are no omissions from the list.

Are there any other abbreviations which are commonly used in your school or college? If so add them to the list in the correct alphabetical sequence.

This passage contains the following errors:

- Six excess words
- Five incorrect words
- Two grammatical errors
- One omitted word
- One punctuation error

Can you identify them all? When you have, word process a copy of the passage correcting the errors that you have found.

> Most word processing systems check your documents for spelling errors by using their main dictionary, which contains most common words. If a word is found which are not in the main dictionary. it will be displayed on screen in a box and a choice of alternatives are offered too enable you to correct the misspelling.
>
> Some words have not have not been included in the mane dictionary, such as names and technical terms. To check the spelling of these words and to prevent your word processor from questioning then if they are spe!t correctly, they car be added to custom dictionary.
>
> Some systems will automatically check the hole document each time the the spell checker is run. Others will give you the option to check only work which have been highlighted. At any point in checking your document, it is possible to stop the process by clicking on the cancel button when the spelling dialogue box is on is on the screen.

Extension material

(a) Word process the following passage correctly extending any abbreviations and correcting any other errors you may find.

> By the following Mon the a/c of the new customer had been opened and the credit rating cheques carried out. They had proved necy because too of the three cheques wh had been used to pay for the goods had been refd back to the person who wrote them. The third cheque was returned because the sig was not a suff match and the bank had become suspicious.
>
> When all this was reported to the cttee, the following month, the decision was taken not to gntee any further bus from this customer until those resp could be traced. The exp of the bank returning cheques had to be payed by the cttee and their was also the immed incon of having to make another visit to the bank on the Tues morning.
>
> It was recom that in future all new a/cs wl be opened and cheques paid in and cleared before any goods are supplied. Recs wl be issued for the money recd and orders will be ackd, but know goods will be supplied.

(b) You work as Office Supervisor for a firm of solicitors and your employer has noticed recently an increase in the number of non-spelling errors in work produced by your staff. Compose a memorandum to your staff advising them of the problem and explaining the types of errors which are involved.

Rearranging material

Modern business offices use a great deal of information, much of which is stored in a computer system. When correctly encoded, stored data can be retrieved and presented in a wide variety of ways. For example, data about sales of a product can be stored by customers' name, by the date the sale was made or by the product code.

Occasionally office staff will need to re-sort information into a different form or sequence. The three main sequences in which data is likely to be required are: alphabetical, numerical and chronological.

Alphabetical sequence

This stores information by surname or company name starting at A and running through to Z. Where individuals have the same surname, data should be stored by surname and then the initial of their first name. For example when filing 'Smiths' alphabetically, the order would be:

Smith	Amanda
Smith	Brenda
Smith	Fiona
Smith	John
Smith	Roger

With company names, the word 'The' should be ignored when present. Where two or more surnames appear in one company name, the first should be used, and if the registered name of a company includes a first name, the surname should be used:

- The Glass Bottle Co. Ltd would be filed under: Glass Bottle Co. Ltd. (The)
- Boulton & Cooper Ltd. would be filed under: Boulton & Cooper Ltd.
- John Cooper & Sons Ltd. would be filed under: Cooper, John & Sons Ltd.

Numerical

Some firms use numbers to reference their data and file information using a numerical format. For example, each new order received by a company may be given a number against which the details of the order will be stored. Alternatively, a firm with many clients may allocate a customer number to each of its clients and store information by customer number. Numbers can be allocated in ascending order – 1, 2, 3, 4, 5, etc. – or in descending order where the next number to be issued is less than the previous one – 10, 9, 8, 7, 6, etc.

Where information is stored as records in a database such as Microsoft Access, a 'key' field, or numeric identity is often generated by the program and data is stored using that as a code. This gives a unique reference for each set of data and still allows it to be sorted alphabetically or numerically on the contents of any other field.

Chronological

This requires information to be stored in order of the date. Hard copies of business letters and memoranda stored in customer files are usually held in date order with the latest communication on the top and the earliest at the back of the file.

Exercises

1. List the three main sequences in which data can usually be stored in a computer system. (3)
2. Explain the rules for alphabetical sorting of company names. Illustrate your answer with examples from real businesses from your local area. (3)
3. Carefully explain, with the help of an example, what is meant by (a) ascending numerical order and (b) descending alphabetical order. (4)
4. What is meant by the term *chronological sequence*? Why might a business require data to be sorted in this way? (3)
5. Explain why a business might sort and store its correspondence alphabetically and its sales invoices chronologically. (4)
6. Why might a business code its data when storing it on an electronic system? (3)

Make a list of all the students in your class. When complete, word process a copy of the list alphabetically by surname. Save the file using the filename ALPHA and print a hard copy on appropriate paper.

Using the copy of the above list printed from file ALPHA, obtain each student's date of birth. Key in the data obtained against each student's name. Group this list in ascending chronological order of dates of birth. Save the new list as ALPHA1 and then print a hard copy.

Extension material

Enter the following list of firms into your database. Check the data for errors and make any corrections.

Customer Number of Last order	Customer Name	Date
006	Westward Builders Ltd.	08.03.1998
009	The Midland Publishing Co. Ltd.	26.10.1998
001	Superior Office Cleaners	14.09.1999
013	Peter Jackson & Sons Ltd.	04.12.1999
035	Concord Glazing Co.	29.03.1998
026	Golden Hill Garage PLC	13.02.1998
094	Primrose Farm Guest House	31.08.1998
091	Avonside Windows	21.08.1999
023	Bristol Engineering PLC	24.07.1999
042	Isobel Sharpe (Dental Surgeon)	07.01.1998
059	Adept Energy Conservation	12.04.1999
102	Sheffield Insulators Ltd.	01.04.1998
044	AB Insurance Agency	26.07.1997
040	Castlemead Knitwear	15.12.1998
024	Bristol Game & Puzzle Co. Ltd.	27.08.1999

Sort the data

1 into alphabetical order

2 into chronological order of the most recent order

3 into descending order of customer account number.

Print a copy of each list.

UNIT 43

Search and replace

Very often prepared text needs to be amended and reprinted. Occasionally some of the amendments are similar throughout the text. For example, a job title may change from 'Office Manager' to 'Administration Manager'. This means that a word processing operator would have to search through the document and find each occasion when Office Manager occurred and then replace it with Administration Manager. This can be a time-consuming process and it is easy for the operator to accidentally miss one or more of the changes, particularly if it is a long document.

Most word processing systems have a 'search and replace' or 'find and replace' option. This enables the operator to identify a word or words they are seeking to change together with the word or phrase they wish to replace it with. Once activated the word processing system will scan through the text and stop each time it encounters the phrase for which it is searching. The operator can then decide to replace that phrase or ignore it and move on to the next.

Alternatively, the system can be set to automatically replace the word or phrase on each occasion it occurs in the document, without stopping. Most

operators, however, prefer to set their system to stop when it reaches the specified word or phrase. This allows them to decide when to replace the text and when not to. This also avoids incorrect replacement with the wrong word. The following sentence is an example that could occur in a staff handbook:

> The Office Manager is responsible for the smooth running of the Sales Office.

If the title Office Manager was to be automatically altered to Administration Manager throughout a document, and the above sentence was a part of this document, when the operator set the system to automatically search and replace 'Office' with 'Administration' the sentence would read:

> The Administration Manager is responsible for the smooth running of the Sales Administration.

Whilst the first change is correct, the second has created an incorrect phrase and so the sentence no longer makes sense.

The search and replace system can also be set to take into account capital letters, or to ignore them. In the previous example the word 'office' may appear with or without an initial capital. The system can be set to select only those words with the same capitalisation.

Exercises

1 Write a paragraph to explain to a new word processing operator how the **find and replace** feature on a word processing system works. (3)

2 Explain when the **find and replace** or **search and replace** facility is useful to a word processing operator. (2)

3 What are the possible disadvantages of using such a facility? (2)

4 List three examples when the **find and replace** facility could be used by a printing company. (3)

5 Carefully explain when a word processing operator would use **find next** rather than the **replace all** facility. (2)

6 What are the disadvantages of automatically replacing a word or phrase in a long document without stopping at each change? (3)

Key in a copy of the following passage in double or one and a half line spacing. Check your work for accuracy by spell checking and proofreading it carefully. Print a copy on plain A4 paper.

GREENWOOD HOTEL

Greenwood Hotel is one of a group of seven hotel complexes run by Thomas Henman Associates. Each is set in fresh, open countryside on the outskirts of a major city where all forms of transport, motorway, air and rail are close at hand.

The latest hotel to join the group is set in beautiful surroundings on the outskirts of Chester. It is this near perfect setting which encourages many of the hotel's guests to return again and again to enjoy the many facilities of the hotel and attached sports complex. Greenwood Hotels have a growing reputation for providing only the best for their clients.

The latest edition of the RAC's Good Accommodation Guide lists all seven of the Greenwood Hotels as being well worth a visit. They are listed as providing their guests with excellent cuisine and good value for money. If you are staying away from home, either on business or for pleasure, make sure you stay where you will be treated as if you are still at home – choose a Greenwood Hotel.

Adapted from a SEG Examination Question, 1994

Using the search and replace function of your word processor, replace the word 'hotel' whenever it appears in the passage with the words 'country club'. Print a copy of the amended passage then save your work.

Key in a copy of the following text in single line spacing. Spell check and proofread your work before printing a copy on A4 paper.

Freshco Supermarkets PLC

The following instructions are for cashiers and are designed to promote the company's new policy of improving client satisfaction

- Be polite and friendly to all clients at all times.
- Under no circumstances should you argue or talk back to angry clients. When faced with a dissatisfied client, always call your supervisor.
- All complaints from clients should be referred to the duty supervisor and written down in the Client Complaints Book which is held at the Customer Service Desk.
- Check each item as you ring it up to ensure it is not damaged or sub-standard in any way. Do not allow clients to leave the store with faulty goods. Always ensure a packer, or other member of staff obtains a replacement for the client. Do not allow customers to get their own replacement products.
- Never guess the price of an item. If you are unsure, or the cost is not clearly marked, do not ask the client, get the supervisor to verify the price from their stock records.
- When serving clients, please refrain from having conversations with the next cashier.
- Dress must always be of an acceptable standard. Large earrings, excess jewellery and high heeled shoes should not be worn during working hours.

Adapted from a SEG Examination Question, 1989

Use the search and replace facility on your word processing system to change the word 'client', which appears ten times, to 'customer' whenever it appears in the above passage. Save the amended passage using the filename CUSTOMER and then print a copy on A4 paper.

Extension material

Prepare an accurate copy of the following passage:

> TREAT YOURSELF TO A VALUE FOR MONEY MARCH BREAK
>
> During March Starline Vacations are able to offer you an opportunity you cannot afford to miss. You can travel to any one of our twenty six European vacation destinations for a refreshing three day break at real value for money prices.
>
> One of the most delightful times to visit Paris, Rome, Venice or any of the major cities of Europe, March weather is warm and pleasant without being too hot – a real bonus for the more discerning traveller. March is also an excellent time to take a second vacation. Choose yourself a short break or a vacation from 7 to 28 nights, the choice is yours.
>
> All our March vacations are based on the same hotel, room type and board arrangements as our summer range of holidays given in this brochure. We guarantee our hotel prices will not be affected by supplements so the price quoted is the price you pay for your vacation. If you choose self-catering accommodation for your vacation, the price for the March breaks is the same as those shown for the low season occupancy.
>
> Child prices are the same as the prices in the last week of March for the accommodation you have chosen for your vacation and providing you book before 1 March this year, we guarantee you will not pay any surcharges.

Use the find and replace facility of your word processor to change 'vacation' to 'holiday' throughout the passage, except in the company title in the first line. Print a copy of your work on A4 paper.

Change 'March' to 'April' throughout the passage except in the last line of the final paragraph, then print a copy of the amended passage.

Moving and merging text

One of the main advantages of using a word processor is the facility the operator has to move and re-order text in a passage without having to delete and re-key in the work. This means that text can be amended and moved quickly and easily without the possibility of introducing errors which may occur when keying it in again.

There are three main methods by which text blocks can be moved: 'cut and paste', 'copy and paste' or 'drag and drop'. All three require that the text to be moved is selected or highlighted using either the mouse or the cursor and shift keys.

Moving text

Cut and paste

Once the text has been selected, click the 'cut' button on the standard toolbar, usually represented by a pair of scissors. This will remove the section of text from the passage and store it in the computer's memory on the clipboard. Now move the cursor to the point in the text to which the passage is being moved and click on the 'paste' button, usually represented by a clipboard, on the toolbar. The section of text should be inserted back into the document in the new position. This is a useful method of moving text from one point to another when the position you wish to move the text to is not visible on the screen. It can also be used to move text between documents, as once the text is 'cut' and stored on the clipboard, it can be 'pasted' into any new or existing document.

Copy and paste

This is a similar facility to cut and paste, but by using the 'copy' button on the toolbar (represented by two pages), rather than 'cut', it leaves the highlighted section of text in its original position in the document, but still stores it on the computer's clipboard. Consequently, the passage can be added into the document in a new position. This facility is particularly useful when using the same phrase or sentence several times in the same document or a number of documents. Once keyed in, it can be copied and then pasted back in at each point it is required.

Drag and drop

Again, the passage to be moved needs to be highlighted or selected. Using the mouse move the pointer onto the highlighted area and click and hold down the left mouse button. Within a second a small, dotted rectangle will appear on screen attached to the mouse pointer. This represents your passage of text.

A small vertical shaded bar also appears on screen. This indicates the point in the document where the passage will be inserted once the mouse button is released. Use the mouse to move the shaded bar through your document to the point to which the text is to be moved and then release the mouse. Your passage should now appear in its new position. This method of moving text is ideal when both the original passage and the point of insertion are visible on the screen at the same time. You may need to tidy up the line spacing between paragraphs after this operation.

The above methods of moving or copying text have been illustrated using toolbar buttons. If these are not available on screen, they can usually be found in the 'Edit' menu on the main menu bar. Clicking the mouse on 'Edit' will call up the following menu on which the cut, copy and paste facilities can be selected using either the mouse or the cursor keys.

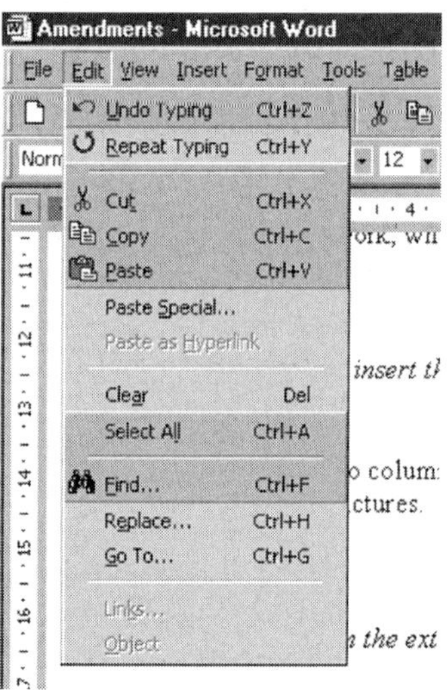

Alternatively, you can carry out the key functions of most word processing systems by using a combination of keystrokes. For example, in Microsoft Word, to copy a section of highlighted text, you would press 'Ctrl' and 'C', and 'Ctrl' and 'V' to paste it into another position in the document. Most of these keystroke alternatives are shown on the drop down menu against the function to which they relate. (See the diagram below.)

Merging text

The ability to move text from one document to another is a real benefit when using a word processor to produce a document. Sections or passages can be moved between one document and another using the cut and paste or copy and paste facilities described above. It is also possible to insert or merge complete documents into others with relative ease. This is a particularly useful facility when several documents have been produced at different times and have been stored on disk prior to being put together in one report.

It is also possible to copy and paste other forms of data, such as graphs or charts, which have been produced in other software. For example, inserting a pie chart produced in a spreadsheet into a word processed document.

Most Windows-based operating systems allow keyboard operators to insert saved computer files into another document. When recalled, these files can be inserted at the cursor point in the new document. When compiling a report from several previously prepared files, it is advisable not to add the other files to the first document. Always create a new file and insert each file in turn into this so as to retain all the original source material unaltered. If anything then happens to corrupt your new document, you should be always be able to recall your original files and recreate the new document, if necessary.

Exercises

1 Explain the three different methods of moving blocks of text in a document. (3)

2 When might the use of **drag and drop** rather than **cut and paste** be more difficult when moving text in a long document? (2)

3 When using **drag and drop** explain how the word processing operator can see what is happening on the screen to ensure it is moving correctly. (3)

4 What are the advantages to the word processing operator of being able to copy and paste blocks of text? (3)

5 Write a paragraph to explain how several separate files could be merged into one single document. (4)

1 Key in the following passage that contains five paragraphs. Spell check and proofread your work to ensure that it contains no errors. Save your work using the file name CAPRI and then print a copy on plain A4 paper.

> Legend has it that the devil stole a slice of paradise, the Island of Capri, and planted it in the Bay of Naples. The island's beauty does credit to the myth and may explain why the island is referred to as 'a piece of paradise which has fallen from the sky'.
>
> Among the first to be struck by the beauty of the Isle of Capri were the Romans. The famous general Augustus stayed here after his victory over Anthony and Cleopatra.
>
> The Emperor Tiberius owned twelve villas on Capri and spent the last years of his life living there with a life style of wine, women and song. Those who displeased him are said to have been thrown from the cliffs, which still bear his name, into the sea below.
>
> Despite its size, the Island of Capri attracts large numbers of celebrities and day visitors alike and is easily accessible being only three miles from the mainland. Regular ferries cross to the island and the journey takes less than forty-five minutes.
>
> Capri town is the capital and is very fashionable with the rich and famous. The town of Annacapri, up in the hills, a little more old-fashioned and less spoilt by tourism, has a chair lift service to the top of Monte Solara, the highest point on the island.

2 Using the cut and paste facility, move the third paragraph to position beneath the fourth paragraph, then move the second paragraph above the first.

3 Using the copy and paste facility, copy the final paragraph and paste it back into the document so it also appears after each of the first three paragraphs. Save your work as the file CAPRIA before printing a copy of your amended document on A4 paper.

1 Key in a copy of the following text. When you are sure your work is correct, print a copy out on plain A4 paper. Save your work using the file name AMALFI.

> A drive along one of Italy's most beautiful coastal roads brings you to this fascinating historic Italian town. Amalfi nestles in a deep, narrow ravine and is protected from the worst of the Italian winter weather. Churches, towers and arched houses are clustered together in attractive irregular squares and rise in steps above a small harbour which is still used by traditional sardine fishing boats.
>
> The town of Amalfi is surrounded on three sides by a dramatic backdrop of wild precipices and thick woodland which is dominated by ancient watch towers. The town's famed harbour now plays host to luxury yachts which can be seen moored amongst the traditional fishing craft.
>
> The greatest treasure of the town is the 9th century Cathedral dedicated to Saint Andrew which overshadows the central square. The jumble of streets are lined with inviting shops and restaurants selling lace and leather goods which are traditionally made in this region of Italy. The more adventurous can hire a boat from the harbour to explore the caves along the coastline and reach otherwise inaccessible beaches.
>
> A ten minute sail down the coast will bring you to the Emerald grotto, an unusual little cave bathed in a mysterious green light.

2 Using the cut and paste and copy and paste facilities, carry out the amendments to your document shown following.

> A drive along one of Italy's most beautiful coastal roads brings you to this fascinating historic Italian town. Amalfi nestles in a deep, narrow ravine and is protected from the worst of the Italian winter weather. Churches, towers and arched houses are clustered together in attractive irregular squares and rise in steps above a small harbour which is still used by traditional sardine fishing boats.
>
> The town of Amalfi is surrounded on three sides by a dramatic backdrop of wild precipices and thick woodland which is dominated by ancient watch towers. The town's famed harbour now plays host to luxury yachts which can be seen moored amongst the traditional fishing craft.
>
> The greatest treasure of the town is the 9th century Cathedral dedicated to Saint Andrew which overshadows the central square. The jumble of streets are lined with inviting shops and restaurants selling lace and leather goods which are traditionally made in this region of Italy. The more adventurous can hire a boat from the harbour to explore the caves along the coastline and reach otherwise inaccessible beaches.
>
> A ten minute sail down the coast will bring you to the Emerald grotto, an unusual little cave bathed in a mysterious green light.

3 Now key in the following as the last sentence in the final paragraph.

The Amalfi coastline in Italy provides us with one of the most exciting holiday destinations in Europe.

Next copy the sentence and paste it in as the last sentence in each of the other paragraphs.

Save your work using the file name ITALYA and print a copy on plain A4 paper.

Extension material

1 Key in each paragraph in the following text as a separate file. When they have been checked for errors save each one using the filenames ITALY1, ITALY2, ITALY3 and ITALY4 respectively.

Special theme nights with guest disc jockeys are advertised on posters and flyers distributed at daytime bars and cafes.

Expect to pay about 15,000 Lire (approximately £5.00) as an entrance fee to each of the clubs. However, this usually includes a free drink except on a Friday or Saturday night when the clubs are much busier.

ITALIAN NIGHTLIFE

Taxis are very expensive in this part of Italy and you are likely to be charged about 80,000 lire (approximately £26.00) for a journey of five miles. The bus services are excellent and very reasonably priced. It is worth remembering that the drivers do not collect any money and you have to buy your ticket in advance from one of the many shops which sell them.

2 Now create another new file and key in the following paragraphs:

The Italians love to spend hours chatting and sipping a drink at one of the many cafes which surround the local piazza or squares. In the warm summer evenings they will often stay up until the early hours of the morning. Clubbing is very much a summer pastime in Italy as many bars and cafes are open air.

Normally bars will close one day a week, with the day varying from bar to bar. More night clubs stay open at weekends during the summer months which stretch from early May until the end of October. In winter they open for fewer days and close earlier.

Most bars offer waiter service, but with the relaxed style and pace of life in this part of the world, be prepared to wait! Even so, it is great fun to just sit and watch others enjoy themselves as you sit and take in the holiday atmosphere which pervades this whole area.

3 Save this file using the filename NIGHTS. Now amend it as shown below and then print a hard copy on A4 paper.

(Merge ITALY3 here as a heading)

The Italians love to spend hours chatting and sipping a drink at one of the many cafes which surround the local piazza or squares. In the warm summer evenings they will often stay up until the early hours of the morning. Clubbing is very much a summer pastime in Italy as many bars and cafes are open air.

(Merge ITALY2 here)

Normally bars will close one day a week, with the day varying from bar to bar. More night clubs stay open at weekends during the summer months which stretch from early May until the end of October. In winter they open for fewer days and close earlier.

(Merge ITALY1 here)

Most bars offer waiter service, but with the relaxed style and pace of life in this part of the world, be prepared to wait! Even so, it is great fun to just sit and watch others enjoy themselves as you sit and take in the holiday atmosphere which pervades this whole area.

(Merge ITALY4 here)

Common correction symbols

When writing a report or a business letter, it is quite common for a draft copy to be produced by the author and then revised and amended to make it more clear and succinct. If the original version has been word processed then the author can return the hard copy to the keyboard operator for amendment and reprinting. However, it is important that any amendments to be made are clearly indicated in the text in an unambiguous way in order to avoid any misunderstanding.

To help with this there is a set of standardised amendment or correction symbols. The use of these symbols makes it quite clear to both the author and the keyboard operator precisely what corrections have to be made. The most common of these symbols, together with their meanings, are given on the next page with examples. Some symbols appear in the text where the amendment should occur, others are included in the left or right margins of the passage.

Correction symbol	Meaning		
⅄	Insert the character or word(s) or punctuation into the text where indicated by the carat sign		
	e.g. ⅄red The girl wore a⅄shirt	becomes	The girl wore a red shirt
⊢⊣	Insert a hyphen between the characters or words where indicated		
	e.g. ⅄⊢⊣ He was the twenty⅄first Member	becomes	He was the twenty-first member
⊢Ⓝ⊣	Insert a dash between the words where indicated		
	e.g. ⅄⊢Ⓝ⊣ Paper 2⅄Foundation level	becomes	Paper 2 – Foundation level
♂	Delete the character or word(s) indicated in the text		
	e.g. ♂ The bikes were ~~all~~ blue	becomes	The bikes were blue
⁀‿	Close up the space between the characters or words where shown		
	e.g. The cup board was empty	becomes	The cupboard was empty
⅄#	Insert the space between the characters or words where indicated		
	e.g. ⅄# He worked full⅄time	becomes	He worked full time
trs	Transpose or change the order of the words as indicated by the lines		
	e.g. ***trs*** It was red and blue	becomes	It was blue and red
lc	Change the indicated character(s) to lower case letter(s)		
	e.g. ***lc*** the North of England	becomes	the north of England
uc	Change the indicated character(s) to upper case or capital letter(s)		
	e.g. ***uc*** Her name was jane	becomes	Her name was Jane
stet	Let the original version stand. Do not omit the word(s) struck out and dotted underneath		
	e.g. The wire was ~~blue~~ (brown)	becomes	The wire was blue
caps	Render the word or phrase indicated in capital letters		
	e.g. ***caps*** The Main Heading	becomes	THE MAIN HEADING
sp caps	Render the word or phrase indicated in spaced capitals i.e. with a space between each letter and three or four spaces between each word		
	e.g. ***sp caps*** The Heading	becomes	THE HEADING
NP //	Insert a new paragraph where indicated in the text		
run on	Remove the paragraph already indicated in the text		

Examples of text correction

The following two passages give an example of each of the above correction signs, firstly as they would appear in the text and secondly showing the text as it should appear once the amendment indicated by the symbol has been carried out.

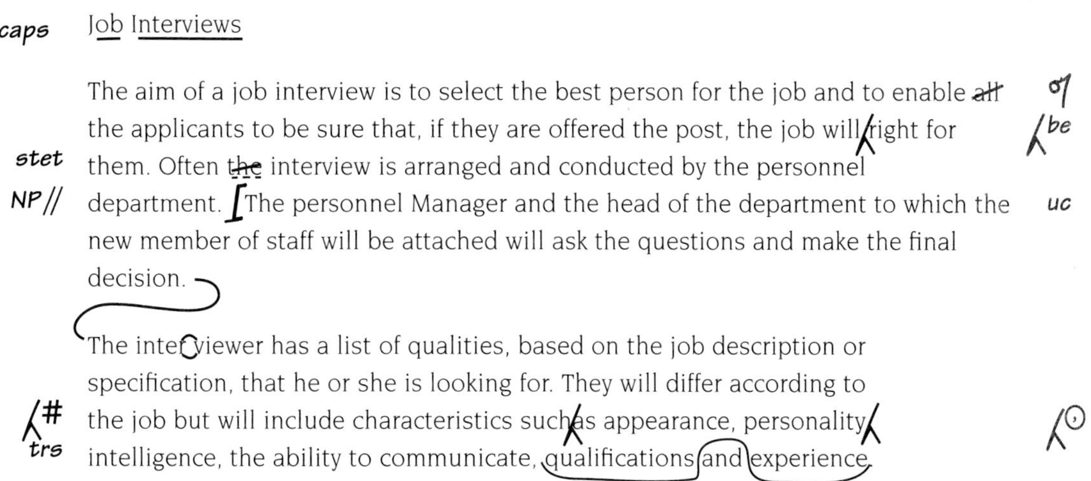

Check carefully how each correction sign has been used to amend the text. The corrected passage should look like this:

> JOB INTERVIEWS
>
> The aim of a job interview is to select the best person for the job and to enable the applicants to be sure that, if they are offered the post, the job will be right for them. Often the interview is arranged and conducted by the personnel department.
>
> The Personnel Manager and the head of the department to which the new member of staff will be attached will ask the questions and make the final decision. The interviewer has a list of qualities, based on the job description or specification, that he or she is looking for. They will differ according to the job but will include characteristics such as appearance, personality, intelligence, the ability to communicate, experience and qualifications.

Exercises

1 Why is a standardised set of correction symbols used in text processing when amending text in business? (3)

2 What do the following correction symbols mean *lc*, *uc*, ⌐ and #? (4)

3 Explain how the following correction symbols could be used in a passage of amended text: *trs*, *stet* and *sp caps*. (3)

Word process an amended copy of the following passage on plain A4 paper.

lc	Every evening they settled down to watch Television together. During the winter
⋀#	it was an enjoyable affair. They closed the door to the fron⋀room and turned the
⌐	fire up to create a warm, ~~and~~ cosy environment.
uc	When easter came everything changed all at once. The lighter evening s meant
trs	that could they spend time in the garden and prepare the flower borders and
	vegetable plot ready for the coming season's plants.
⋀continue	Secretly, however, they would both have preferred to⋀to sit in front of the
⋀t	television but neither voiced their though⋀s to the other and so they continued to
	go out into the garden when they would have preferred to remain indoors.

Key in an amended copy of the following text on plain A4 paper using single line spacing. Save your work using the file name SCHOOL.

caps	Advertising Feature
lc	Do you remember School as 'the happiest days of your life'? Or were you, like many other people these days, in that category of those who did not make the
stet	most best of their opportunities at school? //How often have you thought about what you could have achieved if only you had worked that little bit harder? NP
Run on	Have you ever thought of improving your qualifications?
⁊/e	Ar you one of the many who left work to look after your family and would now like to go back to work but feel you need a refresher course before you start?
trs	We recently have opened ~~our~~ new premises above Marks & Spencer in the High ⁊
/in	Street. Fully equipped with the latest word processors and office equipment, supplied by Optical Computers Ltd, we are able to offer a wide range of
caps	secretarial and business courses aimed at meeting your training needs.
caps	As an introduction to our services, we are offering a free 30 minute introductory lesson starting at 10.00 a.m. and 7.30 p.m. in all of the following classes:
⁊/s	Word procesing for beginners Word processing intermediate/advanced
lc	Spreadsheets for beginners Desk Top Publishing made simple
	Why not come along on Tuesday, Wednesday or Thursday next week and join one or more of our free sessions?
run on	
lc	See what The First Class Secretarial School can do to improve your career prospects – there's no obligation!

Adapted from a SEG Examination Question, 1991

Extension material

Key in an amended copy of the following passage. Spell check and proofread your work. Save a copy of the file to disk and print a hard copy on plain A4 paper.

SHOPPING

THE GALLERIES ⋀ MALL

The latest concept in shopping has arrived in Gloucester. The
uc galleries, now open in the city centre, is the ~~fifth~~ ⋀ in a — ꝺ/⋀ sixth
series of new shopping malls to be established in the Country — lc
towns and cities during the last three years by Meltorn
trs Property Group Ltd.

⋀ a Within the Galleries Shopping Mall there is ⋀ wide range of
retail shop units of varying sizes on four floors ◠ Floors are — close up
stet ~~connected~~ (linked) by three escalators as well as a wide open
NP staircase. [Many of the units open directly onto the
wide and well-lit pedestrian walk ◠ ways ⋀ allowing — close up ⋀ ,
shoppers quick and easy access to many of the shops.
The central feature of the Mall is a water sculpture and
rising ⋀ aqua garden ~~which rises~~ through all four floors and ~~is~~ ꝺ
lit by more than 5000 coloured light bulbs.

Most of the retail units in the Mall have now been leased
and further details of those which remain can be obtained
stet from the ~~developers~~ (builders) – Meltorn Group Property Ltd. The
building took more than two and a half years to
complete, including the underground car park for more
than 200 cars.

Recent research, however, has shown that the opening of
this new regional shopping centre at Cribbs Causeway
on the outskirts of Bristol has significantly affected trade
Run on in the Galleries.

Many of Gloucester's shoppers are travelling the ~~25~~ miles — ꝺ/⋀ 30
ꝺ to Bristol to ~~to~~ try out this 'totally new shopping
experience' in the few weeks remaining before
Christmas.

Adapted from a SEG Examination Question, 1993

Bullet points and special characters

Word processing and desktop publishing systems have the added advantage of being able to provide a whole range of different ways of emphasising and highlighting items within text. Possibly the most common of these is the use of bullet points.

These are the solid dots – rather like over-sized full stops – which appear on the line beside each new point being made. They enable lists and features in a document to be customised, thus improving the presentation of the document and assisting the

All walkers are required to be properly equipped at the start of the walk. Please ensure you have the following with you:

a change of socks
a waterproof jacket
a pair of waterproof trousers
stout walking boots
a map of the area
a whistle
a complete first aid kit

We will stop at the old railway bridge for lunch and return by 4.00 p.m. at the latest.

Without bullet points

All walkers are required to be properly equipped at the start of the walk. Please ensure you have the following with you:

- A change of socks.
- A waterproof jacket.
- A pair of waterproof trousers.
- Stout walking boots.
- A map of the area.
- A whistle.
- A complete first aid kit.

We will stop at the old railway bridge for lunch and return by 4.00 p.m. at the latest.

With bullet points

Before there is a list of bullet points in the text of a report it is likely that there will be a series of paragraphs which all begin at the left margin. The bullet points then stand out more clearly as they appear inset into the document.

- This is an example of a paragraph which has been given emphasis by the use of a bullet point rather than an alternative form of heading. The points make the start of the paragraphs stand out in the body of the text.
- This second paragraph also makes use of a bullet point to give it emphasis and allows the reader to see easily where each new point is being made by the author.

A concluding paragraph can also be used which returns the text to the left margin which gives a more rounded appearance to the whole report.

Paragraphs and Bullet points

reader by drawing their eye to a list of items in the document. How effective this is can be seen in the two examples given here:

The list in Figure 27 uses bullet points for emphasis, which makes the list stand out more clearly. This form of emphasis can also be used to draw attention to paragraphs, and can be used instead of the more traditional method of paragraph or shoulder headings.

Types of bullet point

Bullet points can be produced in a variety of styles. The 'over large' full stop is the most commonly used, however most computer software will now produce a range. For example:

◆ Filled diamonds

➤ Arrows, pointing towards the item

◇ Clear diamonds

* Asterisks

The size of the bullets can also be adjusted to give a variety in the emphasis if required:

➤ this arrow represents an increase in point size to 20 from the one in the paragraph above which is in point size 12.

Special characters

In addition to bullet points, a range of special characters are also available to the keyboard operator to help him or her enhance the quality of the work produced. These can easily be input using the 'Insert Symbols' menu and include the following:

- The copyright symbol – © 2001.
- The degree symbol – 360°
- The acute and grave accents – é, è

A further method of emphasis which seems to be used less frequently these days are leader dots. These are used to draw the eye along a line between two linked pieces of information. They are frequently used on such items as a cast list for a play or the contents of a book, where the chapter title is linked with the page on which it starts. An example of leader dots is given below. Please note that in order to set these out well a space has been inserted following the first item and another before the item to which it is linked. These spaces have been omitted on the last item below to show how it detracts from the appearance of this as a form of display, as the words seem to be directly connected.

John Smith .... Jeremy Irons

Janet Smith .... Margaret Roberts

Anthony Chislett .... Shuheb Khan

Ian Paisley .... Maurice Cotton

Shane Paisley................................ Alexander Briggs

Leader dots can be inserted in patterns if required. An example is given below, however, care should be taken to ensure that the space which precedes the dots is equal to the space which follows them and that the patterns are aligned vertically on the page. This will ensure a balanced look to the presentation.

Chapter 3 ... ... page 45

Chapter 4 ... ... page 56

Chapter 5 ... ... page 66

Exercises

1 Explain how bullet points can help emphasise items in a word processed document. (3)

2 List the different symbols which can be used as bullet points on your word processing system. (3)

3 List as many special characters as you can which could be used to help emphasise text in any form. (3)

4 Explain what leader dots are. (2)

5 How can leader dots be used to emphasise work? Give two examples of when they could be used. (4)

Recall the file CAPRIA that you saved in Task One of unit 42. Insert bullet points at the start of all paragraphs except the first one. Print a copy on plain A4 paper.

Recall the file SCHOOL that you prepared in Task Two of unit 45. Change the list of courses to a single column with single line spacing and insert bullet points using a diamond pattern. Increase the size of the points to 15 point. Print a copy of your work on A4 paper.

Extension material

Word process a list of at least three advantages and three disadvantages of using bullet points in a report rather than numbered paragraphs. Emphasise each item in your work with appropriate bullet points. Print a copy on A4 paper and keep this for revision purposes in your folder of work.

Graphics

Most word processing and desktop publishing systems have the facility to draw in a limited manner using lines, rectangles, ellipses and some freehand shapes. These can all be re-sized and adjusted in proportion and so be used to create simple graphic images when combined.

Simple two-dimensional outline drawings can be very effective when drawn properly. With a little practice you will soon be able to use the drawing facilities of your computer system to create useful diagrams to enhance your text. Each of the drawing facilities has certain properties which are designed to assist you when drawing with them.

Lines

This will create straight lines at any angle from the origin. If you wish to draw a vertical or horizontal line, or one at 45°, hold the shift key down as you pull out the line. This will give the desired effect without having to keep a steady hand or judge a difficult angle. Some systems, such as Microsoft Word, will also allow you to draw lines at 30° and 60° angles. When putting together shapes, such as triangles and rectangles using the line facility it should be noted that, although these completed shapes will look solid on the screen, they will not be

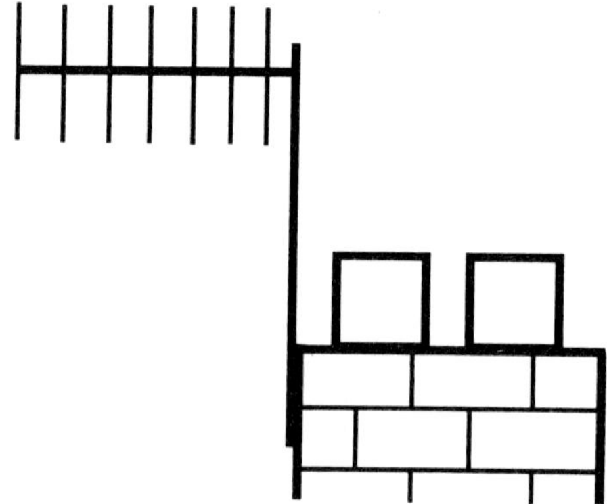

Figure 32 Example of a line graphic

able to be filled or shaded in any way as the computer system still recognises them as individual lines, and not a completed shape.

Rectangles

This function enables you to draw perfect rectangles to any shape or size. They can be used in graphic images or to enclose items of text within a document. It should be remembered however, that if the text is subsequently amended and moves position within a document, the box may also need to be moved. If a perfect square is required, hold the shift key down as you draw out the box. This will cause the height and width of the box to change equally at the same time. The row of terrace houses in Figure 33 has been drawn using only rectangles.

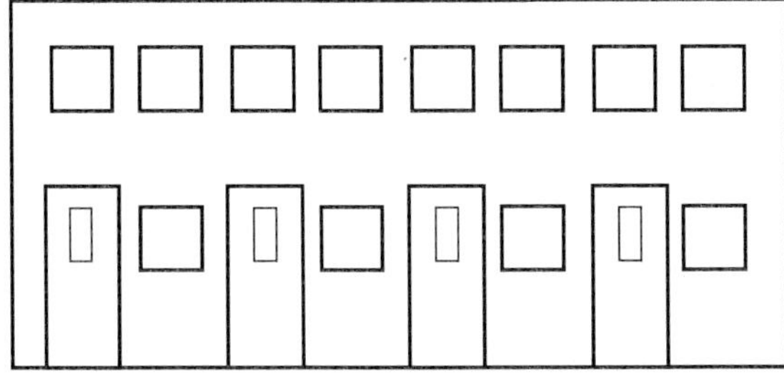

Figure 33 Example of a rectangular graphic

Ellipses

In the same way that rectangles can be drawn to any given size, so can ellipses. They can also be drawn as perfect circles by holding down the shift key when drawing out the ellipse, in the same way the square is created from the rectangle facility. The following diagram showing the orbit of the moon around the Earth, has been drawn using only ellipses.

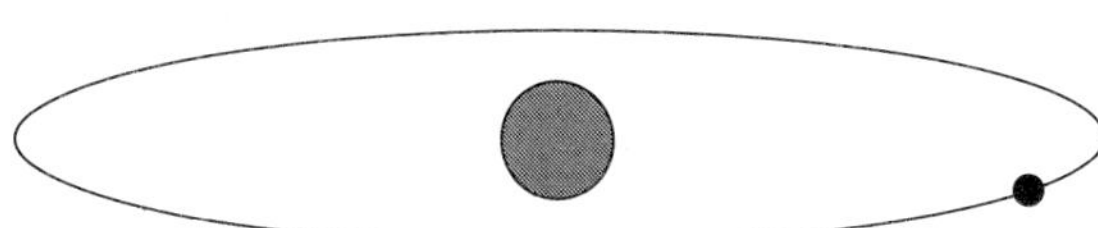

Figure 34 Orbit of the Earth using only ellipses

The circles representing the Earth and the Moon have been filled to give them more emphasis. This is done by selecting the shape to be filled and then selecting an appropriate shading or colour with which it can be filled. The use of filled and unfilled ellipses can also give diagrams a 3-Dimensional effect as in Figure 34.

Other shapes

Some systems allow you to create a free form shape or polyline which can be created to any shape or size you wish, like this fish (see Figure 35)!

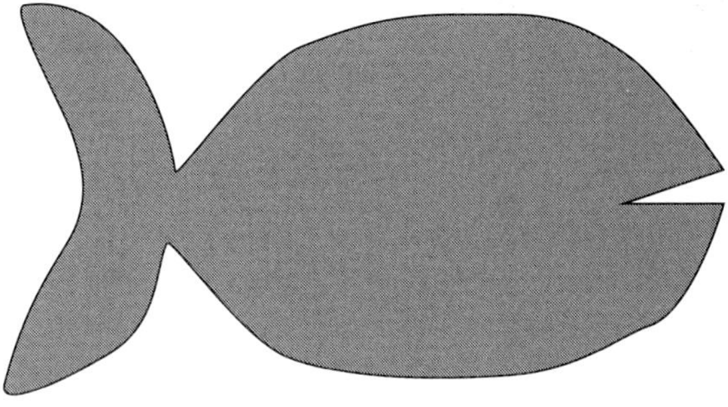

Figure 35 Example of a free form or polyline graphic

Other systems provide pre-formed shapes in which the proportions can be altered, but the shape itself remains fixed (Figure 36).

Figure 36 Pre-formed shapes

The top left hand shape is one of the pre-formed shapes available with Microsoft Publisher. Underneath it has been stretched and on the top right, squeezed, to alter its proportions.

Moving facilities on screen

Once in the document, shapes can be moved into other positions on the page. Just click on the shape with the mouse to make it active (i.e. it shows the eight small black 'handles' which surround it) and it can either be moved using the mouse, or by pressing the relevant cursor key to move it in the required direction. Minor adjustments can be made to the position by holding down either the CNTRL or the ALT key (depending on the program being used) and using the cursor keys at the same time. In this way you can 'fine tune' your diagrams by 'nudging' your shapes into position.

Labelling diagrams

Labelling facilities enable you to itemise features on your diagram to make its purpose more clear. Some systems, such as Microsoft Word, have a 'call out' facility which will create a text box which is linked to a line which can indicate to what the description is related on the diagram. This facility is shown on the diagram of the Moon's orbit below (Figure 37):

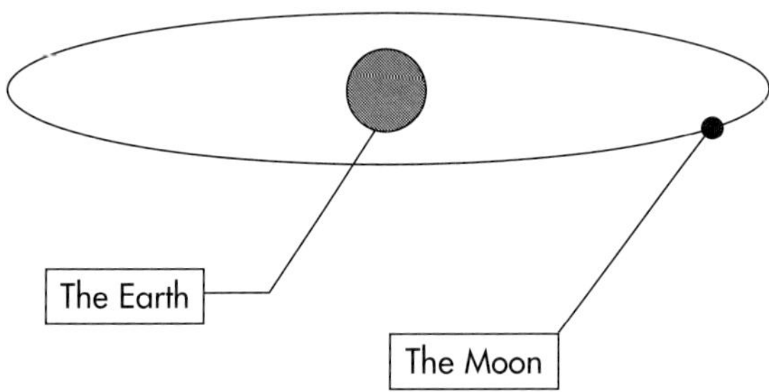

Figure 37 Diagram of the moon's orbit

An alternative form of labelling diagrams is to use a key which describes each shape used. Figure 38 shows a straightforward plan of a manager's office that has been labelled with the use of a key which indicates what each shape represents.

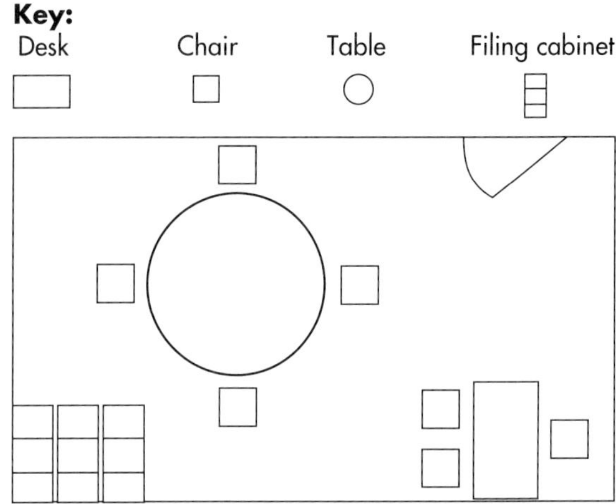

Figure 38 Office plan

Filling drawn shapes

As already demonstrated, the area inside a shape, provided it is fully enclosed, can be filled with either a shading or a colour. This enables you to give a different form of emphasis on your diagrams.

Exercises

1 What is the difference between a two-dimensional and a three-dimensional drawing? (2)

2 Write a paragraph explaining to a new word processing operator how to draw straight lines, perfect circles and perfect squares using either your word processing or your desk top publishing package. (3)

3 Explain how you can fill an ellipse with colour. (2)

4 Why can you not fill a triangle drawn from three straight lines? (2)

5 What is meant by the term polyline graphic? (1)

6 Explain when you would make use of call out text boxes. (2)

Using the drawing facilities on your word processing or desktop publishing system, recreate the diagrams shown in the text for lines, rectangles and ellipses. Try to give emphasis through the use of shading and colour (if you have colour printers available) and make use of call out boxes to label your diagrams.

The diagram of the office shown in Figure 42 makes use of a variety of shapes. Recreate this diagram and shade in the different items of furniture. Either use a key similar to the one shown or make use of call out boxes to label your diagram.

Extension material

You have been asked to draw a plan of the classroom in which you are currently working. Use the drawing facilities of your computer system to complete this task. Make sure you include a key or labels to clarify your plan. Try to make the plan as complete as you can and indicate all doors and windows as well as power points, not just the furniture.

Clipart

Clipart is the term given to previously prepared graphic images, generally available on most modern computer systems, that enhance your work. Most of these images are copyright free, which means you can use them without having to pay a fee to the computer programmer who designed them. You can also purchase disks and CD Roms of images, some with a specific theme, such as sport or music.

Using clipart

It is possible to obtain clipart images by downloading them from the Internet or from disks or CD Roms which are occasionally given away free with computer magazines and journals. This is called 'shareware'. You will almost certainly have seen some of these images and some examples are given in Figure 39 below:

Figure 39 Clipart images

Many of the images are of animals or figures, others are of shapes or patterns that can be used to decorate text and other documents (see Figure 40).

Figure 40 More clipart graphics

Once inserted into a document or page, these clipart images can be adjusted in size simply by clicking on them with the mouse to show the eight 'handles'. These are small black or grey squares. By moving the mouse over one of the squares, the mouse pointer will change shape, enabling you to click and, by holding the left mouse button, change the size of the image to suit the requirements of your document.

Images can also be copied using the copy and paste facility (see Unit 44). Click on the image to show the handles and then copy it into the memory of your computer. Once copied, the image can then be pasted into your document as many times as you wish. The line in Figure 41 has been made up by copying the leaf pattern shown in Figure 40 and inserting the leaves in sequence. It contains the same clipart image, centred on the page, and repeated seven times.

Figure 41 Copy and paste clipart

Advantages

Clipart has a number of advantages:

- It is readily available and so is quick and easy to use.
- Most clipart software is copyright free, therefore there is no cost involved in using it.
- There is a wide range of images from which to choose.
- The size of the image can be easily adjusted to suit your individual needs.

Disadvantages

The disadvantages of using clipart include:

- The use of a clipart image cannot be legally controlled and so if a business adopts a particular piece of clipart for its logo, it would be unable to prevent another company from using that same image.
- As clipart is available to all, it also reduces the impact which a particular image may have.

Despite this, clipart is used extensively by many people and organisations and is very successful. You will undoubtedly see many familiar images on the documents, leaflets and posters which you will come across.

Exercises

1 Explain what is meant by the term *clipart*. List as many sources of free clipart that you can. (3)

2 What are the advantages to (a) an individual and (b) a business of using clipart rather than a personally designed graphic? (4)

3 Why is it unlikely that a business would make use of clipart in its logo? (1)

4 Write a short paragraph to explain how a piece of clipart could be copied and then pasted several times into a document. (2)

Key in the following passage using your word processing system:

> Rashid was uncertain as to what to buy with the money he had been given for his birthday. He certainly wanted to purchase a new CD but would it be better to put the money towards a portable CD player?
>
> His brother had offered to split the cost of a new game for his computer with him but it was a game in which Rashid had little interest. His mother had suggested he might like to buy himself a new pair of jeans and his father would be happy if Rashid put the money into his savings account at the building society.
>
> Rashid was very confused. He had not been helped by the suggestions made to him as none of them had any real appeal. After much thought, Rashid had a brilliant idea. He knew exactly what he would do with his money.

1 Spell check and proofread your work, then save it using the file name MONEY.

2 Select an appropriate clipart image and insert it at the top left of the passage above the first line of type.

3 Select a second appropriate clipart image which can be used as a border or decoration. Click on the image to show the 'handles' and then reduce the image in size. Then, using the copy and paste facility, create a line of pattern at the foot of the passage by repeating the image several times across the page.

Making your own headed notepaper

1 Open a new file on your word processing package and reduce the top margin on your page to 1 cm. Click on the centring icon so that every line will be centred on the page.

2 Select an appropriate clipart file which reflects the image you wish to portray about yourself. Are you an animal lover? A sports person? Do you have musical talent or other artistic trends? Reduce this image so that it is no more than 2 cm tall.

3 Leave a line of space under the picture and then key in your full name in capitals. On the next line key in your full address, including the town and your postcode. Put your telephone number on the next line.

Your finished paper should look similar to this (see the next page). If you wish you can use the mouse or cursor to highlight all or any part of your name and address and put it into bold type, italics or a different font style or point size. Try putting your name in point size 16, the address in point size 10 and the telephone number in point size 9.

ANTHONY BLAIR

14, Crossway Street, London SE22 7JE

Telephone: 0171 650 7421

Extension material

1 Try to create a different style of headed paper, which reflects another of your interests.

2 Why not use a different font style for your name? Or leave the clipart image centred and right justify your name, address and telephone number. There are lots of variations you can try.

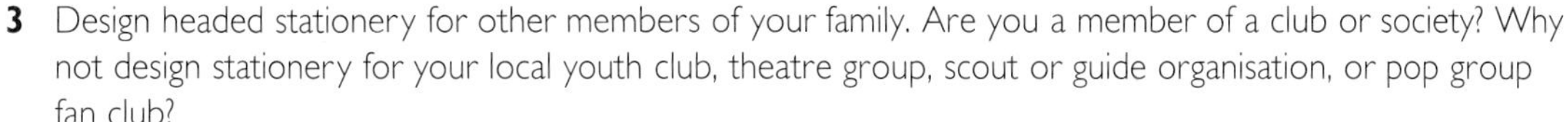

3 Design headed stationery for other members of your family. Are you a member of a club or society? Why not design stationery for your local youth club, theatre group, scout or guide organisation, or pop group fan club?

4 Why not try using the same clipart image more than once, but also vary its size? For example:

Lines and geometric shapes

Most word processing systems display on-screen toolbars that enable you to make use of a wide range of facilities available through the system. If these are not shown on screen they can usually be accessed by clicking on the appropriate icon or button. Alternatively, you may need to go into one of the menus and select the drawings toolbar for display. Desktop publishing systems offer similar facilities. A typical drawing toolbar is shown in Figure 42. It usually includes options to draw shapes, text boxes, arrows, colour filling effects, shadowing, line thicknesses and more.

Once the drawings toolbar is available you can start to use the facilities to draw objects. Most word processors or DTP systems have three main drawing facilities: lines, rectangles and ellipses.

Figure 42 A drawings toolbar

Lines

Select the line drawing button, move the cursor onto your page and click the left mouse button down and drag out a single line. When you release the mouse button the line remains on the page. You will notice that is has two handles: one on each end of the line. By moving the mouse over one of these handles, you can adjust the line length and direc-

tion. It is also possible to move the line to a different position on the screen (or page) by dragging it with the mouse.

It requires a considerable skill to draw a perfectly straight line. Hold the shift key down as you draw out your line. This will enable you to produce a perfect line, horizontally, vertically or at a 45° angle.

Rectangles

These can be drawn in a similar way to the line except that they will have eight handles in the same way that clipart does, and they can be adjusted in the same way. The corner handles will adjust the overall size of the rectangle: those in the top or bottom centre will increase or decrease the height and those on the centre left and right will alter the width. Move your cursor over the handles and see how they can adjust your rectangle. Use the shift key together with the mouse to adjust the sides of the rectangle proportionately.

Ellipses

An ellipse can be drawn and adjusted in the same way as the rectangle. The shift key will also proportionately increase or decrease the size of the ellipse. With a little practice using this and the other shapes, a wide variety of drawings can be created.

Grouping

Once several shapes or lines have been used to create an image or pattern, they can usually be grouped together so that the system will then treat them as one object. This makes copying and pasting objects much simpler and also helps you to move or adjust the size of the object more easily.

Exercises

1 Explain how to use a software application on your computer system to draw a straight line and a perfect square. (2)

2 What is meant by the term *grouping*? Write a short set of instructions to explain how grouping can be used to make a copy of a composite image. (3)

3 Make a list of all the icons on the drawing toolbar of your word processing system together with a short explanation of what each does. (3)

4 Compare the drawing icons on your word processor with those available on your desktop publisher. Carefully explain the use of any additional icons available on your DTP system. (2)

Using the line, rectangle and ellipses copy this simple drawing of an articulated lorry.

Try drawing a picture of the house or flat where you live (see below).

Additional facilities may be available on more advanced systems, such as free form drawing, curves or arcs and pre-formed shapes. Group the items which make up your house together. Then copy and paste them to make up a row of houses.

Extension material

Once you feel confident in drawing using the lines and geometric shapes, try some of these challenges: draw a car, or an animal, or a musical instrument, or a plan of your ideal bedroom, or a stage set for your favourite group, the possibilities are endless!

Précis

The ability to reduce the length of a piece of text without losing the meaning of the passage is a valuable skill which is worth developing.

The word 'précis' refers to the process of cutting down or reducing the number of words in a sentence, paragraph or passage without losing the sense of the text. It is a process that is often used when a piece of text is too long to fit into a certain page area, for example, when preparing a newspaper or when desktop publishing. Look at the sentence below:

The *old ginger tom* cat sat on *the edge of* the mat.

This sentence contains twelve words, however, if it needs to fit into a text area approximately half this size, you could remove the words in italics without significantly affecting the sense of the sentence. The result would be:

The cat sat on the mat.

This is now a less interesting sentence, but still informs you of the main points you wish to make. The words which embellish, illustrate or describe elements within the sentence have been removed. The original sentence gives a detailed description of

SOME PRECIS METHODS ARE EASIER THAN OTHERS!

the cat – he is old, ginger in colour and is a tom. This has been cut from the revised sentence, but you soon know that the sentence is about a cat. Similarly, this applies to where the cat is sitting: it is sitting on the mat. Only the detail of the cat's whereabouts on the mat has been removed!

Examine the following sentence:

The quick brown fox jumps over the lazy dog.

This can be précised to:

The fox jumps over the dog.

Again, the essential information is still included in the sentence, but the descriptive elements have been cut.

Sometimes an alternative word or words can be used to help reduce the length of a sentence. Look at the following sentence:

I look forward to hearing from you within the next few days.

The phrase 'within the next few days' could be replaced with the word 'soon'. Alternatively, you could use the phrase 'next week' to replace the phrase 'within the next few days'. Both of these alternatives would reduce the length of the sentence by one third.

A third method of reducing the number of words in a passage is to change the order in which they appear in the sentence, as well as removing those words which are less essential. For example:

By turning the adjustable spanner slowly, the engineer was able to tighten up the nut.

This could become:

The engineer tightened the nut by turning the spanner slowly.

Once you are sure you have completed your précis, it is very important to read through your revised passage and check that it still gives the same message as the original. It is very easy to omit a vital word or phrase or to change the sense of the passage as you work without realising the effect this may have on the meaning.

Exercises

1 Explain what is meant by the term *précis*. (1)

2 Why is the ability to précis a passage of text a useful skill for a word processing operator to have? (3)

3 What are the three main methods of reducing the number of words in a passage of text? Give an example of each. (3)

4 Explain why it is essential to read through a précised passage when it has been completed and compare it with the original document. (3)

Key in each of the following sentences. Précis each sentence and try to reduce each of them by at least five words. Word process your amended sentence underneath the original.

1 The sun was shining brilliantly when the small girl started to ride her brand new bicycle slowly down the road towards the local playground.

2 Soon all the leaves on the trees in the woods had turned a lovely range of various shades of brown, but it only lasted for a few short days.

3 One by one the adult zebra moved through the clearing towards the water hole but the slightest sound could disturb them and cause them to stampede.

4 They were all very excited by the opportunity which the new swimming pool created for the whole population of the town and surrounding villages.

5 Although Jenny was the last to hear of the exciting new offer available at the shop, she managed to be one of the first through the doors when they opened at 9.00 a.m.

Now try these slightly longer paragraphs. Try to reduce each by at least ten words. Key in the original version first, followed by your précis underneath.

1 The ship sailed slowly and majestically up the meandering river towards the town quay to begin unloading its cargo. There was great excitement amongst the local population as the crates containing exotic oriental spices and herbs were lifted out of the vessel's hold and onto the jetty.

2 One by one the climbers began to notice the increasing need to make use of their oxygen as they moved higher and higher up the craggy cliff face. Several of the less experienced climbers decided not to continue the climb. The remainder, after a short break to regain some of their expended energy, continued the assault on the south face. The thinness of the air became much more noticeable once they were over 5,000 metres.

3 All the children from both the junior and the senior schools had attended the youth centre at some time or another in their lives. Consequently, the youth leader who had worked at the club for more than twenty years knew almost everyone who had attended the recent meeting that had ended in disorder. It took the leader only a few short minutes to make a list of all those who had joined in the demonstration. He was less certain, however, which of the young people had been involved in smashing the windows of the youth centre.

Extension material

Each of the following passages has to be reduced to a maximum of 100 words. Prepare a word processed answer for each of these passages. Remember to read through your work to ensure the shortened passages still make the same sense as the originals. Do not forget to spell check and proofread your work before printing a copy out. The number of words in each passage is given at the end to help you.

1 The one disturbing thing that seemed to affect them all was the way in which several small children from the camp were constantly watching them. Whichever way they looked, there were always at least three of the children with their faces turned towards them with that blank staring look on their faces. At first they spoke to the children and offered them items of food to encourage them to talk. But always they were met with an uncompromising silence, and that blank look. After a few days most of the workers on the site just ignored the children and often forgot they were even there. That was their big mistake. Once the workers stopped watching the children, tools and other items of equipment began to disappear.

(126 words)

2 Before the 1920s there was no free dental treatment and very few working-class people visited a dentist until driven to do so. Thus, bad teeth led to undesirable eating habits as people ate what they could that would cause as little pain as possible. Inevitably, this in turn, led to bad health. One dentist near the old bridge encouraged people to call, on Saturdays only, to have their teeth pulled free of charge. Many of the village people took advantage of this – at least once – even though the treatment was a practice session for student dentists and was carried out without any anaesthetic. By 1929, however, local children could have free dental treatment at the surgery established by the local Sisters of Mercy and held in the back room of the White Horse public house three afternoons a week.

(141 words)

3 It was like walking onto the set of a western. The bar was long, stretching almost the whole length of the saloon bar and had black pull-pump handles which projected from the smooth dark surface of the bar counter. The walls were covered in planking which had originally matched the uncarpeted floor. Over the years rough soled boots had removed any sheen the floor may have had. There was a coal burning stove in the middle of the far wall with a pipe which ascended to the ceiling and then ran back to the door, the length of the room to disappear through an outer wall. This was the only form of heating which I could see in the bar. The whole western image was, however, ruined by the illuminated fruit machine which flashed on and off casting an eerie light around the rather dimly lit room. Even the customers seemed to dress in a rugged fashion, rather like ranch-hands.

(159 words)

PART 6

Finance and Business Structure

Insurance in business

Financial documents

Management structures

Representing groups at work

The impact of change

Insurance in business

If you are thinking of buying a motorbike or a car to get around in, you will also have to take out an insurance policy. The purpose of this policy is to give you protection in two ways:

- Firstly, to cover the cost of repairing or replacing your motorbike or car should you have an accident.
- Secondly, to cover the cost of injury or damage which may occur should anyone else (known as a third party) be involved in an accident.

Not everyone will have an accident and need to make a claim on their insurance. The principle of insurance works on the basis that each individual pays an amount of money or premium into a central fund. This money is pooled to provide a fund from which payments can be made to those who need it (see Figure 43). For example, if the average cost of repairing a car is £500 and one out of every ten cars is involved in an accident each year, the average premium could be calculated as £50. When one of the ten insured cars is damaged then the £500 can be used to repair it.

Problems can arise if more than one car is damaged in any one year, or if the cost of repairing a car is greater than £500. Therefore, calculating exactly

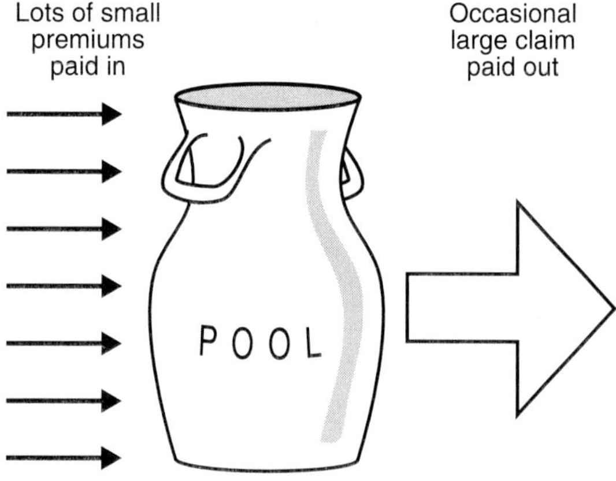

Figure 43 Diagram of the insurance premium process

how much should be paid in insurance premiums is a very complex process and is carried out by a specialist, known as an insurance actuary.

However, some people tend to have more accidents than others, and they will usually have to pay a higher premium as they are likely to make more claims on the central fund than other people.

Insurance principles

Insurance is based on the three principles of **utmost good faith**, **insurable interest** and **indemnity**.

Utmost good faith

Utmost good faith means, quite simply, that you must tell the truth when completing a proposal form and declare any other information which is relevant, to obtain insurance. For example, it would be against the principle of utmost good faith not to declare that you have had a previous motoring accident and to try to get cheaper insurance for your car. If you do this and the insurance company subsequently finds out, your insurance will no longer be valid. This principle also applies to the insurance company – they are obliged to inform you of the main clauses in the insurance policy, any exceptions which may apply and if there are any unusual features contained in the policy.

Insurable interest

The principle of insurable interest requires you to have a personal financial interest should a loss occur, which requires you to make a claim on the insurance policy. Therefore, you could insure yourself against personal accident because you would suffer the loss of no longer being able to work, should you became disabled as the result of an accident. You could not, however, insure your friend against personal accident as you would have no financial interest if he or she were unable to continue working.

Indemnity

Indemnity is the principle that prevents anyone making a profit out of an insurance claim. When an insurance company pays out on a claim, it aims to return the insured person(s) to the position they were in before the loss occurred. For example, if a car stereo is stolen it will be replaced with a similar unit – not the latest top of the range system – so the insured does not make a financial gain from the loss. Some insurance companies now operate a 'new for old' policy, where rather than paying financial compensation, they will provide a new item of comparable quality and value to the original item lost. For example, a three year old carpet damaged by fire will be replaced by a new carpet of the same quality as the damaged one.

Insurance is important to individuals because it allows them to protect themselves and their property against possible loss. Firms also take out insurance as it protects them and reduces the risk of losses which inevitably occur in business.

Types of insurance

Following are the most common types of insurance.

Fire

This covers damage or loss of property and its contents (such as furniture, stocks of goods, machinery, etc.) caused by fire, together with any damage caused in putting the fire out, such as water ruining stocks of goods. This type of insurance often includes any loss as a result of flooding and storms. It may also provide consequential loss insurance, which covers the firm for loss of revenue if, as a consequence, they are unable to continue trading because of a fire or other damage.

Theft

As it implies, this form of insurance provides compensation if property is stolen. It may also include a fidelity guarantee which covers loss resulting from the dishonesty of an employee, such as the theft of cash by a wages clerk.

Employers' liability

All employees have a legal right to work in a safe and healthy environment. Should they suffer injury or contract an illness as a result of their work, they can claim compensation from their employer. This insurance, which all companies must have by law, will provide the business with cover for this eventuality.

Public liability

This provides insurance cover for the firm if a member of the public is injured as a result of an employee's negligence, for example a passer-by being struck by a brick or tile that a builder accidentally drops from some scaffolding. As with employers' liability, this form of insurance is compulsory. It can be extended to include damage or injury caused to customers when using a firm's product if required, such as being electrocuted when using a faulty lawn mower. This is known as product liability insurance.

Motor insurance

Vehicles operated by businesses and individuals are required by the Road Traffic Act (1972) to be insured if they are used on public roads and motorways. There are three types of cover:

- Third party insurance – covers any damage or loss to others, but not to the driver or vehicle itself.
- Third party fire and theft – similar to third party insurance but also includes any loss to the insured vehicle as a result of fire or theft.
- Comprehensive – as the name implies, covers all risks not only to others but to the insured vehicle as well. This is the most expensive form of motor insurance but it provides the highest level of cover.

Marine and aircraft insurance

In the same way that cars, vans and lorries are protected against accident or loss; aircraft and ships can also be covered. However, due to the considerable replacement cost of a ship or aeroplane (often more than £150 million), insurance cover is provided at Lloyds of London by groups of business people, called 'syndicates', who specialise in assessing this type of risk. It is quite common, due to the high cost involved, that should a claim be made, the insurance on any one aircraft or ship will be divided between several syndicates.

Insurance allows those who pay the premiums to obtain compensation if the risk they have insured against occurs. The principle is again based on the pooling of risks, where many small premiums are paid into a fund that is then used to pay compensation to the few who need to claim against it. Insurance companies will only provide insurance for insurable risks, i.e. where reliable statistical evidence of the level of risk can be obtained. This allows them to calculate with accuracy the degree of risk involved and so set an appropriate premium. The higher the risk, the higher the premium which will have to be paid to provide insurance cover.

Advantages of insurance

- Insurance reduces business risk by allowing firms to insure against the possibility of accidents and unforeseen events, and receive compensation when they do occur.
- Whilst employees cannot be protected against

every accident in the workplace, they can receive financial compensation when or if they do occur.

- When members of the general public have to visit business premises such as shops, garages, and offices they can also be protected by public liability insurance against any accidental injury or loss which may occur.
- It enables some businesses to start trading which they would not be able to do if they were unable to insure against certain risks occurring.

Disadvantages of insurance

- Some premiums may be so high, because the risks are very great, that it is too expensive for a business to pay to provide insurance cover.
- Not every risk can be covered by insurance. Some events, such as changes in fashion or the fluctuating tastes of consumers, cannot be assessed and are said to be uninsurable risks.
- The risk of loss on some items may be so small they do not warrant the cost of insurance.

Exercises

1 Explain what is meant by the term *pooling of risk*. (2)

2 What are the three principles on which insurance is based? Give a brief explanation of each. (3)

3 Use an example to explain what is meant by a 'new for old' insurance policy. What are the benefits of this type of policy to the insured person? (4)

4 Why are aircraft and ships insured through syndicates at Lloyds of London? (2)

5 Explain the difference between employers liability insurance and public liability insurance. (2)

6 What are the disadvantages of a business taking out insurance against possible theft? (2)

Find definitions for the following insurance terms. Then word process a copy of the list together with your definitions and include it in your notes:

- premium
- pooling of risks
- third party insurance
- uninsurable risk
- indemnity
- insurable interest
- public liability
- consequential loss
- compensation

Yourself and a friend are considering setting up a business valeting second-hand cars for several local garages before they are put on the forecourt for sale. You intend to use two garages in a block of eight lock-up garages and the open area in front of them to carry out your business. These lock-up garages are just around the corner on the local housing estate that your friend lives on, and the other six garages are used by local residents.

Word process a list of all the different risks you should insure against, giving reasons for your choices. Are there any uninsurable risks that you should consider?

Extension material

Visit your school, college or local library and try to find out more about the work of Lloyds of London.

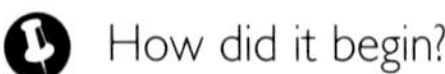

- How did it begin?

- Where is it currently situated?
- What is the exact nature of its business?
- What is a syndicate?
- How can you join a syndicate?
- What risks do syndicate members take when insuring ships and aircraft?
- What is the value of the work of Lloyds to the country as a whole?

Financial documents

When you purchase most goods from a shop you pay for them there and then. Some larger items (televisions, cars, washing machines) may be purchased on credit terms, where you pay a deposit initially and then the balance either weekly or monthly.

Trade credit

In businesses, almost all transactions which take place are based on credit terms. Firms buy and sell materials, components and finished goods using trade credit. That is, they take the goods on the understanding that they will pay for them within 30 or 60 days. Trade credit allows firms to purchase materials, process them and then sell them to their customers before they have to make actual payment for the materials purchased.

Systems

Before goods can be sold in this way, it is important that businesses have a system in place that will enable them to monitor what goods have been sold, to which customers and what money is owed. Large firms will have thousands of customers and hundreds of suppliers, and even small firms may deal with two or three hundred customers who purchase their products on a number of occasions throughout the year. Keeping track of this information can be quite difficult and time-consuming, so most businesses now use a computerised accounting system on which they store their records. Computers are used to produce financial business documents and to remind firms of outstanding transactions and unpaid bills.

Business transactions

The main stages in the process of recording business transactions are given in Figure 44:

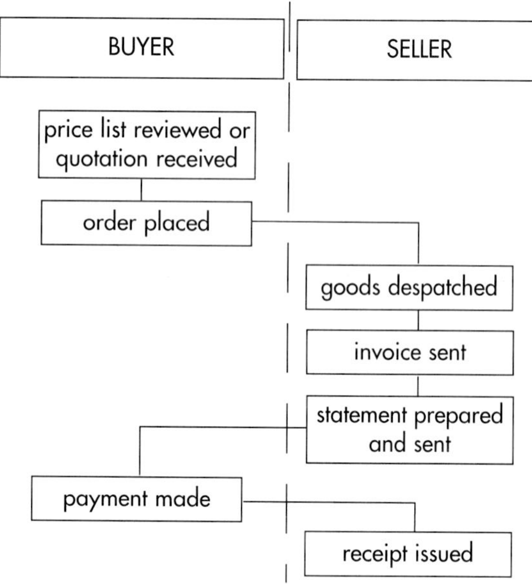

Figure 44 The process of business transactions

Price list

This is the current list of prices that the company is charging for its various products. Very often these are produced separately from catalogues and brochures. This allows the company to amend its prices in response to changes in the cost of components, or as a means of increasing sales through a promotional price. It is considerably cheaper to reprint the price list alone rather than the whole catalogue, which may be an expensively produced colour brochure.

Quotation

An alternative method of pricing goods is for the potential customer to request an estimate from the supplier for the goods or service they require. This method of pricing is often used when it is difficult to know in advance the precise quantity or volume of goods which may be needed. Estimates are commonly used in the building industry where it is difficult to predict how long a job may take.

Orders

A customer purchasing products will place an order with the firm. This will clearly state the name and address of the customer, the address to which the goods should be delivered, the quantity and description of the goods ordered, the price the customer is expecting to pay for the goods and the date by which the goods are expected to be delivered. Once an order is received, a contract exists between the buyer and the seller.

Invoice

Once the goods have been delivered, the supplier will issue an invoice to the customer requesting payment. This gives details of the goods supplied together with the total cost of the order. Should any trade discount or prompt payment discount be allowed, this will be clearly marked on the invoice and deducted from the total due. The invoice will also state the terms of payment, i.e. the date by which payment is expected to be made.

Statement

At the end of each month the supplier will issue a 'statement of account' to the customer. This summarises all transactions that have taken place during the month and will show the amount the customer owes at the start of the month, together with details of all invoices sent to the customer during the month, records of any payments received and the final amount now owed at the end of the month.

Payment

Most businesses still pay by cheque for their supplies. Often these will be produced by a computerised accounting system and automatically posted. Business cheques usually require two different signatures on them – this is a safeguard to prevent members of staff from attempting to defraud the company, and to ensure that the correct amount is being paid to the correct supplier. It also protects those members of staff in a company who have the authority to sign cheques from allegations of fraud.

Receipt

A receipt is issued and sent to the customer to signify that payment has been received.

Exercises

1 Why do most businesses purchase materials and components on trade credit? (2)

2 Explain the advantages to a firm of using a computer-based accounts package rather than a manual system. (3)

3 Explain why some firms have a pre-printed price list for their products whereas others provide a quotation or an estimate. (2)

4 What is the difference between an invoice and a statement? (2)

5 Why do businesses usually require two different employees to sign any cheques which are issued? (2)

6 What is a receipt and why do businesses issue them? Why is it important for a customer paying his/her bill in cash to obtain a receipt? (4)

Using your word processor or desktop publishing system, prepare a copy of the diagram in the text (Figure 48) which shows the relationship between buyer and seller and the documents each will issue when recording business transactions.

Goods are occasionally returned by the purchaser as unsatisfactory and a credit note is issued. At other times, if the full quantity of goods stated on the invoice is not delivered, a debit note may be issued. With the use of reference books, obtain definitions of debit and credit notes. Obtain also a sample of each type of form. Include these two documents in the appropriate place in the diagram you created in Task One.

Extension material

You work for a company called Wonder Bears Ltd. of Worthing, Sussex, BN15 3DG.

1 Using your spreadsheet program set up a template for an invoice.

2 Show the company name and address at the top of your document.

3 Include appropriate spaces for the invoice number, the date and name and address of the firm to which the invoice will be sent.

4 Then set up four columns for quantity, description of goods, unit price and total price.

5 Enter the following items in your template and include the appropriate formulae:

(i) 20 small teddy bears @ £5.00 each.

(ii) ten medium teddy bears @ £7.50 each.

(iii) ten large teddy bears @ £9.00 each.

6 Add a further column for VAT and calculate this for all items at 17.5%.

7 Total up the items above in the 'Total Price' column. Bring down the Total VAT to beneath this Total Price and calculate the FINAL Price. Include a trade discount of 20% and show this on the invoice together with the final amount the customer is due to pay.

Management structures

All businesses have to be managed, but some are managed more effectively than others. So what makes the difference in management? The function of the manager of a business is to lead and to guide others within that organisation. Good managers are able to do this and have strategies to cope with planned and unplanned changes.

Managers

There are several key functions which all managers have to carry out. These are discussed below.

Leadership

There are primarily strategic decisions that must be taken by the management of a business. These establish the long-term aims of the company and set out how they are to be achieved. Leaders need to possess credibility by understanding the nature of the business they manage and be able to persuade others that the decisions they have taken are the right ones for the firm.

Liaison

Here the manager spends time meeting with those in other departments or sections in a firm to find out what is going on in all areas of the business. The manager will also have to meet with those outside the business, such as customers and competitors, to discover what is likely to happen in the market in which the business is operating. This knowledge ensures the manager will be more informed when making decisions that affect the business as a whole.

Information

The manager's key function is effective communication. The manager often provides the 'official' message and also acts as a channel of communication, using the contacts they have established both inside and outside the company in their liaison role.

Decisions

The manager should possess knowledge of what is going on in each area of the business, through their liaison role, and so should have access to more information than others within the company when making decisions. They also have the benefit of being in a position of formal authority, therefore, subordinate employees may be more inclined to accept the decisions that have been made.

Negotiation

A manager often has to negotiate with other members of staff to achieve objectives or to ensure decisions are understood by all those who will have to carry them out. For example, a manager may have to meet with workers and trade union officers to agree appropriate working conditions.

Crisis management

Running a business would be straightforward without the unforeseen occurring. It can be argued that good managers will plan for all contingencies, but inevitably, some things will occur that cannot be foreseen. For example, reorganising production following a factory fire or attempting to renegotiate a sales contract unexpectedly lost to a competitor. All managers will, at sometime, face the need to make decisions without all the necessary information or consultation that they would like to have.

Internal structure

To help with the process of management, businesses can organise their internal structure in a

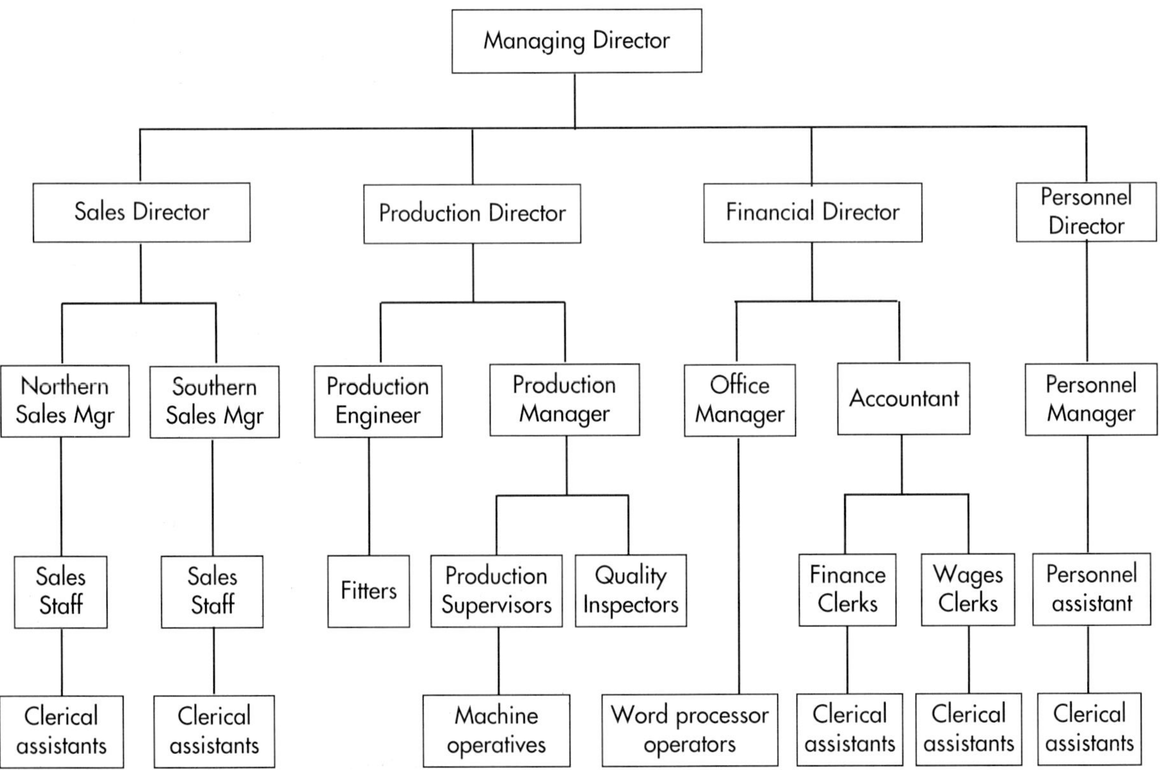

Figure 45 Internal organisation structure

number of ways. Decisions on how it is set up will be based on issues such as who is in charge; who has the authority to make certain decisions; how information is communicated and who carries out the decisions that are made. Internal structure can be set out in an organisation chart such as in Figure 45.

When deciding on how to organise its internal structure, a business should consider three important factors: hierarchy, chain of command and the span of control.

Hierarchy

A hierarchy decides the levels of authority within firms. In Figure 49 there are five levels of authority, which range from the Managing Director at the highest level to the clerical assistants and machine operatives at the lowest level. A company with several levels of management between the most senior and the most junior posts will have less effective communication, as more people will be involved in passing messages between the levels. Today, companies are attempting to reduce the different levels of management that exist and to develop a flatter and more efficient structure.

Chain of command

This illustrates how authority is organised and the path by which decisions and information are passed up and down the company hierarchy. In Figure 49 the chain of command for a word processing operator stems from the Managing Director, down through the Financial Director and the Office Manager.

It is now generally accepted in business that each level of management in a hierarchy will reduce the effectiveness of communication, as information and messages are not passed on or messages are interpreted differently as they are passed through each level of management. Reducing the levels in the chain of command, to improve the communication in a company, is dependent on changing the hierarchy. This may not always be an easy task in a well established business.

Span of control

This shows the range of people within the firm for whom one person has direct responsibility. For example, if the Northern Sales Manager has eight sales representatives working in his region, his span of control is eight. In a company where careful control is needed over employees, for example to ensure that a high level of quality is maintained, then the span of control should be low. This will allow better supervision and easier and more effective communications between small numbers of subordinate employees.

Alternatively, if employees are allowed a degree of independence in their work, such as teachers and lecturers, then the span of control can be higher. This wider span of control allows subordinates more opportunities to make their own decisions, which can lead to greater job satisfaction and help to reduce supervisory costs.

Exercises

1 List the key functions of a manager. Write a sentence about each function to describe what it means. (3)

2 What is an Organisation Chart? What purpose does it serve in (a) a small business employing 20 workers and (b) a larger business employing 5 000 workers? (3)

3 Explain why all businesses cannot eliminate the need for crisis management. (2)

4 Why are modern businesses seeking to reduce the number of levels of their management hierarchy and adopting flatter organisational structures? (2)

5 Explain what is meant by the term *the chain of command*. (2)

6 How is an individual manager's span of control defined? What problems would he/she face with a span of control of 30? (3)

1. Using your word processor or desk top publishing system, prepare a copy of the organisation structure shown in the unit. Use the drawing features on your package to indicate the levels of hierarchy, as well as examples of a chain of command and a span of control.
2. Word process definitions of these three terms at the foot of your chart:
   - hierarchy
   - chain of command
   - span of control.

1. Prepare an organisation chart of your school or college and indicate the levels of hierarchy.
2. Show the chain of command of the pastoral system in your school or college and the span of control of the Curriculum Deputy Head.

Extension material

You work for Holdsworth Engineering Ltd. which manufactures sports equipment. The company has a traditional organisation structure where the Personnel, Marketing, Production and Finance Directors report to the Managing Director who, in turn, reports to the Chairman. In the production department, there is a Production Manager, five technicians, two test engineers, two fitters and twelve machine operators. The marketing department is run by a Sales Manager with seven regional sales representatives and three sales office support staff. Two personnel assistants and two clerks work with the Personnel Director. The finance department is run by an accountant and the Office Manager, who between them supervise a wages clerk, three filing clerks and two word processing operators.

Prepare an organisation chart for the company based on the information given. Suggest ways in which the chart can be altered to provide a hierarchy with fewer levels. Show how this would affect the span of control and the chain of command of the company.

Representing groups at work

In industry today there are a number of organisations who represent the interests of certain groups of workers. Although not part of the actual business, these organisations can have a considerable influence on how firms operate. The most well-known of these representative organisations are trades unions.

Trades unions

These are organisations that represent groups of workers who have a common interest, usually their occupation or trade. For example, the National Union of Journalists (NUJ) or the Amalgamated Electrical Engineering Union (AEEU). One of the largest unions today, with more than one million members, is the Transport and General Workers Union (TGWU). Trades unions are independent of any employers. They are usually affiliated to the Labour Party and the Trades Union Congress, the collective governing body of all trades unions. Unions work towards furthering their members' interests. To do this they perform several functions:

- They negotiate with employers to obtain satisfactory rates of pay for their members.
- They ensure that all workers receive adequate breaks and are not exploited by having to work long hours for low pay.
- They ensure that all working conditions are safe and meet the requirements of health and safety laws.
- They negotiate with employers on behalf of individual members who have a grievance or problem.

Trades unions bargain with employers on behalf of all their members and attempt to obtain the best possible pay and working conditions for them. As the union may represent a large number of workers, they have more strength, or bargaining power, than one individual. Unions with only a small proportion of members within a company will be less effective than those where most or all of the workers have joined the union. Consequently, employers are more inclined to listen and consider the requests of trades unions when they represent a large proportion of the workforce. There are several different types of trades union, detailed below.

Craft unions

Craft unions are the oldest type of union and they developed from the traditional crafts such as weaving and carpentry. Workers with the same skills grouped together to protect their common interests and to prevent unskilled workers from taking their jobs.

Industrial unions

These were formed by groups of employees who all worked in the same industry, such as miners (NUM), railway workers (ASLEF), seamen (NUS) or teachers (NUT/NAS/UWT). Unlike craft unions, members of industrial unions could have different levels of skill and expertise, but simply had to work within the industry.

General unions

General unions were originally founded to represent the interests of workers with many different skills in a wide range of occupations. These unions tend to represent semi-skilled and unskilled workers and are usually much larger than the industrial or craft unions. For example, the General and Municipal Boilermakers and Allied Trade Union (GMB).

Trades union developments

In recent years trades unions have undergone many changes to cope with new employment laws and to provide a better service to their members:

- The amalgamation of many of the smaller unions from similar industries to form larger, more efficient organisations. For example, UNISON, formed from the merger of the public services unions of NALGO, NUPE and COHSE, is now the largest union in the United Kingdom, representing more than one million health and public sector workers throughout the country.
- Some unions have now signed 'no strike' agreements with employers. This benefits the workers, as they will not lose money by taking strike action to enforce their point-of-view on employers, and employers will not have their production disrupted by industrial action. It also promotes a better working relationship between workers and management as it removes the more aggressive practices trades unions have often resorted to in the past, concentrating instead on discussion and negotiation.
- Union negotiations with employers have broadened to include many other issues that affect the workforce, such as facilities for female employees, care of disabled workers, health and safety, in addition to general working conditions and pay. Many of these negotiations now take place at a local rather than a national level, which enables companies to plan their own individual requirements, to meet agreements negotiated with unions and to budget for these costs.
- Unions offer their members an increasingly wide range of services and other facilities. These include: preferential insurance rates, contributory pension schemes, financial and legal advice, discounts on certain goods and services and welfare and sickness benefit schemes. All of these encourage membership and so strengthen the position of the trades union as the representative of the workforce.

The Trades Union Congress (TUC)

This is the organisation that represents the views of all major trades unions. Each member union is represented on the TUC General Council. The TUC acts as a professional regulating body of all trades unions and also acts as a pressure group to advise and influence the government on industrial and labour policies. It is also represented on other important public bodies including the Arbitration and Conciliation Service, the Equal Opportunities Commission and the Commission for Racial Equality.

Other organisations

Staff associations

These provide opportunities for staff members to get together to discuss issues of common interest. They also frequently provide the basis for social activities and in larger businesses may run a sports and social club for staff members and their families.

Professional associations

These are similar to trades unions in that they represent the interests of their members, however they are not actually registered as a trades union. They include organisations such as the Police Federation, which negotiates with the Home Office on all matters affecting the police, the British Medical Association and the Law Society whose members are often self-employed. These associations frequently take responsibility for setting and maintaining professional standards. For example, the Law Society requires all members to hold certain legal qualifications and to act in an ethical and correct manner.

Employers organisations

These represent the interests of employers in a similar way to trades unions. They often provide support to small firms when negotiating with larger trades unions, help with technical and professional support, and provide guarantees to the general public on the standard and quality of the work the firm carries out. For example, many plumbers are members of CORGI, the Confederation of Registered Gas Installers, and most travel agents are members of ABTA, the Association of British Travel Agents. This type of association protects the interests of its member companies but also insists on certain minimum standards in the service or product they provide. They also provide customers with a guarantee of quality.

Confederation of the British Industry

The best known employers' association is the Confederation of British Industry (CBI). Formed in the mid 1960s, it represents the employers' viewpoint in a similar way to the TUC, which voices the opinions of the unions. Its main aims include:

- Helping to influence government policy on behalf of employers.
- Providing legal, financial and economic advice and support to member firms.
- Consulting and negotiating with trades unions on bodies such as ACAS, over issues.
- Promoting the interests of British industry abroad, particularly within the European Union.
- Supporting local businesses through its network of regional offices and support staff.

Exercises

1 List the three types of trade union together with a sentence to explain each. Include an example of each type of union in your answer. (3)

2 What is a no-strike agreement? What are the benefits of such an agreement to (a) employers and (b) employees? (3)

3 What is the TUC? Write a paragraph to explain its role in the trade union movement. (2)

4 List three employers associations and three professional associations. (2)

5 How can a business benefit from having all its employees belonging to a trade union? (2)

6 Explain what ACAS is and how both employers and trade unions can benefit from its work. (3)

1 Use a word processor to make a list of the different types of trades unions, together with an example of each.

2 What are the advantages and disadvantages of trades union membership to:
   (i) an employee, and
   (ii) a company?

Use your word processor or desktop publishing system to draw up an organisation chart illustrating how a trade union is organised. Show the structure from ordinary member to General Secretary, and include the influence of the TUC.

Extension material

1 Using Yellow Pages or a similar directory, find the address of the regional or national office of a trades union. Compose a letter requesting information on membership fees and the facilities and services they offer to their members.

2 When you receive the information read through it carefully and then prepare a summary of the benefits to members of joining a trades union.

The Impact of change

Businesses are constantly changing and, as they form part of the economy of the United Kingdom, the changes that affect them also lead to changes in the economy as a whole.

Technology used in modern offices

In recent years, the most significant change that has occurred in office technology has been the introduction and use of personal computers. This information revolution has allowed businesses to process much larger amounts of information in a far shorter period of time and often also with a reduction in staff. Word processors allow the firm to create and store written communications. If required, these can then be sent by electronic means, such as Email or fax.

Subject to the Data Protection Act, large amounts of data concerning products, customers, suppliers and employees can be stored in databases. Spreadsheets can be used to provide financial information and to answer 'what if' questions in a fraction of the time taken prior to the introduction of computers. Three dimensional designs can be created quickly using Computed Aided Design and products can be produced more easily with the help of Computer Aided Manufacture. Other software applications, designed to carry out specific activities, are also currently in widespread use. These range from holiday booking systems for travel agents to computer scanning of bar codes and EPOS systems in supermarkets.

Customer tastes and preferences

Personal tastes and fashions change frequently. The clothes you wore last year may no longer be in fashion today! Changes in personal tastes and preferences may be met by those businesses that are able to predict what we will want next. Very often, advertising is used to help us decide what the next fashion or trend will be. The range of goods and services customers are now demanding increases and diversifies as they become more wealthy. Wages and salaries are increasing and we also have more leisure time in which to spend our increasing income.

Production methods

The development of computers has produced a considerable increase in the use of **Computer Aided Design (CAD) and Computer Aided Manufacture (CAM)** in recent years. Computers can carry out design tasks much more quickly and efficiently than humans, and difficult and repetitive assembly tasks can be controlled easily by a computer. This allows firms to use less labour and more technology, so reducing the cost of producing goods and increasing productivity. The development of automation in production has the following benefits:

- The quality of computer produced products is more consistent.
- Computers make fewer mistakes.
- Computers do not require meal or rest breaks.

Computers have also allowed many firms to take advantage of new practices that require close monitoring of production methods, but which if successful, will save considerably on the costs of production. The concept of 'Just in Time' production is dependent on a firm being able to obtain new stocks of materials precisely when they are required. Computerised stock control allows this to take place, as it enables a firm to manage its stock levels much more precisely, thus saving money on unnecessary stock holdings, and reducing the storage space required. This also helps to eliminate waste and the possibility of storing obsolete stock that is damaged because of frequent handling in the warehouse.

Many firms that have to cope with either high volumes of goods such as the chocolate industry or large product ranges such as supermarkets, have used technology to improve their product handling. The introduction of computer-automated warehousing, which uses computer systems to record and monitor stock movements and conveyor belts to move it, makes the firm more efficient and reduces labour handling costs.

Figure 46 Loyalty Card

One of the more recent developments brought about by computers has been the introduction of customer loyalty cards by major retailers. By scanning a customer's card with their shopping, the retailer is able to compile a profile of each customer and their shopping habits. For this, the retailer offers small savings on purchases through tokens based on sales, which can only be redeemed at the shop. Consequently when the customer receives their discount, the retailer can also target them with other promotional offers, knowing what they purchase regularly. For example, young families may receive money-off offers on nappies and other baby products, single people may be sent vouchers to save money on ready prepared meals or music CDs and cassettes.

Social attitudes

There have been many changes in social attitudes that have affected the demand for firms' goods and services. For example, the sale of animal fur products has declined dramatically due to the action of groups such as those campaigning against hunting and seal culling. Similarly, social pressure has been imposed on smoking as an anti-social activity. Advertising and sponsorship by tobacco companies of sporting activities has been banned and many public areas are now smoke free zones.

Despite the positive effects that computerisation can bring, many people are resistant to change. The main reasons for this are as follows.

Fear and insecurity

New methods of working are often rejected in preference to old, tried and tested ways. There is a natural fear for some workers that they will not be able to cope with new processes and equipment. This in turn may generate a feeling of insecurity in no longer being in control of their jobs.

Personal factors

The introduction of new modern processes alters employment patterns and working conditions. This may mean the learning of new and unfamiliar processes and at worst it may cause a worker to have to move from one area to another, leaving behind friends and family.

Loss of status

New computerised techniques in industry can lead to a loss of status or power for an individual, as the hierarchy within an organisation becomes flatter and levels of middle management are removed. This may have an effect on wages and salary levels as well as causing a loss of self-esteem, particularly among older workers.

Ignorance

Many individuals reject the possibility of change due to ignorance. Workers who are not made aware of, or who are not prepared to consider the benefits of change, can stand in the way of development. This is generally a problem that can be resolved by management communicating more effectively, to keep its workforce more in touch with the need for, and benefits of, change.

The effects of change

Despite resistance to change, the information technology revolution is here to stay and will continue to affect both those in work and those seeking employment. New skills are required by all workers in order to cope with modern work practices that involve the use of computers. Unskilled, repetitive tasks are now largely carried out by computerised systems within industry. Consequently, workers need a higher level of skill and education to cope adequately with these changing processes.

New computerised industrial processes allow businesses to reduce their workforce and reduce the length of the working week. Some employees are being encouraged through financial incentives to retire early; others are working shorter hours. All of this gives individuals more leisure time in which to spend the increasing incomes they are earning.

However, greater leisure time also has its disadvantages. Workers in many service industries now need to work hours that are less sociable so that the majority can enjoy the leisure facilities. Restaurants, sporting events, concerts and shopping are all examples of service facilities that have required their workforce to break away from the traditional Monday to Friday, 9.00 a.m. to 5.30 p.m. concept of work.

The process of change in industry is increasing, and many of the more traditional jobs are now no longer required because they have been automated. Modern workers must be able to cope with this rapid change and develop transferable skills that allow them to move from one occupation to another – something our parents and grandparents would have considered quite alien.

Exercises

1 Explain how the EPOS system works in a supermarket or large retail store. (3)

2 What are the advantages and disadvantages of using an EPOS system to (a) the retailer and (b) the customer? (4)

3 How has the introduction of modern office technology helped businesses in recent years? (3)

4 Explain how our increasing wealth, in the form of higher wages and salaries, can help businesses. (2)

5 Explain the difference between CAD and CAM. How can these processes benefit industry? (3)

6 What is meant by the term *Just in Time* or JIT? How can computers help businesses manage their levels of stocks of materials and finished goods? (4)

7 How have social attitudes changed in recent years? Explain, with the help of examples, how these changes can affect a business. (4)

8 What are the negative effects which may arise from social change? Illustrate your answer with examples. (4)

You work for a company that distributes 40 different product lines to more than 500 retail outlets throughout the United Kingdom. Your employer is considering introducing a computer-controlled stock control system to manage warehouse stocks, and has asked you to consider how this new development might affect the 16 workers who currently manage the warehouse stock. Word process a short report itemising the problems that you think the new system may create. Suggest ways in which each of these problems can be overcome.

Make a list of all the ways you can think of in which computers and information technology are used to make your life easier. What are the benefits of this to you? Are there any other areas that would benefit from the use of information technology which do not at present?

Extension material

Define the terms: Electronic Point of Sale, Computer Aided Design and Computer Aided Manufacture. Find out all you can about these concepts and then prepare a short report to show how they have benefited modern industry. Include examples from local firms to illustrate your report.

PART 7

Student Study Guides

Examinations

Revision

Skills check list

Keyboard skills

Keyboard skills: testing your speed

Examinations

Examinations are very stressful. This stress, however, can be reduced by being fully prepared and knowing what the examiner is looking for before you sit the examination. This means not only knowing the subject content well, but also understanding the structure of the examination and the purpose behind the different types of questions asked.

Examination structure

The Business and Communication Systems examinations set by Assessment and Qualification Alliance (AQA) Examinations Assessment Board, and that of Edexcel, contain both theory and practical questions. Students following the AQA course will sit a separate one hour theory paper and a two hour practical session. Edexcel candidates will sit a two hour examination which contains a mixture of theory and practical tasks. OCR candidates will sit a 1¾ hour foundation paper or a 2 hour higher tier paper in all examinations, all questions set are compulsory. Make sure you check with your teacher the full details of the structure of the examination you will be taking.

Both Examination Boards provide a choice between foundation and higher tiers of entry. The decision as to which tier you will be entered for will be taken by your teacher or lecturer who will use their professional judgement, based on how you have performed in lessons, mock examinations and practice questions in class and for homework. It is important therefore, that you work hard and do your best from the start of your course. Each piece of work you complete provides evidence that may be used to decide on your examination entry level.

Foundation tier candidates may be awarded GCSE grades from C down to G. Whereas higher tier candidates may gain a grade from A* down to D.

Whichever tier you are entered for, it is important to make sure you are properly prepared to do your best and to score as highly as you can in the examination you sit. To do this you need to be aware of the way the papers are set out.

The questions are set around a scenario, which is printed at the beginning of the paper. It is very important that you read this carefully as it may affect the way in which you respond when answering some of the questions. For example, if the scenario is about a job you are assumed to hold, working for a garage, then you need to frame your answers as a garage employee rather than a school or college student. This may help you direct your knowledge to the application the examiner is looking for, rather than providing a more generalised response which will earn fewer marks.

Theory questions

It is important to be properly equipped for the examination. Remember that the theory paper will be sat under formal conditions in the examination hall. You will be required to supply your own pens, pencils, ruler, rubber and calculator. Do not forget to include a spare pen and pencil. Remember to check the instructions printed on the front of the examination paper and read each question carefully before starting to write. The time allowed for the paper prevents the use of free response or essay style questions and so you will find there are two forms which theory questions take: multiple choice or short answer.

Multiple choice questions

These aim to test your knowledge and application. Each question gives a statement or 'stem' followed by a choice of possible answers, of which only one is correct. These questions can be set out in either of two ways:

1 In order to copy a printed photograph into a file on a computer, it would be best to use a:

laser printer   scanner   keyboard

In the above case you would be required to circle or underline the correct answer. Alternatively, you may be required to write down the letter which corresponds to the correct answer.

2 Businesses which use computers to talk to and see their customers at the same time would use:

A personal contact

B video conferencing

C networking

D telephones

Both types of question are asking you to respond to a similar stimulus, but the answers are recorded in different ways. If the answer is obvious, these questions seem easy! However, if you cannot immediately spot the correct answer you need to start by eliminating any answers that are obviously wrong. This will reduce the choice you have to make and (hopefully) increase your chances of selecting the correct answer. Remember, always answer **all** multiple choice questions. If you leave the question blank you will score nothing. If you attempt the question, even if you are not sure of the correct answer, you may get it right. You lose nothing by attempting every question.

Short answer questions

These questions are designed to get you to think and to respond to a given situation. The questions may be broken down into two or more parts, thus providing you with a structure to guide your answers. There are two further guides to help you answer these questions effectively. Firstly, the marks allocated to each part of the question are given. This should provide you with an indication of how you should allocate your time. For example, spending ten minutes on a question which has a maximum of two marks can only give you two marks, regardless of how comprehensive your answer is. Alternatively, if you only spend two minutes on a question with an allocation of ten marks, this does not give you the time to write down all the information the examiner is seeking to enable you to gain maximum marks.

Secondly, the space provided in the answer book gives you a strong indication of the length of answer required. As a rule of thumb, to answer a two mark question you will be provided with three blank lines. However, you do not have to use all the lines – being concise in your answers is a good practice to develop. Remember you do not have to reply to every question in full sentences. Some questions require only a word or phrase, others a list of points.

You should read each question carefully. Within it you will find one or more key words that tell you how to respond to the question. These words are always given in the context of the question and that is particularly important. Sometimes the words are linked together, which may alter what is required from you. For example, 'explain' asks you to provide knowledge, but when linked with the word 'why' you will be expected to provide further analysis or an evaluation in your answer. The most commonly used key words are listed below together with their meanings:

Key words

Explain This requires a detailed and clear coverage of the subject matter, giving clear reasons that support your answer.

Describe This is a relatively easy task which requires you to give a straightforward account of the subject. Ask yourself: 'what do you know?'

Outline This asks you to give the important features and a general idea about the topic of the question. This instruction implies that you should be brief when answering.

Compare This requires you to weigh up the arguments for and against a topic or course of action and to suggest a possible conclusion or solution to the problem posed.

Analyse This suggests a detailed answer is required, which involves breaking down a concept or topic into its component parts or essential features to examine or determine their relationship.

Evaluate Here you are required to judge the worth of a topic or statement and to reach a conclusion as to its value. You should not be concerned with seeking a 'correct' answer but in weighing up evidence to support your conclusion.

Illustrate This is asking you to support or clarify your answer through the use of examples. Remember, it is good practice to do this even when not specifically requested to do so.

Short answer questions differ from multiple choice questions in four key ways:

- They may require you to explain or analyse an idea or concept.
- You may have to apply a general principle to a specific situation.
- Your answers need to be constructed to show your ability to communicate.
- They are used to assess your command of spelling, punctuation and grammar.

Unlike multiple choice questions, which test what you know, these questions allow you to demonstrate and apply that knowledge to given situations. They are frequently set to incorporate an 'incline of difficulty' where more straightforward questions based on the data are followed by more demanding ones. They can also include open-ended questions that give you the opportunity to demonstrate your knowledge and understanding more fully through a short piece of free response writing. An example of such a question might be as follows:

> Other than tea and coffee making facilities, what additional features would improve working conditions for employees? Give reasons for your choices.

A short answer question asks you to provide some further knowledge – a rest room, staff canteen, social club, etc – but then requires you to provide analysis of why these facilities would improve working conditions. A good candidate may also include here examples of local firms of which they are aware, who provide such facilities, and then give an evaluation as to which of the facilities they have listed would have most benefit for the employees.

Practical questions

These require the use of a computer work station for each candidate. As with the questions in the theory paper, they are also based on a scenario but require you to actually use the facilities of your work station to prepare and print answers to the tasks set, rather like an 'in-tray' assignment.

You will need to ensure that all the equipment in your work station is functioning correctly before the examination, and that you are confident in its use. Make sure you check the procedure for printing hard copies of documents and the storage arrangements for your completed work. You need to be certain that you can use the software for each application and know how to recall any material stored for your individual use during the examination. You are allowed to use manufacturers' instruction manuals if you wish but remember that it is not always easy to find what you are looking for in them, especially when under pressure of time during an examination.

Ensure that you spell check and proofread all work prior to printing to remove possible errors. Do not simply look for errors that you may inadvertently have keyed in when preparing material – remember the examination questions themselves may contain some deliberate errors for you to identify and correct.

Finally, make sure you always key in your name, candidate number and centre number on each document you produce. This is the only way to be certain that you will be credited with all the work that you complete.

Quality of written communication

In all GCSE examinations a small proportion of marks are reserved for the assessment of spelling, punctuation and grammar. These aspects are assessed in both theory and practical examinations. In the theory paper they are assessed separately; whereas they form an integral part of the marking scheme for the practical paper.

Approximately 5% of the marks are awarded for correct spelling, punctuation and grammar and so the importance of spell checking and proofreading your examination work should not be underestimated.

Revision

There is no substitute for hard work, and revision is an important and integral part of your learning. It is not something which can be left until a few days before the examination if you want to achieve real success. Revision cannot begin too early in the course. For example, reviewing your notes to make sure you understand the work covered after each lesson is a form of revision and is a good habit to develop.

You will have become aware that you are preparing for an examination as soon as you start your course, therefore try to revise as the course progresses. Make sure you prepare a summary of your notes for each topic as you complete them. Consider setting aside a short part of your homework time each week for revision. One of the benefits of the Business and Communication Systems course is that you can use the practical elements of the syllabus to prepare material and answers to theory questions.

Revision guidelines

1. Ask your teacher to discuss revision with you early on in the course. Do not leave it until a few days before the exam, by then it will be too late to have any real effect.
2. Consider revising with a friend. This can make it more interesting and seem less of a chore – but do not let your revision degenerate into a chat session!
3. Remember to plan your revision carefully, to make it more effective. Try to be realistic in what you can learn. Attempting to do too much revision is as unhelpful as too little.
4. Make sure you do not concentrate too heavily on weak areas of knowledge. Try to alternate between easy and more difficult topics to give you some variety in your work.
5. Make sure that you 'self-test' regularly. Revision is of little value unless you can remember it later.

6 Do not try to learn new material immediately before the examination. Concentrate on what you already know.

Revision techniques

The aim of revision is to assist you in your learning and to help you to remember information for relatively short periods of time with the main objective of passing your GCSE examination. Remember that revision techniques are not substitutes for continual hard work during your GCSE course.

Plan your revision

To get the most out of your revision you will need to plan your work carefully. It is worth spending some time each week planning out what you intend to revise, when you will do it and what books and other materials you will need. Then make sure you have your notes and other resources ready for you to start.

Divide the session into manageable units of time and plan breaks between them. Always set a fixed amount of time for your revision. Be realistic – these periods should not be too long, but neither should they be too short. You should be able to sustain your concentration for two hours, but only if it is broken down into three thirty minute sessions, with a ten to fifteen minute break between each one. For example, if there is a favourite television programme you want to watch, or a friend you would like to telephone, plan this into your schedule as a break. This will give you something to look forward to as you work. You will want a break, so always plan them into your schedule of work before you begin revising.

Mnemonics

This is the term used to describe the process of memorising information by using the initial letters and forming them into a more easily remembered phrase. One of the most well known examples of mnemonics is used to remember the colours of the rainbow:

Richard	Of	York	Gave	Battle	In	Vain
Red	Orange	Yellow	Green	Blue	Indigo	Violet

Mnemonics can be set up for many topics where you need to remember lists of details or other information. Those that incorporate humour or personal association are often the best remembered. However, mnemonics allow you to recall knowledge quickly and easily. You will still need to develop analytical and evaluative skills to ensure you gain the higher order marks for many questions.

Rewriting your notes

This can be helpful when revising a topic that you have not studied for some time. It is, however, time-consuming and poses the danger of you writing without really thinking. To avoid this occurring, rewrite your notes by making them briefer. Better still, summarise your notes by trying to fit a whole topic onto one side of A4 paper. Record summaries of your notes on index cards or postcards and carry them around with you. You can then read these whenever you have a spare moment.

Diagrams

Try to convert your written or word processed notes into diagrams. Identify the key words, which can then be used as prompts. Again, these can be recorded onto postcards that can then be carried around and read whenever time allows. Diagrams on cards are easier to handle than folders of notes and can be slipped easily into a bag or pocket.

Question spotting

This is something of a gamble. Preparing skeleton answers to anticipated questions, can be fraught with difficulties, especially if the topic fails to come up on the examination paper. There is also the danger that when you see the topic on the examination paper, you will answer the question you have prepared rather than the one the examiner has asked.

Rote learning

This involves memorising large amounts of factual

material and possibly some model answers. It is one method of preparing for an examination, but unless it is linked with developing the skills to analyse and evaluate your answers, you are not likely to achieve a high grade. Make sure you build into your plan opportunities to develop analysis and evaluation techniques in the way in which you revise.

Practice

It is essential that you practise answering examination questions. Only through practice will you get used to the way in which the questions are worded, and to preparing good concise answers in a limited amount of time. Have the questions you complete marked by your teacher or lecturer and make sure you understand why you achieved the grade or mark you are given. Ensure that you understand what the examiner was looking for in each of the questions you answer. In this way you will then be able to go into the examination with more confidence as to what to expect and in your ability to do your best.

Checking your revision

Revision is of little use to you unless you can remember what you have revised. Checking your work after you have revised is as important as planning it. Try this system of revision checks:

- Write down everything you can remember about a topic before you start to revise it. You can then check this against what you can remember when you have finished.
- Check the points you have remembered for accuracy against your notes. There is little use in remembering something incorrectly!
- Skim through the topic in your notes and jot down the key points on a fresh sheet of paper.
- Read through your notes carefully, writing down anything based on the key points you have identified. Allow a maximum time of fifteen minutes for this.
- Test what you know about the topic you have just covered. Try drawing a diagram or perhaps using a cassette recorder to save writing everything down. Alternatively, get a friend to test you, but be warned, revising with friends can be a big source of distraction.
- Finally, test your knowledge of what you remember of the topic the following day.

Skills check list

The following check list of skills is designed to help you make sure you have all the necessary skills required to complete the examination. Indicate the date on which you successfully achieved the skill and make a note of the practical evidence to support each statement. This will also help you build up a coursework portfolio if you need one.

Skill	Date Achieved	Evidence
FILE MANAGEMENT		
Create files		
Save files		
Retrieve files		
Edit files		
Print files		
Copy/move files to directories		
Create new directories		
Create new sub-directories		
Import data		
Export data		
ACCURACY OF DATA		
Key in with accuracy		
Use of upper and lower case		
Centre work on the page		
Display tabulated work		
Use of consistent spacing		
Use a variety of line spacing		
Alter margins		
Left/right alignment of text		
Centre text		
Justification of text		
Use of closed/spaced capitals		
Use of bold/italic text		

Skill	Date Achieved	Evidence
Use of a variety of fonts		
Use of a variety of point sizes		
Create headers and footers		
Insert page numbers		
Amendments to typescript		
Amendments to manuscript		
TEXT PROCESSING		
Accuracy keying in data		
Insert text		
Delete text		
Save text		
Print text		
Edit text		
Centre text		
Display in blocked style		
Display in indented style		
Move text blocks		
Cut text blocks		
Paste text blocks		
Import text		
Use of correction symbols		
Use of special characters		
Correct unmarked errors		
SPREADSHEETS		
Create a spreadsheet		
Recall existing spreadsheet		
Save spreadsheet		
Print spreadsheet		
Insert rows		
Delete rows		
Insert columns		
Delete columns		
Resize columns and rows		
Enter text strings		
Enter numerical data		
Enter formulae		
Print formulae		
Edit cell content		

Skill	Date Achieved	Evidence
Format cells as currency		
Format cells as integers		
Format cells as decimals		
Replicate formulae		
Replicate values		
Export data into document		
DATABASES		
Create a data capture sheet		
Create a database		
Recall existing database		
Insert records		
Delete records		
Save database		
Print database		
Insert additional fields		
Delete fields		
Edit field headings		
Edit field width		
Edit field content		
Sort data by a given field		
Sort data by two or more fields		
Sort data in ascending order		
Sort data in descending order		
Search database on one level		
Search database on two levels		
Search database on three levels		
Import data from spreadsheet		
Export data into document		
CHARTS		
Import data from spreadsheet		
Import data from database		
Create pie chart		
Create bar chart		
Create line graph		
Save charts		
Print charts		
Insert title		
Insert data legends		

Skill	Date Achieved	Evidence
Insert axes descriptions		
Amend charts		
GRAPHICS/CLIPART		
Create freehand shapes		
Draw geometric shapes		
Edit using cut, copy, paste		
Save graphics/clipart		
Print graphics/clipart		
Use brush techniques		
Use fill techniques		
Edit line thickness		
Use different line styles		
Add text to graphics		
Add pull-out text boxes		
Insert clipart		
Move clipart		
Resize clipart		
Align objects		
Group objects		
PAGE DESIGN		
Create page format		
Recall page format		
Edit page format		
Save page formats		
Print page format		
Use of more than one column		
Set up text frames		
Edit/move text frames		
Set up picture frames		
Edit/move picture frames		
Set up tabulated data		
Edit/move tabulated data		
Set up graphics/chart frames		
Edit/move graphics frames		
Create headings/subheadings		
Create borders on whole page		
Create borders on given areas		
Import data/graphics files		
Export data/graphics files		

Keyboard skills

Almost everyone today has used a computer keyboard. In today's society its use as a method of entering data into a computer is an everyday part of life. However, few of us have developed the necessary skills to enter data. Many of us still use only one finger on each hand and cannot key in data at a speed faster than that at which we write.

It is essential that anyone who will be working with computers in a business environment should also learn keyboard skills, if they are to be able to key in data into their computer system at a reasonable speed. A great deal of time can be lost by inexperienced operators keying in data too slowly. To learn good keyboard skills requires discipline and practice. You need to practise keying in simple data for at least twenty minutes every day during the first few weeks, as it takes time to learn the keyboard thoroughly. Without this practice you are less likely to be successful and certainly will not be able to touch-type.

Before you start

Firstly, check that your computer work station is correctly positioned, and that you are sitting properly. It is important, when you are using a keyboard for any length of time, to ensure that you are sitting comfortably. Adjust the height of your chair so that you sit in a natural and easy position. Your body should be directly in front of the computer and your feet should be resting flat on the floor. Make sure your back is upright and supported by the seat rest. Forearms should be parallel with the floor with straight wrists, and your fingers should be curved downwards over the keyboard. With your head held upright, your eyes should focus on the top half of the screen which should be about 70–90 cm away from you.

Remember to adjust the angle of the screen and move the keyboard on the desk to a position that makes it more comfortable for you to use.

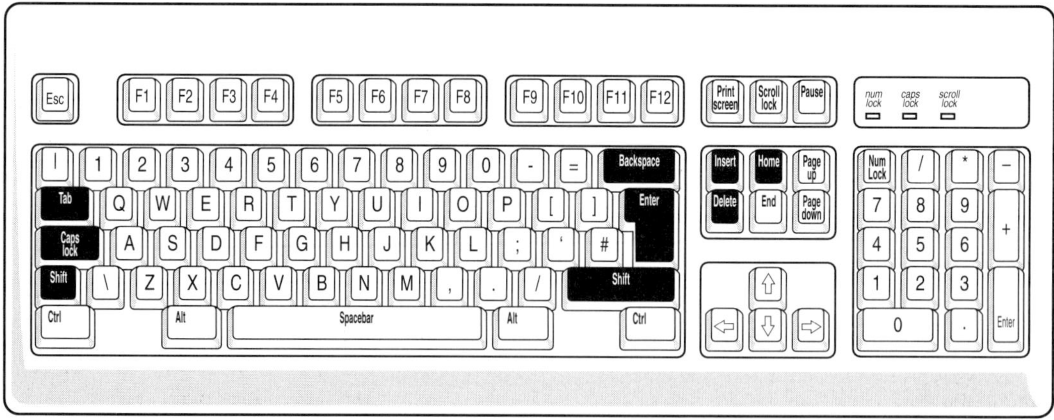

Figure 47 Diagram of a keyboard

The keyboard

You will undoubtedly be familiar with the keyboard of your computer. Although some of the minor keys vary from machine to machine, most will be in a standard position. Make sure you can identify the following keys on your keyboard (see Figure 47):
shift, caps lock, backspace, delete, insert/overwrite, enter, tab, home keys.

There are six rows of keys on a standard computer keyboard. The bottom row contains the space bar and the alt and control keys. The next three rows contain the alphabetic keys, as shown in Figure 51 above. The row above these keys contains numbers and some special characters. The top row of keys usually set slightly above the rest of the keys, consists of the 'function' keys. These carry out specific tasks or call up various menus for the particular program you are using. There is also a numeric keypad to the right of these keys that duplicates the number keys and may be easier to use when entering large quantities of numerical data. Make sure you are familiar with the layout of all the keys on your keyboard.

Touch-typing

This is the process of keying in data whilst not watching your fingers on the keyboard. At first this will seem difficult to achieve, but once learnt, touch-typing is a skill you will never forget (rather like riding a bicycle). It is worth persevering with this if you want to be able to key in data quickly and accurately.

Learning to key in data by touch rather than by looking at the keys requires self-discipline and practice. Whilst it may seem a struggle at first, and is sometimes slower than using one finger on each hand, it will save you a great deal of time in the future. Being able to keep your eyes on the text you are keying in, rather than on your fingers and the keyboard itself, will make you a more accurate word processing operator. You will also be able to build up your speed at keying in data and may soon find it quicker to key in data rather than writing it down.

Learning the keyboard

The home keys

The second row of alphabetic keys contain the home keys. These keys provide a guide for the four fingers of each hand, each one covering a letter. If you look at the **F** and **J** keys, you will notice that there is a small raised bump on these letters. These help guide your index fingers into the correct position to start to touch-type.

Place your index finger of the left hand on the **F** key and the other three fingers should cover the **D**, **S**

Figure 48 Diagram of home keys

and **A** keys. Similarly, place the index finger of the right hand on the **J** key and the other three fingers should now cover the **K**, **L** and **;** keys. Figure 48 shows the position of the home keys.

Try to keep your arms parallel to the floor and your wrists straight. Curl your fingers so that they are just touching the home keys. You should then be able to strike the space bar with the thumb of either hand.

To practise, you could try touch-typing the text below. Placing your index fingers on the **F** and **J** keys and the other fingers of each hand on the remainder of the home keys, key in the following text using the appropriate fingers. Key in each line twice before going on to the next. Remember to look at the text you are keying in, not at what your fingers are doing.

The middle row of keys

By now you will have realised that you have fewer fingers than there are keys on the keyboard! This means that each finger has to operate more than one letter, and as you increase the number of letters you can key in, it is important that you avoid watching your fingers. So before you start keying in a new letter it is important for you to practise the movement your fingers are going to make from the home key to the new key, and back again. It is only by returning to their original position on the home keys that you will know where your fingers are on the keyboard, without having to look down at them.

To complete the middle row of keys, the left hand index finger will also key in the letter **G** and the right hand finger the letter **H**. Practise moving each index finger in turn to the right or left, and then returning it to its original home key. Remember to try to keep your other fingers covering their appropriate home

asdf jkl; asdf jkl; asdf jkl; asdf jkl;
asdf ;lkj asdf ;llkj asdf ;lkj asdf ;lkj

dad lad dad lad dad lad sad fad sad fad sad fad
all sad all lad all sad all lad all sad

lass; alas; lass; alas; lass; alas; lass; alas;
fall; asks; fall; aska; fall; asks; fall; asks;

fall alas fall lass fall alas fall lass fall
asks alas asks fall asks alas asks fall asks alas

salad falls salad falls salad falls salad falls
falls salad falls salad falls salad falls salad

ask a dad; ask a dad; ask a dad; ask a dad; ask a dad;
a lad falls a lad falls a lad falls a lad falls

a lass asks dad; a lass asks dad; a lass asks dad;
a sad lass asks dad; a sad lad asks dad; a sad lad asks a dad;

jj hh jj hh jj hh jh jh hj hj jhj jhj hjh hjh jj hh jj hh jj hh jh jh hj hj jhj jhj hjh hjh
ff gg ff gg ff gg fg fg gf gf fgf fgf gfg gfg ff gg ff gg ff gg fg fg gf gf fgf fgf gfg gfg
jj hh jj hh jj hh jh jh hj hj jhj jhj hjh hjh ff gg ff gg ff gg fg fg gf gf fgf fgf gfg gfg

keys. Once you feel comfortable with the movement of your fingers and know where they are on the keyboard without looking at them, you could key in each of the following six lines twice, for practice.

Now practise using these ten letters by keying in the following lines below. Practise each line at least three times, remembering to maintain a good posture and not to look down at your fingers as they move on the keyboard.

Try not to rush your work – speed is far less important than accuracy. If you make a mistake in a line practise it again until you can key it in without error – and without looking.

The top or third row

The top row of alphabetic keys introduces you to the rest of the vowels and several more consonants. These keys are reached by moving your fingers from their position on the home keys, up to the left, diagonally, except for the T for which you move the index finger from the F up to the right. This movement is shown in Figure 49 below. When a letter in the top row is keyed in you should move your finger up to the key required and then back to cover the home key. The movement of your fingers is: up to the left and then back down to the right.

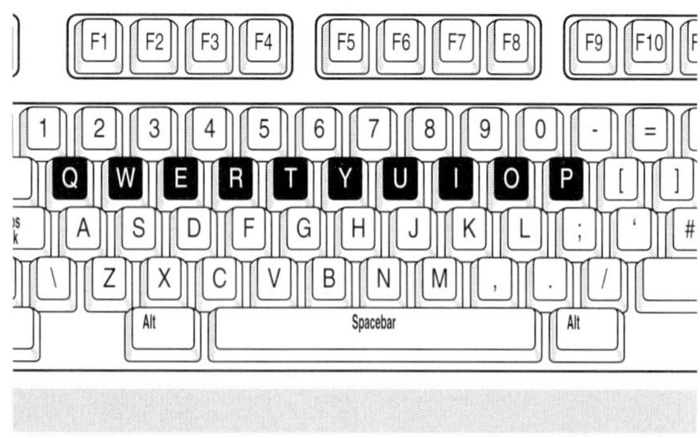

Figure 49 Top row typing movement

dad ada dad ada dad ada dad ada dad ada
sad lad sad lad sad lad sad lad sad lad

all all all all all all all all all all
fad had fad had fad had fad had fad had

sag gas has ash jag sag gas has ash jag
lass alas lass alas lass alas lass alas lass alas

Key in each of the following lines twice. As you key in the letters, try to do so with a steady rhythm, taking the same length of time to press each key. Speed is less important than accuracy at this stage.

1 ff tt ff tt jj uu jj uu ftf ftf juj juj ftf juj ftf juj

2 ff rr ff rr jj yy jj yy frf frf jyj jyj frf jyj frf jyj

3 dd ee dd ee dd ee dd ee ded ded ded ded ded ded

4 kk ii kk ii kk ii kk ii kik kik kik kik kik kik

5 ded kik ded kik ded kik ded kik ded kik ded

6 jtf jtf krf krf drf drf srf srf arf arf

7 grt grt hrt hrt krt krt lrt lrt ;rt ;rt

8 jui jui hui hui dui dui sui sui aui aui

9 fat sat hat kat fat sat hat kat fat sat hat kat

10 tall fall sall gall hall tall fall sall gall tall

a Key in each of the following lines twice, maintaining a steady rhythm, as in Task One.

1 rug jug hug tug lug dug rug jug hug tug lug dug

2 stay tray rule sale kale stay tray rule sale kale

3 tall full sall sale stay hall tall tray sale gall rule tall

4 dull full hull dull full hull dull full hull dull full hull

5 stray stuff stray stuff fluff gruff fluff gruff stall drall stall

6 rust rusty rust rusty dust dusty dust dusty just justy just justy

7 rig fig rig fig rig fig rig fig dig hig dig hig dig hig dig hig

8 ear the ear the ear the ear the hid did hid did hid did hid did

9 rate rail rate rail rate rail trail flies trial flies trial flies trail flies

10 kites seeds kites seeds kites seeds fears hears fears hears fears hears

11 the kites fly at the sky; the kites fly at the sky; the kites fly at the sky

12 they eat all the figs; they eat all the figs; they eat all the figs

13 ask if they had the jug; ask if they had the jug; ask if they had the jug

14 all keys are at the hall; all keys are at the hall; all keys are at the hall

b Key in each of the following lines twice, again maintaining a steady rhythm.

1 ask if they had a key; the hat is at the house; try to eat the salad

2 she tried a full glass; she is at the seaside; she had a flat fish

3 that is the day they tried to eat a jaffa salad at the hall

4 that is the day they tried to take the lass a large glass

5 eat a jaffa salad at the hall; take the lass a large glass

6 the red jug is still here at the hut; the red jug is still here at the hut

7 their father had a large fish at the hall; their father had a large fish at the hall

8 their aircraft has left the airfield; their aircraft has left the airfield

9 ;; pp ;; pp ;; pp ;; pp ;p; ;p; p;p p;p aa qq aa qq aa qq aa qq aqa aqa qaq qaq

10 ss ww ss ww ss ww ss ww sw sw sws sws ll oo ll oo ll oo ll oo lo lo lol lol

11 dd ee dd ee dd ee dd ee kk ii kk ii kk ii kk ii ded kik ded kik ded kik ded kik

12 lot lop lot lop pot lot pot lot post stop post stop post stop

13 saw was saw was saw was saw was pole lope pole lope pole lope

14 quay quip quay quip quay quip queue queer queue queer queue queer

Extension material

Key in the following sentences three times. Try to do this without making any mistakes.

1 try to fillet the flat fish while all the lasses look out for the ship

2 what other people said was to persuade her to look after the dog

3 those fresh pies are part of the last lot they took to the fish quay

4 the poor people are all at the party today so are to share this food

5 please persuade the workers to post their letters at the right time

6 they were worried as the dogs rushed past the last of the pupils

7 grass has started to grow at last; all the fields look a lot fresher these days

8 when the earthquake started all the girls rushed out of the old town hotel

9 she was the first lass to walk past the old part of the walled town this year

10 as we queued we were told that there was a good supply of apples at the shop

Figure 50 Diagram showing the 'qwerty' keys

Figure 51 Diagram showing bottom row

The bottom or first row

The bottom row introduces the remaining alphabetic keys. Keys are reached by moving your fingers from their position on the home keys, down to the right diagonally, except for the N for which you move the index finger from the J down to the left. This movement is shown in Figure 51. Remember to move your finger back to the home key once you have keyed in a letter on the bottom row. Ensure that you practise each of the finger reaches before you start to key in the data. Avoid looking down at your fingers, keeping your eyes on the text you are copying rather than the keyboard.

Key in each of the following lines twice. Concentrate on accuracy rather than speed. If you make a mistake on any one line repeat it until you can key it in without errors.

1 jj mm jj mm jj mm jmj jmj jmj jmj ff vv ff vv ff vv fvf fvf fvf fvf

2 ff bb ff bb ff bb ff bb fbf fbf fbf fbf jj nn jj nn jj nn jj nn jnj jnj jnj jnj

3 dd cc dd cc dd cc dd cc dcd dcd dcd dcd kk ,, kk ,, kk ,, kk ,, k,k k,k k,k k,k

4 ss xx ss xx ss xx ss xx sxs sxs sxs sxs aa zz aa zz aa zz aa zz aza aza aza aza

5 dan jan dan jan dan jan dan jan fan lan fan lan fan lan fan lan

6 bay boy bay boy bay boy bay boy nib nab nib nab nib nab nib nab

7 boys girls boys girls boys girls boys girls boys girls boys girls boys girls

8 bank sank bank sank bank sank bank sank lank hank lank hank lank hank lank hank

9 blue boat blue boat blue boat blue boat begin began begin began begin began

10 mad mat mad mat mad mat mad mat view visa view visa view visa view visa

11 live move live move live move live move love mine love mine love mine love mine

12 value every value every value every value every never women never women never woman

Key in each of the following lines twice, as in Task One.

1 the boys never took the old blue bus to the station except on their birthday

2 she has borrowed a small green badge to show that she is a visitor to the house

3 the men are now able to use the brown paint on the walls of the manor house

4 when the band was playing by the river the students were able to read their notes

5 our van driver arrived late this morning but was soon lost from view

6 the new moon was shining on the flowers in the park garden all night

7 all of the children came to watch the new ship when it was being launched

8 all of the adults were surprised to be given free tickets to watch the circus

9 not everyone was able to stand up in the terrible winds which followed the storm

10 many people were hurt badly when they were knocked over by the severe wind

11 many new members joined the drama club after seeing their latest play at the theatre

12 very few people were able to remember the last time so many members had attended.

Extension material

The following sentences also include the use of the comma and full stop keys, which are keyed in using the second and third fingers of the right hand. Practise keying these in without error.

1 they all listened to the band playing while they sat together on the bank.

2 one by one the tired, dusty elephants walked past the old watering hole.

3 she was unable to borrow the blue blouse from her sister so wore the yellow one.

4 the dog was so angry after it had been shut up, nobody was able to control it.

5 the sailors decided to take the boat out into the open sea despite the poor weather.

6 it was several hours later before the coastguard was called and told of the accident.

7 she tried to cancel the order for the food, but it was too late, it had already been cooked.

8 when the cat reached the top of the stairs, she waited and watched for several minutes.

9 all of the children who had performed in the play were taken out to tea afterwards.

10 none of the boys wanted to be lost in the caves, but nobody knew where the exit was.

11 everyone was going to go to the concert by car, then the committee organised a coach.

12 having reached the summit, the last climber stopped and looked at the wonderful view.

Shift keys

The shift key allows you to key in a capital letter. If you look carefully at the keyboard you will see that there are two shift keys: one on each side of the bottom row of keys. To key in a capital letter you need to press and hold down the shift key and then press the letter you require. Releasing the shift key automatically returns to keying lower case letters. It is normal practice to hold the shift key down with the little finger on each hand.

If you wish to key in a capital letter normally entered with the left hand, you should depress the right shift key with the little finger on the right hand. Similarly, if you wish to key in a capital letter entered with the right hand, you should depress the left hand shift key with the little finger on the left hand. This takes a little practice.

The shift key will also allow you to key in the characters above the numbers on the top row of keys. For example, to key in an asterisk (above the 8 key), depress the left hand shift key and use the index finger on the right hand to press the 8 key. Try the following practice exercises for entering capital letters.

Right shift key

aA; sS; dD; fF; gG; qQ; wW; eE; rR; tT; zZ; xX; cC; vV;

Ann, Sue, Dave, Fred, Gemma, Queen, Walter, Erica, Roger, Tony, Zoe, Carl, Victor.

Andover, Salisbury, Durham, Farnham, Glasgow, Walsall, Exeter, Reading, Truro, Colchester, Ventnor, Aberdeen, Southampton, Derby, Fulham, Gretna Green, Wolverhampton, Edinburgh, Runcorn, Tenby, Carlisle.

Left shift key

lLa kKa jJa hHa pPa oOa iIa uUa yYa mMa nNa

Louise, Katie, John, Henry, Peter, Olive, Ian, Ursula, Yvonne, Mary, Neil

Leicester, Kettley, Japan, Hull, Paris, Oban, Ilkely, Uttoxeter, Yale, Madrid, Nice, Liverpool, Keighley, Jarrow, Humberside, Peterborough, Ormskirk, Inverness, Utrecht, Yorkshire, Manchester, Newcastle.

Shift lock/caps lock

The shift lock or caps lock is used when keying in more than one consecutive capital letter. It changes all alphabetic characters into capital letters when the keys are depressed. Numerical characters remain unchanged. The shift lock or caps lock key is located above the shift key on the left hand side of the keyboard. When it is depressed an indicator light on the keyboard will come on. To release the shift or caps lock, this key should be depressed a second time and the keyboard will revert to lower case characters.

It is a common fault to depress the caps lock key to key in a single letter. This can only slow the operator down, as the key then needs to be struck a second time to release the caps lock; whereas with the shift key, as soon as it is released, the keyboard reverts to lower case letters.

For practice, key in the following sentences using the shift key or the caps lock where appropriate.

The first train stopped at BIRMINGHAM NEW STREET on Sunday morning.

The boys were able to see the film TITANIC at the Curzon cinema.

One member of the BASKETBALL squad was unable to play.

All of the teams were entered in the HEAD OF THE RIVER race at Henley Regatta.

John was unable to save the QUEEN ELIZABETH from being towed to New York.

The BOYZONE concert was to be held at the ALBERT HALL in London.

He was not sure if it was an IBM or a TOSHIBA computer Sheila was using.

The INDIAN ELEPHANT is smaller than the AFRICAN. It also has smaller ears.

Warm up practice

Once you have mastered the alphabetic keyboard the following sentences may help you to practise your skills. Each sentence contains most of the letters of the alphabet at least once.

As she gazed at the pieces of exquisite jewellery in the window of the shop, she began to wonder if she could ever afford them.

Maxine was quite concerned that she would have jeopardized her chances of obtaining the autograph of the author by keeping quiet.

She required a pair of size sixteen jeans to allow for shrinkage although she has always claimed to be only a size twelve.

When the zip on her new boots jammed, she was quite sure they would be exchanged the next time she went down to the town centre to shop.

The walk to the town square was extremely breezy and by the time she got there she was glad she had decided to put on her warmest jumper.

Individual letter practice

If you are finding it difficult to key in one or more particular letters, use the following exercises to practise until you become more competent and accurate with each letter.

A

date what said many mail make take case race that rate have than
back bank save each fact half have past able last lass pain cane mane
All the animals are able to have a last chance to have their coats and stalls cleaned today.

B

bin ban bed bag beg bob boy box but buy best been both bath bill ball
bell bull blue bill bust busy back baby book bank black blank build built
The boys brought the blue boat up to the big old beech tree beside the broken barrier.

C

car can cut cur co cot care came case cave cure curt curl curb cast cost
come comb cash cosh club cube could claim clear clean cloud close cheer
Cabbages and cauliflowers could be cultivated in the cool clear cold frames by the canal.

D

did die due day dry dot dear dean does dose draw drew dray down dawn
read dear road paid made said done door dress drake drill delay dated desire
Daniel decided to deliver the dangerous package despite the decision to delay the deadline.

E

ear dew wet hen den bed led red wed let get met net set each else even ever
early eight equal error enjoy agree enough effect except expect evening enclose
Everyone educated in Exeter was excluded from entering the exciting weekly entertainment.

F

fur fat fun fin few far fir fit fen fan fee fed feel feet fire firm food four five file
fact fear fall full farm firm free face fire fine find fund funny first family favour
For all farming families the festival of fresh fish was a feast they had to finally forget.

G

gun gin gag gig gap gas bag big bog bug dig dog dug fig fog give gave good glad
girl game gold gone thing going young agree again along bring great guard grade
George grinned when he glanced at the giant before having to give the green jug to Gerald.

H

her him has had hid hod hat hit hop hip hut hum his has have hard help here head
happy hippy house homes dash hush dish ship shop show shall these there their
Having held the horse by its halter for an hour, Harriet was hoping to have a ride on him.

I

dig pig wig fig big rig lid lip rid rip nip sip fir sir kit lit pit sit kind mind find rind
mine line life wife right might bill fill income living writing lighting fighting
In the individual diagrams the Indian ink was used to indicate the weight of the insects.

J

job jib jab jog jig jug jam jar jet jot jut jaw joy just junk join just jest joke juke
jilt jolt jeep jeer jerk jive jilt jade jolly jelly judge joint juice jeans jingle jangle
Jenny jumped off the jetty into the jumble of junk in her jeans, jumper and jacket without injury.

K

kit kid key sky ask ink key knob know knit knot kill kilt kilo kiln kiss king kilo
kite kate kept kerb knock knack knife think thank stock check quick quack speak
Knowledge was the key to knowing how he kept the kind market traders keen to talk back.

L

lot let low law last list lost loss less left lift line link lint life live long lung love late
lady dale hale male pale foal fail local large leave light could would allow small
The little local old lady was allowed to fill the small well with large leaves until it was full.

M

met mat men man many made make male most must mist mast more move much
form firm some same seem name game meet mile mill miss mere month mouth music
Most of the money was made at the market by the many mothers who came from home.

N

not not now new net man men ten tin tan ton need near note next nice mine main
line lane once only many mind night never newer doing going down dawn gone gain
Northern nannies did not notice the many men who were alone in the morning and evening.

O

our out old off too top ton tor own owe once over only open other order offer
book took come some home tome cost lost host post sold told cold fold bold gold
One good job was the order obtained from the old doctor who was not following the book.

P

pit put pet pat pot put pin pan pun pad pod pip pop pup paw paid page post poor
upon open play ploy part tape person people please proper prompt present perhaps
The principle operatic player was on the ship in place of the poor person who had passed on.

Q

quit quay quiz quid quiet quite quick quire query queer quote queue quota quire
squib squid squire square squash squeal quack quail quench quaint request require
The queen was quizzed on the quest and the quota or quantity she was required to request.

R

run rum rut rub rot rat rob rod roe rot road room real rest arm car far fir for bar
from form four firm fire free foam ford work were wire wore worn warn card cord
The room rate was remarkably reasonable considering the regular work the firm required.

S

set sat sit say sir she has his was saw use sue ask said same sane sign sigh sure
lost loss last list seem seam sell save side sold miss must most rest rust puts stop
The sturdy sailing ship was sure to be last as it steered using only the set of its single sail.

T

ten net bit but get got let lot out too two put pot pit pat this than than they them
must most meet meat both best beat beet rate rest stay stop sent sunk sank with what
It was almost time to meet the three tailors at the top of the path by the little statue in the city.

U

up us use sue you our fur but cut buy due cue run four full hour must just sure
much such sure pure trust truth house mouse cause pause pound found round mound
Usually it lasted until the music caused the young guard to run out of the busy club house.

V

vet vat van vow have gave rave save pave cave vote verb vent veal vein vale
visa vice vine view vase very love dove move wove leave serve verve value valve
Never before have the five villagers vowed to serve vegetables in various very vivid vases.

W

who why was win won war way will well were work with what when went town
wait warm want went week weak where while which whose whole worth waste water
They waited when the weather warmed up to waste words with the weak woman who knew.

X

box fox cox fax fix tax axe sex mix axis axle next text exit exam flex flax hoax coax
mixer fixer extra relax exist expert expel exile exact extend export except expect excuse
The experts excited by the extra mixture, had to explain the hoax was an excuse to relax.

Y

any may fly sky try ply bay day ray say hay may bay way toy boy year yawn yell
play ploy lady pity city delay apply every enjoy fully happy sorry hasty today forty fifty
Any delay in the lady replying to your happy and enjoyable play would only apply today.

Z

zoo zip zap zeal zest zinc zoom zone daze gaze raze haze doze quiz fizz buzz jazz
amaze glaze maize breeze sneeze freeze frieze puzzle dazzle razzle muzzle puzzle squeeze
Zac gazed at the crazy zebra in the zoo but was puzzled when the breeze caused him to sneeze.

Keyboard skills: testing your speed

When measuring speed of keying in a standard five character word is used. Each key pressed is a stroke; five strokes make up one standard word for measuring speed.

As an example, if you can key in the following sentence twice in one minute, you are keying in data at an average speed of 20 words per minute. However, if you make any errors, these should be deducted from the 20 words. For example, if you make four mistakes your keying in speed is 16 words per minute (i.e. 20 standard words keyed in one minute, minus four errors, equals 16 words per minute).

the vessel was tied up just past the old fish quay

How well did you do? Why not try this next sentence? It contains 12 standard words. Keying it in twice without error in one minute gives a speed of 24 words per minute.

the quality of the quartet was so good other players clapped

Finally, try your hand at keying in the following sentence twice without error. This will give a keying in speed of 30 words per minute.

as we queued we were told there was a good supply of apples at the new shop

Practise these three sentences whenever you have a spare few minutes. They will help you build up a good keying in speed.

Each of the following sentences contains 25 standard words. Practise each one three times, and then time yourself to see how many times you can key in the sentence in one minute without error.

1 Each week for the past year, the dustbin had been emptied on Friday and so it was a surprise to come home and find it full.

2 Kevin had told his mother that he would be late home from school because he was playing rugby. In fact he was in detention.

3 Soon all the leaves on the trees in the woods had turned a range of shades of brown but it only lasted for a few short days.

Next use the following sentences to improve your speed. Each contains 25 standard words. Practise each sentence three times before seeing how many times you can key it in without error in two minutes.

1 Turning the screw slowly, the optician was able to tighten it up sufficiently for the customer to wear the spectacles again.

2 Quite a lot of people had already gathered around the injured man by the time the surgeon arrived to see how she could help.

3 By the time the machine had finished its second cycle, the clothes from the previous wash had dried in the blustery weather.

4 One by one the adult giraffes moved through the clearing towards the watering hole. The slightest sound would disturb them.

Extension material

Now try this short paragraph. Practise keying it in once, and then allow yourself five minutes to see how much you can complete without error. The passage contains 125 standard words.

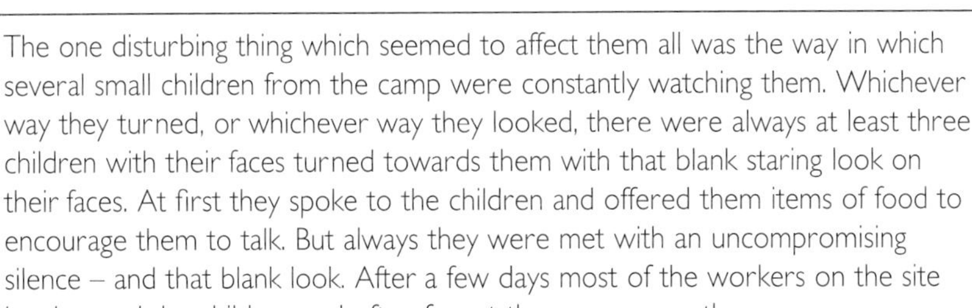

The one disturbing thing which seemed to affect them all was the way in which several small children from the camp were constantly watching them. Whichever way they turned, or whichever way they looked, there were always at least three children with their faces turned towards them with that blank staring look on their faces. At first they spoke to the children and offered them items of food to encourage them to talk. But always they were met with an uncompromising silence – and that blank look. After a few days most of the workers on the site just ignored the children and often forgot they were even there.

Adapted from an SEG Examination Question, 1996

Index